W9-BSM-656

Love Online

"Computers have changed not just the way we work but the way we love. Falling in and out of love, flirting, cheating, even having sex online have all become part of the modern way of living and loving. Yet we know very little about these new types of relationship. How is an online affair where the two people involved may never see or meet each other different from an affair in the real world? Is online sex still cheating on your partner? Why do people tell complete strangers their most intimate secrets? What are the rules of engagement? Will online affairs change the monogamous nature of romantic relationships?" These are just some of the questions Professor Aaron Ben-Ze'ev, distinguished writer and academic, addresses in the first full-length study of love online. Accessible, shocking, entertaining, enlightening, this book will change the way you look at cyberspace and love for ever.

AARON BEN-ZE'EV is Rector of the University of Haifa, Professor of Philosophy and Co-Director of the Centre for Interdisciplinary Research on Emotions at the University of Haifa. He has published extensively on emotion, most recently *The Subtlety of Emotions* (2000).

Love Online

Emotions on the Internet

AARON BEN-ZE'EV

CAMBRIDGE UNIVERSITY PRESS

PUBLISHED BY THE PRESS SYNDICATE OF THE UNIVERSITY OF CAMBRIDGE
The Pitt Building, Trumpington Street, Cambridge, United Kingdom

CAMBRIDGE UNIVERSITY PRESS
The Edinburgh Building, Cambridge, CB2 2RU, UK
40 West 20th Street, New York, NY 10011-4211, USA
477 Williamstown Road, Port Melbourne, VIC 3207, Australia
Ruiz de Alarcón 13, 28014 Madrid, Spain
Dock House, The Waterfront, Cape Town 8001, South Africa

http://www.cambridge.org

First published 2004

Printed in the United Kingdom at the University Press, Cambridge

Typefaces Minion 10/12 pt and Formata *System* LaTeX 2_ε [TB]

A catalogue record for this book is available from the British Library

Library of Congress Cataloguing in Publication data

Love online: emotions on the Internet / by Aaron Ben-Ze'ev.
p. cm.
Includes bibliographical references and index.
ISBN 0 521 83296 9 (cloth)
1. Love – Computer network resources. 2. Man–woman relationships – Computer network resources. 3. Mate selection – Computer network resources. 4. Dating (Social customs) – Computer network resources. 5. Internet.
HQ801.A3L68 2004
306.7′0285′4678 – dc21 2003055129

ISBN 0 521 83296 9 hardback

To Ruth, my real love

Contents

Preface

> Paradise is exactly like where you are right now . . . only much, much better.
>
> Laurie Anderson

Nowadays, one of the most exciting social, as well as romantic, sites to visit is cyberspace. At any moment, millions of people across the globe are surfing that space, socializing with each other or having romantic affairs. Their number is growing by the minute. What is the lure of the Net? Why do people feel compelled to leave the comfortable surroundings of their actual world and immerse themselves in this seductive space? Why are emotions so intense in this seemingly imaginary world? Are we witnessing the emergence of new types of emotions and romantic relationships? What is the future of romantic relationships and prevailing bonds such as marriage?

In this book two topics are analyzed: cyberspace and emotions. Whereas emotions have been at the center of our everyday life throughout the development of human beings, cyberspace has been accorded such a central role only in recent years. Many thinkers have contributed to various debates about emotions, but the more systematic study of emotions has only recently become the focus of substantial academic investigations. Cyberspace is itself a relatively recent phenomenon and the academic community has just begun to collect and publish data and to formulate theories about it.

In my book, *The Subtlety of Emotions*, I presented a comprehensive framework for understanding emotions in our everyday life. The present book seeks to apply this framework to the rapidly growing instances of online relationships. It focuses upon a few central emotions that occur in cyberspace, and in particular romantic love and sexual desire. I examine the nature of these emotions in cyberspace and compare them to their counterparts in offline circumstances. There is no doubt that intense, real emotions are present in online affairs – otherwise, such affairs would not be so popular. However, the reasons for the generation of such emotions are not readily apparent.

The Internet has a profound impact upon the extent and nature of romantic and sexual relationships. Describing this impact may be helpful in coping with the online romantic and sexual revolution and in predicting the future development of these relationships.

Acknowledgments

In writing this book I have been helped by many people. In particular, I would like to thank Deb Levine and Azy Barak, both experts on the topic of online personal relationships, who read the whole manuscript and generously gave both their time and invaluable advice. I am grateful to my two research assistants, Anat Lewinsky and Oren Livio, who contributed greatly to the various ideas presented here and who provided me with essential research materials. I thank Marion Ledwig, Nicola Doering, and Monica Whitty for reading the whole manuscript and for their useful and pertinent comments. The following people read various chapters of the book and gave me helpful feedback: Oz Almog, Sholamit Almog, Yair Amichai-Hamburger, Oded Balaban, Avinoam Ben-Ze'ev, Ruth Ben-Ze'ev, Michael Keren, Eva Illouz, Daphna Lewy, Fania Oz-Salzberger, Ruth Sharabany, Saul Smilansky, Ada Spitzer, and Daniel Statman. Special heartfelt thanks are due to my language editor, Glendyr Sacks, who has made the manuscript comprehensible regarding not only its style but its content as well. I am also deeply grateful to my editor at Cambridge University Press, Sarah Caro, who has always believed in this project. I am grateful to Leigh Mueller for the excellent editing work. I would like to thank Lady Shelby, Starchild, Tina, Lisa, Armand, Cabe, and all the many other anonymous people whose account of their online relationships I read with much interest. Earlier versions of parts of chapters 5 and 7 will be appearing in *Computers in Human Behavior*, **19** (2003), 451–467; and in *Convergence*, **10** (2004). Finally, the debt I owe my beloved wife Ruth, and my two wonderful sons, Dean and Adam, goes far beyond words.

1 *The seductive space*

> The most exciting attractions are between two opposites that never meet.
>
> Andy Warhol

The appearance of computer-mediated communication has introduced a new type of discourse and consequently a new type of personal relationship has developed. There are various kinds of computer-mediated relationships that differ in some significant aspects: one-to-one or group communication formats, interrelating with real people or fantasy personas, interrelating with anonymous or identified people, and communicating in synchronous or asynchronous formats. Such types of communication can be text-based, voice-based, video-based, or a combination of any of these. My main concern is with those types of communication that facilitate romantic relationships. Foremost among such types are email, which is asynchronous text-based communication that can be one-to-one or one-to-many, and chat or instant messaging that allows for synchronous text-based communication, either one-to-one or many-to-many. These types of communication take place between real people who, while not completely anonymous, may have not fully disclosed their identity: in most cases, you cannot see or hear the other person.

The interactive revolution in imagination

> We waste time looking for the perfect lover, instead of creating the perfect love.
>
> Tom Robbins

Cyberspace is a psychological and social domain. It is not tangible and some of its dimensions, such as distance, and location, are not measured by physical parameters, but by psychological content. This often imaginary reality is not limited to the private domain of a specific person; rather, it is shared by many people. Such a novel psychological reality is supported by sophisticated technology, but it is not defined by this technology; it is defined by the various psychological interactions occurring in it.[1]

Cyberspace is virtual in the sense that imagination is intrinsic to that space. In many online relationships, you can imagine your cybermate in whatever way you wish to and you can describe yourself as you want to be seen. When people are asked why they engaged in sexual relationships online, the most common reason given is that they have specific fantasies and desires that are not being fulfilled in their offline relationships.[2] However, in another important sense cyberspace is not virtual: online relationships are conducted between actual, flesh-and-blood people. Although this relationship involves many imaginative aspects, the relationship itself is not imaginary. Cyberspace is a part of reality; it is, therefore, incorrect to regard it as the direct opposite of real space. Cyberspace is part of real space, and online relationships are real relationships. The term "actual" may be slightly more accurate than "real" in denoting the opposite of "virtual" – although it raises certain difficulties, too. Another term that I will use often to denote the opposite of "online" is "offline."

People typically consider the virtual, or imaginative, nature of cyberspace to be its unique characteristic. Although cyberspace involves imaginary characters and events of a kind and magnitude not seen before, less developed virtual realities have always been integral parts of human life. All forms of art, including cave drawings made by our Stone Age ancestors, involve some kind of virtual reality. In this sense, cyberspace does not offer a totally new dimension to human life. What is new about cyberspace is its interactive nature and this interactivity has made it a psychological reality as well as a social reality. It is a space where real people have actual interactions with other real people, while being able to shape, or even create, their own and other people's personalities. The move from passive imaginary reality to the interactive virtual reality of cyberspace is much more radical than the move from photographs to movies.

Most other types of virtual realities are essentially one-dimensional: the person may passively receive the informational content from outside (as in art), or create it by herself (as in imagination), but there is no actual interaction among the participants – the interaction is purely imaginary.

Communicating through writing letters or speaking on the phone involve actual interaction, but none of these involve a comprehensive virtual environment – the participants in such communication are typically fully immersed in their own ordinary, non-imaginary environment. Cyberspace provides a whole virtual environment in which such actions take place. The closest imaginary reality to the virtual one associated with cyberspace is that elicited by phone sex. Actual interaction is also part of phone sex, but the imaginary environment is limited to a certain sexual activity only. Hence, its impact is limited as well.

Interactivity is a crucial element in the psychological reality of cyberspace. The greater and the more profound the interaction is, the greater degree of psychological reality we attach to it. Thus, psychological reality is perceived to be greater if what we send and what we receive consist not merely of words that we type, but also of voices, pictures, and body movements. The outputs we send are of greater psychological reality for us the more their execution seems natural to us; for example, the less effort we need to control them. The psychological reality of the inputs we receive is determined by features such as the speed and frequency of the responses that express the sender's psychological attitude toward us. An immediate response is psychologically more exciting, just as live broadcasting is more exciting. Similarly, instant messaging is psychologically more real than corresponding by email. The more similar the inputs and outputs are to offline interaction, the more real they are typically perceived to be.[3]

The greater interactivity of cyberspace implies that we have greater control over our personal relationships. For example, when we so desire, we can either slow them down or increase their pace. If someone surprises you – say, by expressing her love for you – you have time to consider your response. You do not have to rely merely on your spontaneous responses. In this sense, it is easier to cope with online relationships. The sense of greater control is often central to enjoyable experiences.[4]

Cyberspace is similar to fictional space in the sense that in both cases the flight into virtual reality is not so much a denial of reality as a form of exploring and playing with it. One crucial difference between the two is the interactive nature of cyberspace. In cyberspace, people do not merely read or watch a romantic affair undertaken by others, but in a sense they are actually participating in it. As one woman says: "It's almost as though you were reading erotica, except you are also writing the erotic story, and you don't know what's going to happen next."[5] Karl Marx once said that people "make their own history, but they do not make it just as they please."[6] In cyberspace, they can finally make it exactly as they please.

In cyberspace, we are more actively involved than we are when we read novels, but, in addition, online communication touches upon more personal and specific aspects than does reading novels. As one woman writes: "I love reading about sexual things. When I know that the writer is thinking of me specifically, it is completely, absolutely thrilling. And when I find someone who enjoys the same level of explicitness I do and has similar writing skills, it's particularly alluring."[7] Since the personal aspect is of special importance in stimulating intense emotions, cyberlove and cybersex are typically more exciting than reading novels or watching television.

When reading fiction or watching a movie we enter the imaginary world even if we remain aware of its imaginary nature. We suspend disbelief and though, on one level, we accept the fictional reality of the characters, on another we recognize that the situation is make-believe. In cyberspace this recognition is often absent.

The imaginary journey into the fictional reality of novels or movies is not usually condemned unless it is perceived to have a negative influence on our everyday life. The moment that such negative impact is present, as in the case of violent movies, the effect of the imaginary reality is condemned. The interactive nature of cyberspace makes it more susceptible to moral criticism, as its practical impact is greater. As one man argues: "Cybersex is closer to having a hooker than plain pornography because there is a real and active person involved on the other end. People are touching each others' minds in a mutual and cooperative way that silent fantasy does not permit."[8] Indeed, in a survey of Internet users, 75% stated that they would find it acceptable for their significant other to visit an adult site, whereas 77% said that it would not be acceptable for their significant other to participate in an adult one-on-one online video conversation with a member of the opposite sex whom they do not know.[9] Due to the interactive nature of cyberspace, virtual activities on the Net are accorded moral significance.

Cyberlove and cybersex

> Online sex is a wonderful invention. Now, if only everyone could type faster.
>
> Unknown[10]

The interactive element in cyberlove and cybersex has made these options very attractive. The nature of cyberlove and cybersex will be explored throughout the book. In this section, I characterize some of their salient features.

Cyberlove is a romantic relationship consisting mainly of computer-mediated communication. Despite the fact that the partner is physically remote and is to a certain extent anonymous, in one important aspect this relationship is similar to an offline romantic relationship – the emotion of love is experienced as fully and as intensely as in an offline relationship.

In a broad sense, cybersex refers to all types of sexually related activities offered in cyberspace. In this sense, the viewing of sexually explicit materials on the Internet is also a type of cybersex. Since this book is concerned with personal relationships, I am less interested in this type of cybersex and will use the term in the narrower sense, referring to a social interaction between at least two people who are exchanging real-time digital messages in order to become sexually aroused. People send provocative and erotic messages to each other, with the purpose of bringing each other to orgasm as they masturbate together in real time. These messages are typically sent via a private communication, such as an email or instant message, but can also be part of a public chat room – in which case, they could be considered as public sexual activity. The messages may be of various types – video, audio, and text-based; here I mainly refer to text-based cybersex. In cybersex (or in slang, "cybering"), people describe body characteristics to one another, verbalize sexual actions and reactions, and make believe that the virtual happenings are real. Cybersex requires the articulation of sexual desire to an extent that would be most unusual in face-to-face encounters. In cyberspace, that which often remains unspoken must be put into words.[11]

When people are involved in cybersex, they cannot actually kiss each other, but nevertheless the kiss they may send is emotionally vivid and its emotional impact is often similar to that of an actual kiss. Our active role in cyberspace makes this environment more exciting and seductive than that of daydreams, erotic novels, or X-rated movies; hence the temptation to engage in sexual activities is greater. A married man whose wife of fourteen years is having cybersex, reports: "I offered a compromise and suggested that she read adult stories or look at pictures instead of a one-to-one chat. She refused. I even suggested that while she's cybering, she types, I do the things the other person describes, but she flatly refused and told me that it was a personal chat and is nothing to do with me."[12] The personal interaction, rather than the mere aspect of imagination, is what excites his wife. Since the line separating passive observation from full interaction has already been crossed in cybersex, it becomes easier to blur the line separating imagination from reality.

Participants in cyberlove take the reality of cyberspace seriously. Thus, people speak of their cybermates or even their online husbands or online wives. People have even got cybermarried and vowed to remain faithful to each other. One woman wrote that what attracted her to respond to the first message sent by her online lover, with whom she is now deeply in love, is that he asked her to cyberdance with him.[13] Some women have claimed that they do not want to engage in cybersex with the first person who asks them, since they want to save their virtual virginity for the right man. Similarly, some say that they do not want to have a one-night cyberstand, but rather wish to have a more extended and meaningful online sexual affair. A man who often participates in cybersex writes:

> I love to cyber; I think it's great. The only thing is I can't cyber with someone I have never talked to before. Someone sent me a message and went right into cybering without asking my name or if I even wanted to. I know it's probably silly since the person you cyber with is a stranger, but I would just like to have a regular conversation first. I guess some reality does play a part here, because I would not have sex (in real life) with someone whose name I didn't even know.[14]

People complain that they now have the added pressure of faking cyberorgasms too. In one survey, 36% of Net surfers who had engaged in cybersex said they had reached orgasm; 25% said they had faked it; and the rest neither reached orgasm nor faked it. (The percentage of people faking orgasms in offline circumstances seems to be somewhat greater: in one survey, 56% of women and 23% of men claimed to have faked an orgasm.)[15] One married woman described her online sexual partner: he was "self-centered on his part and not very exciting and I found myself faking an orgasm over the computer and thought I had totally lost my mind."[16] The illusory nature of cyberspace does not diminish the need to resort to the same illusory methods used in offline circumstances.

The presence of interactive characteristics in the imaginary realm of online relationship is a tremendous revolution in personal relationships, as it enables people to reap most of the benefits associated with offline relationships without investing significant resources.

The interactive revolution in online romantic and sexual relationships has promoted both greater social interaction and more solitary activities. In comparison with standard fantasies, online relationships involve more social activities with other people. However, in comparison with offline relationships, many romantic activities are performed while someone is all alone sitting in front of a computer. Take, for example, cybersex. Compared with offline masturbation, cybersex (like phone sex) is a much more social interaction, as it is done while communicating with another person. While in offline masturbation, orgasm comes courtesy of the person's own hands and mind, in cybersex, orgasm also comes courtesy of another person's mind. Cybersex narrows the gap between masturbation and offline sex, as it involves the active contribution of another person. However, compared with offline sexual relationships, cybersex is less social and it can in fact reduce the need for actual social interactions.

Letter, telegraph, and telephone

> Pardon me, but I am writing a phone book – can I have your number?
>
> Unknown

Online romantic relationships are not the only kind of romantic relationships that use communication to overcome spatial limitations. Other examples include relationships that are based purely on conventional letters, telegraph, or phone conversations.[17]

Falling in love through letter writing is not a new phenomenon: it has been going on for hundreds of years. It has been particularly prevalent during prolonged periods of war when men were far away from home and the only way to communicate with them was through letters. Writing love letters is also common in peacetime when the two lovers are in different places. Online relationships are based upon an improved version of an old-fashioned way of communicating: writing. In the new version, the time gap between writing, sending, receiving, and reading has been made almost instantaneous – the sender can receive a reply while still in the state of emotions in which she sent the original message. This difference, which may appear merely technical, is of great emotional significance, as emotions are brief and involve the urge to act immediately. In this sense, instant messaging is better than email. A man comparing the two methods remarks: **"I think I prefer the IM's. I have had cybersex once or twice, and it's nice to have that instant feedback from the woman (God, I hope they're women) that you're with."**[18]

Writing romantic letters to a person you hardly know and online romantic communication have certain aspects in common: for example, the scanty amount of information the partners have about each other at the beginning of the relationship, the significant role of imagination, the reliance on writing skills and verbal communication, the spatial separation, discontinuity of communication, and marginal physical investment. In both types of relationships, people fall in love with individuals who are almost strangers to them and about whom they know only what they glean from the written word. The information we rely on when we write letters is often greater than that available through online communication. When we write a letter, we usually know the real name and address of the recipient. If the letter is being written under special circumstances, such as during a period of war, we may be able to detect further details – that the person is a soldier, his rank, his probable age, and a rough idea of his present situation. Some information can also be gathered about the sender from the type of paper she writes on, her handwriting, and her name.[19]

Even this amount of information may be absent in online relationships: we have neither the real address nor the real name of our online friend, and there are usually no special circumstances that can provide further information. Of course, the name our partner chooses to use or the type of chat room we are in can provide some clues, but these are typically insufficient and unreliable. Thus, if the name of the chat room is "Married & Flirting," you can assume that most participants are married people who would like to have an affair, but even this meager information may be unreliable. It should be noted, however, that most sites now offer online profiles from which you can gather a reasonable amount of identifying and personal information about someone; sometimes even photos are included.

The presence of partial information, and hence the need to fill the informational gap, explains the significant role of imagination both in letter writing and in online communication. When someone is not physically present, imagination takes on some of the functions typically fulfilled by vision but people have to be careful about their underlying assumptions.

Letter writing and online communication are based on writing skills and verbal communication and not on external appearance. In offline affairs, two partners can have sex or go to a restaurant without talking too much to each other. In online affairs, every activity consists essentially of verbal communication. The emphasis on verbal communication forces the participants to enlarge or deepen the scope of their mutual interest. Extended communication between two partners cannot be limited to sexual messages; other aspects must be explored as well.

The great temporal gap between one letter and another does not suit the impetuous nature of romantic affairs. A snail-mail affair is also less immediate in the sense that you cannot just speak your mind; you need to find an envelope, a stamp, and a postbox before (slow) communication can take place. Other features distinguishing online communication from conventional letters are related, for example, to convenience, ability to copy the message and send it to other people, a possible use of multimedia, and a convenient manner in which incoming and outgoing messages can be stored.

Telegraphic communication between private wireless operators who made Morse contact with other operators is similar in many respects to cyber communication. Both cases involve online exchanges between people who do not meet face-to-face. In both types of communication, speed and writing style are more important than external appearance. One significant difference between the two types is that, whereas access to cyberspace is open to almost anyone, telegraphic communication was limited to a closed, exclusive community of telegraph operators. Another difference concerns the lack of privacy in telegraphic communication, as opposed to the anonymity typical of cyberspace communication.

Despite the apparently impersonal nature of telegraphic communication, it generated profound and intimate romances; some of these came to an abrupt halt when the two parties met for the first time. Accordingly, at the end of the nineteenth century, several articles and even a book were published on telegraphic romances, bearing titles such as "Romances via the telegraph," "Making love by telegraph," "Wired love," and "The dangers of wired love."

The powerful romantic impact of the written communication that is typical of cyberspace is clearly expressed in telegraphic communication as well. Thus, an article discussing a love relationship by telegraph describes a man who was involved in "a red hot row" with a young female operator. After some time, he started to feel in love with the woman, realizing that "nothing short of an angel could work that wire." After meeting face-to-face, they married and remained happily married for a long time.[20]

Limited access, limited vocabulary, the expense involved, and lack of anonymity are among the main reasons for the limited impact of the telegraph upon romantic affairs. In this sense, the introduction of the telephone has been much more significant.

Interpersonal relationships conducted exclusively via phone conversations have some features in common with online relationships. Telephone conversations often involve sincere self-disclosure, as do online relationships. Like cybersex, phone sex involves no fear of unwanted pregnancy or sexually transmitted diseases. In both types of sexual activity, external appearance is not significant.

Phone communication, however, is closer to face-to-face communication than online communication is. Phone sex does not involve typing but engages with the other person's real voice, whispers, sighs, moans, groans, and other sexually arousing sounds; it involves the immediacy of face-to-face interaction.[21] Phone conversations involve a lesser degree of anonymity – typically, your gender and approximate age are detectable – and hence imagination has a lesser role in such communication. Phone communication is also more expensive than online communication and this may influence the length and thus the content of the conversation.

Another important issue in this regard is that of continuity. The ability to call the other partner whenever one wants to may prevent the participants from disconnecting themselves from this relationship if they want to end the affair. Unlike online communication, in which you choose when and how to respond without immediate time or psychological pressures, phone communication is more intrusive and insistent. The telephone forces you to respond at a time and in a manner that may be inconvenient for you: it induces a sense of obligation and urgency that is hard to ignore. Moreover, since most telephones do not have off switches, this further enhances the sense of urgency in replying to the phone's ring. This sense is even more pronounced in the case of the telegraph.[22]

It is easier to avoid or defer responding to unpleasant questions in email communication than in phone conversations. An obsessive romantic partner can intrude upon our everyday routine much more by phone than by online communication. Merely pressing a button cannot end intimate phone relationships. If you do not pick up the phone and merely respond to messages on an answer machine, communication by phone may be less intrusive, but then it loses some of its advantages, such as immediacy. Today, with the extensive use of mobile phones, there are even fewer opportunities to escape incoming calls. However, mobile phones do have off switches that enable you to mark the boundary of your private zone and so can be less intrusive.

In many chat rooms and instant messaging communication, there are buddy lists that enable people to know when you are online. This increases the continuity aspect that is more problematic in email relationships. Even when taking into account this feature, phone communication is still more intrusive and less anonymous than online communication. The latter provides, therefore, a greater degree of safety. Hence, it is more likely that a woman will give a strange man her email address, rather than her phone number. A man who presents himself as an expert in these matters argues: "I've found that getting an email address is not only easier, but it gets more positive responses later on. And I've found that emails are answered FAR more often than voicemail messages."[23] Indeed, giving someone your email, then your phone number, and finally your address, represents increasing levels of trust in the other person and your commitment to the relationship.[24]

The greater similarity of phone conversations to face-to-face communication increases the reality of such conversations. This is nicely expressed in the following description by a 26-year-old woman who has engaged in both cybersex and phone sex:

> I met lots of men, and eventually I had cybersex with many of them. This did not seem promiscuous to me. I would never have sex with so many men in real life. After three months of this, I met

someone online who really intrigued me. We started having phone sex, and for me this seemed very real because I could hear his voice. Now, if I had phone sex as often as I had cybersex, I think I would feel promiscuous because phone sex seems more real.[25]

In a similar vein, people testify that it was easier for them to say "I love you" in online communication than on the phone – even when the phone conversation took place after this statement was communicated online. It is still harder to utter these words in a face to face meeting. The same goes for flattery (and criticism), which is easiest to express in cyberspace and hardest in face-to-face encounters. In all these cases, the less real nature of online communication reduces the pain of a hostile response.

Another reason why some people prefer phone sex over cybersex is that it can provide "hands free" stimulation – it does not have to be done while the person is typing with one hand. A married woman, who had little sexual contact with her husband, said she had tried computer sex but found it "too difficult to be into it when typing . . . phone sex is better, you don't have to use both hands to talk with."[26] (You can even turn the loudspeaker on, so that you have both hands free.) For some people, it is really difficult to get turned on while typing; for others, communicating by typing about mutual sexual activities is very stimulating. People get quite proficient at typing with one hand and masturbating with the other. Moreover, when they reach an orgasm, they often just bash their hands randomly on the keyboard, which does not take a great deal of precision.[27] If, in the good old days, an ideal desired person was tall and beautiful, in cybersex the ideal is a smart person who can type fast with one hand. The mechanics of cybersex are not entirely clear to everyone. Thus, one person writes: "I don't get it. If you're trying to masturbate, how do you keep up with yourself and the key board? Anyway, boys and girls, at least give them credit for being coordinated; I could never do it."[28] It should be noted, however, that most cybersex does not involve one-handed typing; it involves people typing, and reaching orgasm sequentially – in such cases, fast two-hands typing will suffice as well.

The form of one's response – for example, its length and speed – is left more to the discretion of the respondent in online communication than in letters or phone communication. In this sense, too, online communication has some advantages over relationships conducted by letters and telephone. Thus, instant messages can be very short – even one word and often one sentence – whereas such a short message is rare, and thus considered rude, in the other types of communication. In email communication, such extremely short messages are also considered rude. Online communication offers the immediacy of the telephone, but, as in letters, it is up to the respondent to choose when to respond – the response does not have to be spontaneous if one does not so wish; this may reduce the stress on the participants.

A face-to-face relationship is the most profound type of relationship we experience. In evaluating other types of relationships, we should consider their affinity to this relationship. If it is too close to a face-to-face relationship it may keep most of the advantages of the latter, while failing to avoid its disadvantages. When the similarity is more superficial, the ability to retain the advantages of a face-to-face relationship is considerably reduced.

Relating by merely writing letters or phone conversations cannot present a real alternative to conventional offline relationships. Accordingly, these means typically supplement such relationships – when those are not feasible or desirable – but do not replace them. Online relationships do not merely supplement offline relationships, when those are not feasible or desirable, but in some circumstances can present a real alternative to them. In this sense, an online relationship, rather than one conducted via telephone conversations, is "the next best thing to being there." Sometimes an online experience is even better than being there. Thus, a 57-year-old married woman, who frequently has cybersex, comments about her offline ("real") sex: "When I have the real thing, I am thinking of my (online) experiences."[29] Indeed, many people testify that their virtual cybersex is much more active and intense than their actual offline sex.

Computer usage is often compared with that of television, but the similarities are superficial. Indeed, both media entail a visual screen and sound, but whereas television is essentially passive – viewers watch what is offered to them – computer communication is interactive, presenting an exchange of information and a range of social relationships.[30] Although nowadays there are attempts to make television more interactive, this aspect is insignificant in television when compared to interaction on the Internet. The interactive nature is an essential reason why the Internet, rather than television, has gained tremendous momentum as a primary communication medium.

The impact of television on our social life is mainly negative: watching television has reduced social participation as it keeps people at home; the introduction of the telephone, on the other hand, has enhanced social participation. The major reason proposed for the decline in social participation as the result of the introduction of television is time displacement, that is, the time people spend watching television is time in which they are not actively socially engaged. Excessive watching of television, which keeps people at home and leads to reduced physical activity along with reduced social activity, results in diminished physical health and psychological well-being.[31]

Using the Internet also involves physical inactivity and limited face-to-face social interaction, but, like the telephone, it involves social interaction; active interpersonal communication is the dominant way in which the Internet is used at home: much of the time spent online involves social activity as people correspond with other people. In this sense, the social and psychological impact of the Internet is more like that of the telephone than that of television.[32] A social disadvantage of the Internet in comparison with television is that the former is less likely to be used as a group activity, while several people often watch television together. When people watch television, it can easily be relegated from the foreground of attention into background noise, thereby allowing social interaction to continue; when people surf the Internet, however, it is less possible and hence unusual to treat it as a background to social interaction. In comparison to watching television, time spent online involves more social contacts with friends and colleagues, but less social interaction with close family members, such as children. Overall, Internet users spend more time in conversations and sleep less than do television watchers.[33]

There are conflicting findings concerning the social value of the Internet. Some indicate that the Internet facilitates shallow and aggressive behavior as well as loneliness, depression, and lower social support and self-esteem. In contrast, other findings indicate the profound nature of online relating as well as a decrease in loneliness and depression and an increase in social support and self-esteem.[34]

These contradictory findings reflect the complex nature of the Internet and the difficulty in defining a typical Internet user. Thus, there may be general and individual differences in social value when reference is made to cyberlove, sex sites, or online support groups – such as groups for specific chronic illnesses, for weight loss, or for bereavement. The Internet suits most types of personalities, even though it is differently associated with each type. Despite the various prognoses, it may turn out to be the case that people with more extensive offline social contacts will use the new medium more frequently than shy people who have fewer contacts; however, the latter are more likely to achieve more intimate relationships.[35]

The Internet can have a particularly harmful impact in the case of heavy users who often behave in a compulsive manner that makes it difficult to sustain personal or social relationships. However, in cases of more moderate use, the social value of the Internet is evident. Indeed, recent studies indicate the social value of the Internet, while suggesting that its use is most socially beneficial when online interaction supplements, rather than replaces, offline interaction. There is evidence that online social contact supplements the frequency of face-to-face and telephone contact.[36] Online communication can be characterized as a social activity performed alone. This seeming contradiction aptly sums up the unique nature of online communication: communication is a social activity, but online communication is conducted through the privacy of one's computer.

Mobile texting

> When a Roman was returning from a trip, he used to send someone ahead to let his wife know, so as not to surprise her in the act.
>
> Michel de Montaigne

Modern technology continues to improve the methods available for distant relationships. One such recent technological innovation is Short Message Service (SMS), which is a kind of mobile texting. Other types of mobile texting are those made available by Palm Pilots or even mobile computers; here I focus upon mobile phones, which are the most typical and prevalent kind of mobile texting. SMS allows text messages to be sent to and received by mobile telephones. The text can comprise words or numbers or an alphanumeric combination. Mobile texting is essentially similar to paging, but SMS messages do not require the mobile phone to be active and within range, as they are held for a number of days until the phone is active and within range. The SMS is a storing and forwarding service; short messages are not sent directly from sender to recipient, but via an SMS center. The SMS also offers confirmation of message delivery: senders can receive a return message back notifying them whether the short message has been delivered or not. Short messages can also be sent and received simultaneously in voice mode. Furthermore, users of SMS rarely, if ever, get a busy or engaged signal.[37]

The kind of information and style of communication typical of mobile texting is somewhat similar to that of phone conversations. The means of communication in both cases is a phone and the communication is basically in the form of live conversation. The written form of mobile texting requires shorter sentences than those usually employed in phone conversations. Accordingly, a whole new alphabet has emerged because SMS messages took too much time to enter and appeared quite abrupt, as people attempted to say as much as possible with as few keystrokes as possible. Abbreviations such as "C U L8er" for "See you later," which started in online communication, have become more popular and even fashionable in mobile texting. Consider the following message: "AAR8, my Ps wr :-) – they sd ICBW, & tht they wr ha-p 4 the pc&qt . . . IDTS!! I wntd 2 go hm ASAP, 2C my M8s again." The message actually says: "At any rate, my parents were happy. They said that it could be worse, and that they were happy with the peace and quiet. I don't think so! I wanted to go home as soon as possible, to see my friends again." Children's frequent use of SMS shorthand as their first choice of written communication may impede their educational progress in spelling and grammar.

Mobile texting continues the text-based revolution of computer-mediated communication, but uses mobile phones instead of personal computers. In both cases, we are reading a text rather than talking. As compared to mobile texting, online messages are longer, more detailed and profound, and less similar to continuous conversations. In this sense, online communication is closer than mobile texting to letter writing; mobile texting seems to be closer to face-to-face conversations. In comparison to online communication, mobile texting is more continuous, available, immediate, and spontaneous. Like online communication, mobile texting is not intrusive, but it is less anonymous and less detached.

Mobile texting is quite common among teenagers who consider it a more convenient, direct, and private mode of connection. They see email as mostly useful for interactions with adults, whereas mobile texting is a more casual connection, useful for a brief chat or gossip. Mobile texting with its character limit for a text message is seen as a plus because short abrupt messages are perfectly acceptable. Mobile texting is also discreet as messages can be sent and replied to silently, and can therefore be used in public places or late at night in bed. It thus allows them to communicate without the surveillance of parents.[38]

When using mobile texting, people are "always on" – they are always available to their friends or partners. Mobile texting extends the time and location in which people carry out tasks or recreational activities. Thus, it enables them to interact with friends while moving or while on a train or in a crowd. The constant interaction increases participants' sense of belonging to a social group and makes them feel that others are thinking about them. This is one aspect of the social value of mobile texting. On the other hand, valuable social boundaries are blurred when one is always on call. One significant boundary that may collapse as a result is the line between our private and public lives. The privacy of home is no longer protected from the invasion of work obligations, colleagues, friends, or lovers. In a private situation, the intrusion of those from our public life can disturb or unsettle our social or private life, as the sudden "presence" of an outsider may switch our attention from close relationships to distant ones.[39]

Mobile texting is also most useful for communicating matters that one has not the courage to do by talking. Thus, it is easier to express interest in a potential romantic partner via mobile texting as this is a more neutral medium and one thus avoids the possibility of face-to-face rejection. Sending a bland message, such as "That was a nice party," can test the other's attitude – the other can ignore the initiative and hence signal disinterest, or respond and thereby express interest.[40] Online communication is similar in this regard, but, since mobile texting is closer to everyday conversations, the latter is a more neutral vehicle.

Mobile texting is a very useful and convenient means for flirting, as it suits the superficiality and brevity that characterizes flirting. It also has practical uses that regular online communication lacks. Thus, "interpersonal awareness devices" have been evolving recently. Such devices send a text description of potential romantic matches who are nearby at that moment. The just-in-this-time, just-in-this-place matchmaking service illustrates the greater integration of mobile texting into ordinary everyday life than of online communication. This makes mobile texting more susceptible to actual hazards. In a sense, the mobile telephone is evolving into a kind of remote control for people's lives; those controlling the remote control can easily harm us.[41]

Mobile texting provides the modern and light version of written flirtatious communication. Indeed, a sizeable proportion of SMS users choose SMS for asking someone out on a date.[42] It is highly likely that in the future the use of mobile texting and online communication for romantic purposes will be significantly greater.

The egalitarian space

A woman without a man is like a fish without a bicycle.
Gloria Steinem

The interactive nature of cyberspace has a profound impact upon its social structure. The ability to shape your virtual society eradicates many social constraints, particularly status differences. One does not have to be the product of many years of evolution, personal development, and luck in order to share the advantages enjoyed by handsome and rich people. In the virtual reality of cyberspace, these advantages are open to everyone.

Cyberspace is indeed an egalitarian medium – theoretically, everyone can have access and everyone is treated equally regardless of personal characteristics such as external appearance, gender, color, religion, race, age, disability, social status, and income level. People are connecting on the basis of what they have to say, and what is on their mind. While income level, education, and place of abode can clearly limit the access of everyone to the Internet, decreases in costs of computers and advancements in the developing world's education and infrastructure are projected to make the Internet increasingly more accessible to many more people. The digital divide is indeed shrinking.[43] There are, however, other characteristics, such as creativity, intellect, interests, wit, a sense of humor, and the ability to respond quickly in a witty manner, that give an edge to those who possess such skills, and this makes the Internet less egalitarian. As a married man who has a cybersex relationship notes: "I'm a good writer and a fast typist so my partners seem to enjoy themselves."[44]

The egalitarian nature of cyberspace is also expressed in the fact that the demographic characteristics of cyberspace users increasingly resemble those of the general population. This is particularly striking concerning gender differences. In one comprehensive study conducted in the USA in 1994, only 5% of those in cyberspace were women; in 1998, nearly 39% were women, and now women outnumber men online.[45] Physical gender differences are less significant online as people can choose to present themselves as a member of the opposite sex. Consider the following statement:

> I've been playing in Lesbian chat rooms for almost 5 months now. I present myself as a 30-something lesbian single mom. I have pictures of a very attractive young woman that I am willing to share. The only problem is they are not me. I'm a middle aged, married male and this has been one of the most powerful experiences of my life. The Internet is a real gender blender.[46]

In cyberspace, gender differences are limited to the mental realm where boundaries are much more flexible.

Age differences are also less important in cyberspace. As one woman wrote about her online lover: "He was a few years older than me, but I figured age didn't matter if we have a good chat."[47] Indeed, people of all ages interact with each other, and this can have negative as well as positive consequences. There is particular concern over the ease with which pedophiles can take advantage of this and lure children into online sexual activities and then into face-to-face activities.

Another important egalitarian aspect of the Net is that specific sectors of society such as those who are physically disadvantaged, sick, older, younger, shy, unattractive, homosexual, bisexual, and transsexual, may find the Net a very attractive place to initiate and maintain romantic and sexual relationships.

The fact that the properties assigned to "netizens" (people who frequently use the Internet) are essentially self-described properties makes cyberspace egalitarian in yet another respect: some properties that netizens claim to possess are remarkably similar – especially those that improve their image. Thus, before becoming involved in cybersex, most women report wearing a thong, a garter belt with black stockings, their best Wonderbra, and a pair of high heels. Men report simply that they are naked and wearing just a smile. Similarly, Gloria Brame wrote that one day she received the following message: "I have a big one 4U: 9½ inches." Later on, she found many other similar men: "To my surprise, a breathtakingly large percentage of men who cruised the chat rooms were similarly blessed. Could it be that the magnetic rays from monitors are causing men's genitals to mutate?"[48] In a similar manner, Sherrie Schneider claims that online male lovers are alike in yet another characteristic – they seem to be very caring for their parents during the weekend: "You have never seen so many men with elderly sick parents who have to be visited on Saturday nights. It is unbelievable! But that doesn't mean that on Tuesday or Thursday night, he won't try to sleep with you."[49]

In light of its egalitarian nature, cyberspace is somewhat similar to a huge commune – a kind of mentally nude commune. People feel free to strip off their mental mask and unload their secret desires. Imagination, which paints cyberspace in more intense and seductive colors, also helps people satisfy some of their profound desires. This does not mean, however, that personality differences or differences relating to gender, race, and age completely disappear,[50] as such differences are connected to psychological, social, and physical differences that are not automatically eliminated by online communication.

The lure of the Net

So many men, so little time.

Mae West

The major features responsible for the great romantic seductiveness of cyberspace are imagination, interactivity, availability, and anonymity. The first two features indicate the major benefit stemming from the nature of cyberspace – the chance to conduct exciting, interactive engagements. The other two features refer to the agent's connection with this space and in particular to the possible cost of this connection – availability indicates the low cost in engaging in online activities, and anonymity the low risk in doing so.[51]

Imagination, which plays a major role in cyberspace, makes this space seductive since it can free us from the limits imposed by our bodies and by our contexts.[52] As I indicate in the detailed discussion of imagination in chapter 4, imagination has hardly any practical constraints, and it enables one to depict oneself and the other in a most positive and seductive light – much better than in reality. Online imagination can also complete, in an exciting manner, details upon which our online companions might remain vague. Imagination can, therefore, entertain our wildest fantasies. As someone who has participated in cybersex says: "Just as in personal fantasy, you don't have to worry about mechanics – your legs stretch as wide open as you wish, there are no unseemly smells or tastes or textures, and your partner looks precisely as good as you want him or her to look."[53] The imaginary nature of cyberspace makes it easier to idealize the other; and idealization is an essential element in romantic love.

Interactivity is what distinguishes cyberspace from other imaginative realities. In cyberspace people are not merely imagining themselves to be with an attractive person, they are actually interacting with such a person. Indeed, the reported actions are sexually more daring and exciting. As one woman remarks: "With cybersex, you can let your fantasies run wild. I've done things in cyberspace that I would never have done with someone in real life."[54]

The interactivity of cyberspace fosters a crucial aspect of romantic relationships: reciprocity. Mutual attraction is the most highly valued characteristic in a potential mate – this is true for both sexes.[55] People like to hear that they are desired. It is easier to express reciprocity in cyberspace, as it requires fewer resources or real actions, and self-disclosure is greater.

Cyberspace is an alternative, *available* environment providing us with easy access to many available and desired options. It is easy and not costly to reach desired partners and easy to perform desired actions. It is easier to find romantic partners in cyberspace than at bars, shopping malls, or supermarkets. Cyberspace is also highly available in the sense that it is highly accessible (for the time being, more so in the Western world than in other parts of the world). Connections to cyberspace are everywhere – home, work, hotels, and even cafes – and logging in is simple and inexpensive. The great accessibility and convenience of cyberspace make people feel comfortable about entering this space and staying there. One does not have to do much or invest significant resources in order to step into this imaginative paradise. Millions of people are eagerly waiting for you on the Net every moment of the day. They are available and it is easy to find them. (You must remember, however, that, as is true in offline life, most of those people will not suit or interest you.) The great availability is associated with frequent novel changes, and this makes cyberspace more dynamic, unstable, and exciting. In this sense, online communication combines features of both interpersonal and mass communication.[56]

The *anonymity* associated with cyberspace reduces the risks of online activities. Such anonymity decreases vulnerability and the weight of social norms, and hence makes people feel safer and freer to act according to their desires. In offline circumstances, the fear of harmful consequences is one of the major obstacles to conducting many romantic affairs and to significant self-disclosure in those that are conducted. Because of the greater sense of security, self-disclosure is also more prevalent in cyberspace – this in turn increases intimacy and, accordingly, the seductiveness of online relationships is further enhanced.

The above features of cyberspace increase the lure of the Net and make people feel more excited, comfortable, free, and safe while engaging in an online romantic affair. A woman notes: **"I experienced cybersex for the first time and I have never been so turned on in my life! It gave birth to and brought out my 'animal.' We reveled in fantasyland. It was a constant daily fever – what a rush."**[57] It has been claimed that cyberspace enables one to have more sex, better sex, and different sex. Since many moral and practical constraints are lifted in the Net, people can more easily make sexual contacts when and with whom they want. Cybersex can be more intense, relaxed, and satisfactory – it may also be conducted with people who are not available for offline sexual activities.[58] Cyberspace provides an easy and desired alternative to the difficult circumstances of real life. When attempts are made to transfer this alternative to offline affairs, some of its advantages may disappear. As Lisa remarks:

> I personally have only had cybersex with one person – and although I was alone, it was probably the best sex of my life. Would I want to have real sex with this guy? Of course I think I would, but I'm smart enough to know that it is the separation of reality and fantasy that makes the whole cybersex thing so sexy.[59]

The risky space

> One can find a woman who never had one love affair, but it is rare indeed to find anyone who had only one.
>
> La Rochefoucauld

The great seductiveness of cyberspace and the ease of becoming involved in online affairs also entail risks: people are easily carried away and underestimate the risks of surfing the Net. Moreover, cyberspace does not merely satisfy needs, but creates novel needs that often cannot be met. Thus, the apparent ease of finding true and everlasting love in cyberspace creates the need to have such "perfect" love. Of course, that is far from simple to achieve. Online affairs are like a new toy with which the human race has not yet learned how to play. People may confuse the toy with reality and ruin their life.

Cybering is similar, in a few significant senses, to taking drugs. Both provide easy access to pleasure, which is often based upon virtual realities. In both cases, the tempting results can make people dangerously addicted to the method; people want more and more, but satisfaction is limited and becomes more costly to achieve. An unfulfilled craving for drugs and cybering can cause great distress. Once the first steps are taken in online affairs or drugs, the situation can often run its own course, almost involuntarily. Whereas drugs artificially stimulate pleasure centers in the brain, online conversations artificially stimulate pleasure centers in the mind. Artificial stimulation may appear to be easy and cheap; however, the price can be dear in terms of our overall performance and, in particular, in terms of the price that those close to us in our offline lives might have to pay. The "high" that many people receive from online interaction quickly fades and is replaced by the more dull and routine aspects of everyday life. Moreover, as with drugs, getting "high" online may require more and more doses of imagination – which in turn may further increase the gap between actual reality and cyberspace. Thus, Elaine reports:

> When my husband started having cybersex, at first it turned me on and he let me watch. Afterwards we would have great sex! Then after a while he started doing it behind my back. I caught him several times and he promised he would quit. Of course he did not. I believe he is truly addicted to cybersex. I think it is an addiction just like drugs.[60]

The risk of compulsive behavior in using the Internet may be considered to be even greater than that of drugs in the sense that with drugs, the danger is apparent and well known, and accordingly a large portion of the population does not use them. The Internet is used by almost everyone and its risks are not obvious, so one may fail to take precautions against them.

A significant advantage of cyberspace is that it is different: it provides desirable situations over and above those found in offline circumstances. It is not an advantage however, if people are unable to draw the lines between online and offline worlds. Blurring the lines is dangerous as it abolishes the advantages of each world. Learning to live within two worlds is difficult as well. The price of the greater freedom available online is the risk of being captured by your own desire. As the Eagles put it in their "Hotel California": "we are all just prisoners here of our own device." Cyberspace should complement, rather than substitute for, offline life. Accordingly, people should be moderate in their use of the Internet; thus, they might limit the amount of time they spend online. In light of the great lure of cyberspace, such limitation is hard to achieve.

The lack of practical and social constraints in online relationships increases the frequency and intensity not merely of positive emotions, but also of negative emotions. The intense love experienced in cyberspace involves the risk of intense disappointment when the online love affair is abruptly ended. Consider the following account, in which a woman describes her relationship with someone she met in a chat room:

> I was falling madly in love with this man, though we had never met. He cheated on me with another Internet partner, met her and married her. It has been three years and I still cannot get over him. I feel my heart has been permanently damaged because I have never felt that way about anyone before or since him.[61]

In the same way that some people express their sexual desires online in ways that they would be unable to use face to face, some people may express their hatred or anger online in ways that they never would in a face-to-face encounter. Similarly, while many people in cyberspace are ready to help someone they do not know and are unlikely to meet, other people express extreme aggression and violence toward people they do not know.

It is quite easy to spread anonymous slander and offensive rumors in cyberspace. This may pose a real risk to the democratic nature of our society. When a slander appears in a newspaper, one can deny it in the same newspaper; when slander is spread in cyberspace, there is no way of reaching all the people who encountered it. The Internet increases the risk of social polarization as it makes it easy for like-minded people to interact and hence push each other into extreme and hateful attitudes. The risk of avoiding rational deliberations and surrendering to popular pressure increases in such circumstances.[62] The huge amount of information available on the Net may be morally negative and psychologically stressful if there is no way of evaluating the credibility of the information.

The apparent safety of cyberspace may be illusory – harassment and risky activities are also common on the Net. Thus, a recent survey has revealed that one in four children in the United Kingdom have been bullied or threatened via their mobile phone or personal computers. Children as young as eleven are being faced with taunts or threats from an often-anonymous source. They either do not tell anyone and suffer in silence, or confide in people who themselves do not know how to deal with this effectively. In extreme cases, such harassment may even lead to suicide.[63] The realm of online opportunities also tempts people to do things that are dangerous for them, for example, losing money, falling victim to various types of fraud, and forging connections with criminals. People who are depressed or undergoing a personal crisis are particularly vulnerable when surfing the Net. Thus, one father reported that his son, who was a soldier, spent a lot of time on the Internet. His military service severely depressed him, and one day he took his rifle and committed suicide. After his son's death, the father entered the sites that his son had visited just before his suicide and found that some of them encourage visitors to commit suicide and even provide specific directions on how to do so successfully.

The four factors that enhance the lure of the Net – that is, imagination, interactivity, availability, and anonymity – are associated with risk. Imagination may lead to blurring the distinction between reality and fantasy. Interactivity is associated not merely with greater excitement but also with actual dangers that the other person may inflict upon us. Great availability of a variety of options may result in mental stress associated with a "saturated self" who is unable to make practical choices.[64] Anonymity makes it much easier to practice deception.

The risks associated with the great lure of the Net should not prevent us from surfing there, but should make us behave more carefully and moderately while we are online. As a 48-year-old married woman, who had an online affair, notes: "Cybersex can enhance your home life experiences but you must be careful not to make it a priority." Another woman having an online affair has a similar view: "I guess my advice to others would be to TAKE IT SLOW!! Sometimes you get carried away, and it seems like a fantasy."[65]

Summary

> Nobody in his right mind would call me a nymphomaniac. I only have cybersex with witty men.
>
> Unknown

Cyberspace is a psychological reality in which imagination plays a crucial role. Imaginative activity is not a new feature; imagination has always been an integral part of human life. The novelty of cyberspace lies in the magnitude of the imaginary aspect and in particular in its interactive nature. Such interactivity has made this psychological reality a social reality as well: imaginary actions have become common practice for many people. This has revolutionized the role of imagination in personal relationships and has promoted imagination from being a peripheral tool used at best by artists, and at worst by dreamers and others who, it was considered, had nothing better to do, to a central means of personal relationship for many ordinary people who have busy, involved lives, but prefer to interact online. Although some areas of cyberspace can be regarded as electronic bedrooms, in other areas different types of personal relationships flourish.

Online communication is significantly different from other types of remote communication, such as phone conversations and writing conventional letters. Online communication is easier to pursue, as it requires no paper, envelope, stamp, or mail box as letter writing does; it does not require the other person to answer the phone, nor does it risk calling at an inconvenient time for your partner. Online communication is more immediate than writing letters and more voluntary and less intruding than phone conversations. Relationships that are conducted merely via letter writing or phone conversations are too close to conventional face-to-face relationships and hence cannot present a real alternative to them. Accordingly, such means typically supplement face-to-face relationships – when those are not feasible – but do not replace them. Online relationships seem to be the first real alternative to face-to-face relationships.

A further development of modern communication is SMS (Short Message Service) in which text messages are sent to and received by mobile telephones. Such a kind of mobile texting continues the text-based revolution of computer-mediated communication. When it comes to flirting, mobile texting provides a more lightweight and superficial version of written communication.

The interactive nature of cyberspace has a profound impact upon other characteristics of this space. Two such characteristics are its egalitarian and seductive aspects. Cyberspace is egalitarian in the sense that many features that are significant in everyday life, such as external appearance, age, gender, race, and religion, are scarcely relevant in online relationships.

The main features contributing to the great seductiveness of cyberspace are imagination, interactivity, availability, and anonymity. The first two features indicate the major benefit of such a space – that is, being engaged in exciting, interactive deeds. The other two features refer to the low cost and decreased risk of engaging in online activities.

We should be aware of the downsides of online relationships – in particular, of the possibility of becoming addicted to cyberspace, in the way that people can become addicted to drugs. In both cases, there is artificial stimulation of the pleasure centers, and the distinction between reality and illusion is blurred. Online relationships also involve the dangers of meeting unscrupulous people and of experiencing disappointments that could shatter the dreams of the people involved.

2 *The paradoxical nature of online relationships*

I date this girl for two years – and then the nagging starts: "I wanna know your name . . ."

Mike Binder

After discussing some of the novel aspects of cyberspace in the previous chapter, I turn now to discuss the nature of online relationships. I will show that such novelty, and in particular the interactive nature of virtual reality, offers us a new type of personal relationship. Such relationships characteristically have features typical of both close and remote offline relationships. The coexistence of these opposing features cannot be found in offline relationships. Although my discussion is focused upon heterosexual relationships, most of the claims are valid for homosexual or bisexual relationships as well.

Detached attachment

If it weren't for the fact that the TV set and the refrigerator are so far apart, some of us wouldn't get any exercise at all.

Joey Adams

A friend of mine told me that when he was married to his second wife, he met a wonderful woman and fell deeply in love with her. He did not know how to solve his difficult situation and after long deliberations he came up with the following brilliant idea: their relationship, he suggested, would be that of detached attachment. The woman replied that this was not close enough for her. He then got divorced and married this woman, with whom he still lives happily.

Detached attachment (or "detattachment") is indeed difficult to conduct offline, as a romantic relationship is typically characterized by direct, continuous contact – settling for less is painful. However, what seems to be an obvious paradox in actual-space – that is, intimate closeness at a distance – can prevail in cyberspace. Sometimes an intense online romantic attachment is between people who are physically separated and who are committed in some way or another to a different romantic relationship. The other commitment and physical separation make the relationship detached, but the intense emotions sustain the great attachment.

Human beings have never before had access to such an ambivalent type of romantic relationship. This possibility presents an entirely different ball game in the field of personal interactions. In this exciting, novel game, the rules and consequences are also different.

The following are major opposing aspects of online romantic relationships:

1. distance and immediacy;
2. lean and rich communication;
3. anonymity and self-disclosure;
4. sincerity and deception;
5. continuity and discontinuity;
6. marginal physical investment and considerable mental investment.

Distance and immediacy

One of the advantages of living alone is that you don't have to wake up in the arms of a loved one.

Marion Smith

In typical, offline relationships, two intimate friends are geographically close, and, when they are not together, they are generally aware of each other's approximate location. Online relationships exist between people who are spatially separated. This separation can consist of great physical distance, and the two online friends may not even know each other's exact geographical location. Physical distance becomes irrelevant in cyberspace; some people even speak about the death of (physical) distance. Although each person uses the Internet from different locales, while they are in cyberspace they are actually in the same space.[1]

Online personal relationships are immediate in a temporal sense – two lovers can communicate with no significant time delay – and in the sense that there is no human third party that mediates the conversation. In cyberspace, physical location is of less importance – we could say that this space enables a person to be in two places at the same time, or at least to be detached from her physical context. Despite the spatial separation, everything is close in cyberspace: everywhere is just a typing distance away if you have a modem or high-speed Internet access. Although your lover may be 3,000 miles away, it feels to you as if he or she is just next door, or even inside the room. As one married woman testifies: "We also have a very wonderful time when we chat, so wonderful that it actually feels like we are in the same room doing the things we are typing."[2]

In light of the temporal immediacy, emotional immediacy is present as well: people can express their spontaneous, authentic emotional reactions, as is done in offline relationships. However, in online relationships, people also have the choice of postponing their reaction, in order to allow time to moderate their response. This option seldom exists in offline relationships where the person is in front of you and you are expected to respond at once.

Together with its temporal immediacy and speed, cyberspace enables people to lose track of time and space and to be drawn into an alternative, imaginary environment where the speed of time and the spatial location are more malleable. On the one hand, in this alternative world, time may slow down in the sense that people do not rush to do things; they take their time. On the other hand, while chatting online, time goes by at an amazing pace. In such experiences time seems to pass differently to the way it usually does.[3]

The anonymity and safety of cyberspace enable netizens to be more explicit and direct than they are in offline situations. An online affair is not only shaped by our own fantasies and is therefore less likely to disappoint us, but it is also free from criticism of a third party. While in the actual world our attraction to another person is altered by the way other people view this person, in cyberspace we do not see them through the critical eyes of other people and this allows a more direct interaction.

The direct manner of interaction is evident concerning sexual relations and other intimate matters – such as whether they have children, their marital status, or drinking habits – that many people consider significant but that are usually not explicitly discussed in initial face-to-face meetings. Such anonymity is particularly valuable for shy people or for social groups (such as women) who are expected, according to social norms, to display shyness or modesty.[4]

Further technological inventions may be able to offer online relationships some features of offline relationships that are currently not available online. Thus, whereas nowadays cybersex consists of written messages, future developments may enable people to transmit tactile sensations. There is already a cybersex suit, which interacts with a DVD recording, and can deliver sensations to various parts of the body at the command of specially adapted adult movies. It is plausible to assume that further developments may enable such sensations in one-to-one interactions. NASA has actually developed a similar system in order to enable astronauts in space to conduct virtual sexual relationships with their partners.

Online relationships can be considered direct in another important sense: the participants are engaged in a direct, intimate conversation about issues they care about. They do not have to beat around the bush. Accordingly, superficial politeness is less common on the Net; emotional sincerity is more important. It is not necessary to be polite and respond to every message that is sent; if you do not want to pursue a particular online relationship, you can simply not respond to the writer. No excuses or avoiding strategies are required: you can just say "No" or say nothing. An online romantic relationship is direct because it is more to the point; in this sense, it is emotionally purer, having less "noise" stemming from traditional norms or practical constraints. Indeed, people often consider online sexual relationships as "just pure pleasure."

Imagination enables people to perceive themselves as detached from their body and this sets them free to perform activities they would not do if they were in the actual physical vicinity of their online partner. A great emotional intimacy is achieved since the body, which is the source of moral and mental constraints in personal relationships, does not interfere; the possibility of leaving their bodies at home makes it easier for correspondents to reveal their thoughts and minds. The lack of any physical contact has certain purifying aspects – it appears as though pure spirit travels faster through the modem.

Cyberspace allows each person more breathing space. However, this space still allows two lovers to feel as if they are directly connected – as if their bodies do not interfere, allowing their minds to be in direct communication; they feel as if their minds are melting. As one woman writes: "I don't know what it's like to touch this man, yet he has touched me a thousand times in my dreams." Accordingly, the two partners often describe each other as part of their soul, as "soul mates." Thus, one woman says: "I believe he is my soul mate, even though I can't see him, I feel him near me." Getting to know each other online is considered to be an almost spiritual enterprise in which a deeper and purer kind of interaction takes place: "You don't have all the distractions of how someone looks. It's mind to mind and spirit to spirit talking." Accordingly, cybersex may not seem pure enough: "We started to engage in cybersex, but he stopped it saying that he sensed something special beginning and didn't want to ruin it."[5] The physical separation forces the online relationship to maintain its freshness and spirituality; in this sense, it is like a continuous period of courtship. Hence, online affairs may keep their high intensity even if they persevere over a long time.

Lean and rich communication

Your mind is what interests me the most.

Bumper sticker

Face-to-face communication relies on many sources of information in addition to the verbal one: facial expressions, voice, posture, hands, gaze, focus, and so on. Such sources provide crucial signals for communicating our emotions and understanding the other person's attitudes. Online communication relies on fewer sources and is often based merely on written messages. The lack of visual content seems to be a particularly significant deficiency. Our eyes are of central importance in revealing our emotional attitudes. Sometimes, one look in the eyes conveys more profound information than many words. We say, "A picture is worth a thousand words."

Some online communications use icons – termed "emoticons" or "smilies" – to signify the emotional state of the sender. Although these icons may substitute detailed descriptions of present emotions, they still constitute information which senders are aware of and deliberately convey. Nonverbal communication often involves information that the subject is not fully aware of and does not always want to convey to other people.

The lack of nonverbal information in text-based online communication led some researchers to claim that such communication is leaner and hence online relationships are less involving, less rich, and less personal than offline relationships.[6] It is true that not all types of information available in face-to-face communication are also available in online communication; in this sense, the latter is leaner. However, this does not mean that online relationships are necessarily less involving, less rich, or less personal than offline relationships.

Fewer vehicles of communication can provide richer information than a greater number of communicative vehicles; in this sense, less can mean more. Quality does not merely derive from quantity. In a certain type of communication, people may be ready to provide more profound information than they would in communication based on a greater number of communicative vehicles (which is thus potentially richer). Text-based communication with a sincere person may provide richer information than a face-to-face meeting with another person. Indeed, as compared to face-to-face communication, online communication involves higher proportions of more intimate questions and lower proportions of peripheral questions. Online interactants seem to make more attributions from fewer cues.[7] Although in some cases online impressions of the other, and hence romantic relationships, may take longer to develop, over time they can become as profound and as intimate as in offline circumstances.[8]

Although involving fewer communicative vehicles, online communication has one feature that is absent from offline communication: multi-conversing, that is, the ability to conduct a conversation simultaneously, but nevertheless privately, with a few people at the same time.[9] This type of communication, which prevails in chat rooms and instant messaging, further increases the ability to conduct several romantic relationships at the same time.

In both offline and online romantic relationships, understanding your partner's mind is complex and involves much more than merely reading faces or messages; it involves paying attention to many subtle cues. This is especially true in online communication, where there are fewer sources of information. Reading your partner's mind in online communication consists of reading both the lines and between the lines. The kinds of words chosen, the speed of the response, the length and frequency of messages are all cues to your partner's perception of the type and quality of the relationship. Thus, a fast response indicates great interest, whereas a slow response suggests lack of enthusiasm.

This kind of reading sensitivity is so developed in online communication that people often say that their online lovers can read their mind better than their spouses can. Detecting, for example, that someone had a difficult day at work is often easier for an offline partner than an online partner. This is so since in offline relationships people must communicate with each other even if they have had a difficult day. However, the online lover, lacking many types of sensory information, must be sensitive to every signal conveyed by the other person – otherwise, their relationship cannot develop further. We may say then that, whereas in offline marital relationships seeing one another daily may make each spouse take the other for granted – and hence become blind to the other – in online relationships the inability to see the other prevents both partners from taking the other for granted and this enables each to perceive the other more clearly.

Online communication is often so profound that people maintain that it almost feels unnecessary since the correspondents seem to have the same thoughts, feelings, and dreams. Thus, a married woman writes about her communication with a married man: "We both knew what our hearts were feeling at the time without having to say a word. I feel like I've known Rob all of my life." Another married woman testifies about her online affair: "We knew what we thought before we spoke it." Maggie, an Argentinean woman having an online affair with Walt, an American man, writes: "We know what each other is going to type before the other has the chance to. We even argue like an old married couple." Ruth writes: "Many times we had written the same ideas at the same time. He was even able to know the perfume I wore without me saying a word about it to him, and it is not a usual fragrance either!"[10] Hence, people sometimes say that they feel as if the words on the screen actually touch them.

The different types of communication typical of offline and online romantic relationships influence the type of information conveyed. In face-to-face meetings, people have little control over a large portion of the conveyed information. This is particularly true concerning the physical aspect that is a significant part of it. In online relationships, self-presentation is carefully chosen and the physical aspect is considerably less significant.

The reliance of online relationships on one type of communication may sometimes lead to negative emotions due to misunderstanding. Thus, something that is intended ironically may cause the other person to feel insulted and angry. In offline relationships, other cues carried by eye contact, facial expression, or tone of voice may clarify and contextualize the irony or humor, so that the intention behind the words becomes obvious; in online communication, such balancing factors are absent. The lean communication of online relationships may also generate intense positive emotions because the negative aspects of the correspondent tend to remain concealed.

Brenda Danet suggests considering online typed communication as being both an attenuated and an enhanced means of communication in comparison to speech and writing. It is attenuated writing because the text is no longer a tangible physical object; it is enhanced writing since it is more immediate, interactive, and dynamic than ordinary writing. Online communication can also be viewed as attenuated speech, because it is a kind of attenuated conversation; it is enhanced speech since, unlike ordinary speech, it leaves traces, and can therefore be re-examined for a long time afterwards. Email communication is characterized by a distinctive combination of oral and written styles. The new medium invites informality even in business or official contexts. It is a kind of "interactive written discourse."[11]

The different mediums of communication online give rise to different depths in online relationships. Some of these relationships are highly random, shallow, and last less than a few minutes; others are serious, intensive, and last for months or years. It is not the case, however, that a leaner medium is also associated with a shallower relationship. Despite the usually lean nature of online communication, it gives rise to profound personal relationships. What is important in this regard is the nature of connectivity rather than the content.

A means of communication that enables richer content to be sent is not necessarily preferable to a leaner means of communication. Thus, when videophones eventually become as cheap as telephones, they will not necessarily become more popular than phones are. Similarly, email is the most popular online communication despite the presence of other richer means of online communication. In certain circumstances, people prefer the use of leaner types of communication. Such circumstances include instances when richer communication might threaten the impression that the agent wishes to give or when a leaner type of communication might enhance that impression. Thus, the leaner nature of communication might be preferred when one's external appearance could be an obstacle to forming a meaningful relationship or when one's sense of humor can be more readily demonstrated.[12]

So far, online relationships have mainly been based upon text-based communication. However, it is already possible to add visual and audible information to such relationships. In the future, it is likely that other sensory information, such as tactile and olfactory information, will be included as well, thus closing the gap between offline and online relationships. Such developments will make online relationships more attractive, but will also eliminate their advantages. In order to avoid losing these advantages, people will need to be able to introduce various types of sensory information at their own pace, according to their own choice. For some people, introducing visual information at the beginning of the relationship may be suitable, while others may prefer to continue the relationship via written messages alone, until the relationship has matured.

Anonymity and self-disclosure

> Women might be able to fake orgasms. But men can fake whole relationships.
>
> Sharon Stone

Two seemingly contrasting features of online relationships are: greater anonymity and greater self-disclosure. Anonymity is associated with concealment, which is contradictory to self-disclosure. However, greater anonymity typically facilitates greater self-disclosure, and in turn increases familiarity and intimacy.

Self-disclosure is significant in online relationships. As one man said: "when you're on a one-on-one with somebody, people really reveal a lot of their soul to you. And you are entrusted to keep what you have there as sacred property, because they share a piece of theirselves with you."[13] Indeed, several studies have found that there is faster and more profound self-disclosure in online communication than in face-to-face meetings.[14] This may be attributed to several major reasons: (a) greater anonymity and reduced vulnerability, (b) lack of "gating features," (c) lack of other means to know each other, and (d) greater ease in finding similar others.

(a) Greater anonymity and reduced vulnerability

In online relationships people can be partially or fully anonymous: people can conceal their true identity or important aspects of it. Anonymity in online relationships facilitates self-disclosure as it reduces the risks involved in disclosing intimate information about oneself. People can express themselves more freely since they are more anonymous, less accountable, and hence less vulnerable. Because of our sensitivity regarding our loved ones, the person closest to us may never know our deepest secrets or desires.[15] A woman may be nervous about telling her spouse her sexual fantasies – for fear it may ruin their relationship. However, she may readily tell her online lover about such fantasies without fear of repercussions. A 33-year-old married woman, who loves to cyber, writes: "Sometimes there are things you like to fantasize about that you can share online and don't feel comfortable sharing with your significant other."[16]

In offline personal relationships, such as marriage, there is less room for mistakes: one or several significant mistakes may wound the spouse in a way that will terminate the relationship or severely harm its quality. Although marriage vows state "for better or for worse," and marriage is held to be a life-long commitment, a few mistakes – or even a single significant mistake – may still jeopardize the whole relationship. You risk profoundly insulting your spouse if you describe your fantasies of having an extramarital affair or if you reveal your dislike of some elements in the spouse's external appearance. Indeed, the perceived threat to an intimate relationship is the most commonly cited reason for not discussing one's sexual needs and preferences with one's partner.[17]

Such great vulnerability, which stems from sincere self-disclosure, is less typical of online relationships for various reasons. First, there are fewer practical ways in which the online partner can actually harm you: the fear of actual retaliation or mental disapproval is not significant. Second, it is less likely that the online partner will be insulted by fantasies, as the whole relationship consists of fantasies. Third, even if the online partner is insulted and consequently terminates the relationship, the harm can often be undone, as there are many other available partners. No wonder many participants in online affairs often declare that they have told each other "absolutely everything"; they speak about things online that they have never revealed to anyone else, including their spouses. It is often just like talking to a best friend. As Ruth, a single mother of four daughters, writes: "In this man, I found not only romance and love, but also a best friend."[18]

The conflict between openness and closedness (revealing–concealing, expressiveness–protectiveness) is typical of offline personal relationships, especially for stigmatized groups, such as those involving homosexuality, HIV-positive status, AIDS, sexual abuse, drug addiction, alcoholism, mental illness, and epilepsy. This conflict is considerably reduced in cyberspace. Take, for example, homosexuals who may experience anxiety in disclosing their sexual orientation, and yet for whom failure to disclose this endangers their true self.[19] In the anonymity of cyberspace, disclosing one's true feelings is much easier. Accordingly, it is more likely that in cyberspace the process of self-disclosure will be linear, moving in a unidirectional and cumulative fashion from nondisclosure to near full disclosure. In offline circumstances, the opposing urges to reveal and to conceal makes people oscillate between guarded self-concealment and candid self-disclosure.[20]

Writing to a stranger is in a sense similar to writing in a diary.[21] In both cases, you can freely express your thoughts and such self-disclosure does not make you vulnerable. The advantage of online relationships over writing in a diary is their interactive nature: your thoughts will be read by a real human being, who is ready to offer some comfort or advice for coping with difficult circumstances.

Online self-disclosure also resembles the "strangers on a train" phenomenon, where people sometimes share intimate information with their anonymous seatmate.[22] Since anonymity in cyberspace is greater than on a train, revealing intimate personal details is more common in cyberspace. Online relationships enable people to hide behind a form of communication that is somewhat "removed from life." It is easier to open up to a faceless stranger that you do not have to look at while revealing your secret or to see the next morning. For similar reasons, priests remain concealed when they hear confessions. All these cases support the notion that fear of being embarrassed or being the object of contempt is considerably reduced when the listener is not present or is not seen, or is unlikely to be seen again.

In other circumstances, the listener can be present and seen, but he or she is in a position that cannot hurt you. This is the case, for example, of a therapist, lawyer, or a priest. In the professional presence of such functionaries, you can freely express your emotions and whatever is on your mind without risking hurt. Hence, standard offline rules that guard and limit your behavior and emotional expression are suspended. This freedom enables you to open up and become closer to these functionaries. It is not surprising that people often fall in love with their therapist, lawyer, or priest. Online relations are similar in this regard: people can freely express their emotions and become emotionally close without being vulnerable. Accordingly, it is also easier to fall in love on the Net.

The connection between anonymity and vulnerability also explains why voicing your honest negative opinion about a certain person is easier when you do not have a personal relationship with that person or when he or she is not in your physical vicinity and therefore is unable to harm you. Anonymity and lack of practical implications greatly facilitate the sincere expression of attitudes.

Despite the reduced vulnerability in cyberspace, the online agent can be hurt as well. In this regard, two major aspects are significant: (a) most of the many high hopes that cyberspace generates are not fulfilled – thereby causing frequent and profound disappointments; and (b) profound self-disclosure leaves the agent's mind naked, without any masks to protect her – and this is a highly vulnerable position for anyone.

In online communication, people can disappear the moment they so wish. This ability facilitates the disclosure of intimate information. Online relationships enable people to disclose personal information when they feel ready to do so and in the manner in which they choose. In offline relationships, the manner and pace of self-disclosure are, to a great extent, less voluntary and hence are associated with greater emotional and social tension.

Online relationships typically have fewer practical implications than have offline relationships; hence, participants in these relationships are less vulnerable. Indeed, in offline relationships, people tend not to reveal much intimate information until they feel safe. In cyberspace, people are ready to disclose more intimate information since they assume that anonymity and spatial distance reduce the risk of harmful consequences. Sex in cyberspace is safe not only in the physical sense, since viruses cannot travel in that space, but also in the psychological sense that is provided by being anonymous. Since feeling safe is a major precondition for sexual arousal, the safety provided by cyberspace may explain the vast interest in cybersex.[23]

Cyberspace also provides the opposite conditions that are often involved in sexual arousal: novelty, risk, and unpredictability. In this sense, the great excitement of cybersex may be connected to the not-so-unusual desire to have sex in strange or public places, such as a park, public toilet, spa, parked car, office, or airplanes. Both cybersex and public sex involve these features of novelty, risk, and unpredictability. Having cybersex in a workplace or at your home while your partner is around may also be considered as public in a sense, and it involves the above features that increase sexual excitement.

The impression of reduced vulnerability may be illusory, as online communication often leaves more traces than offline communication: the written messages can be retrieved and become public, whereas spoken conversations cannot (unless they are being tapped). Sitting alone in front of the computer enhances the illusion of being completely alone and hence there is a tendency to underestimate the risk of revealing confidential, personal information.

Anonymity in cyberspace can be compared to wearing a mask: in both cases, the sense of anonymity is powerful and makes you feel different.[24] Great anonymity, however, often prevents closeness and the feeling of authenticity. Accordingly, as an online relationship develops, participants take off some elements of their online masks and reveal more of their true identities. This act of trust in turn further facilitates self-disclosure, but at the same time increases vulnerability.

(b) Lack of "gating features"

The greater tendencies toward self-disclosure in cyberspace can also be explained by a lack of the usual "gating features" – easily discernible features such as unattractive external appearance, stereotypic characteristics, visible shyness, or social anxiety – which might be an obstacle to the establishment of any close relationship. These gates often prevent people from developing relationships to the stage at which disclosure of intimate information could begin. Such barriers are typically absent in cyberspace and hence do not obstruct the early stages of potentially rewarding relationships.[25] As one woman wrote about her online affair: "The best part of meeting someone this way, is there is nothing between you but personality. No physical, cosmetic or material barriers. And after all, aren't those things honestly unimportant?"[26]

We may also speak about internal gates. Whereas external gating features, such as external appearance, prevent *others* from initiating romantic relationships with an individual who possesses these features, internal gating features, such as shyness or traditional norms, prevent *the agent* from initiating romantic relationships with someone else. Cyberspace is useful in overcoming these gates as well. Online anonymity gives these internal gating features lesser weight. Moreover, many people may not have the courage to initiate a romantic relationship, but they can maintain such a relationship once they are more familiar with the other person. Cyberspace provides the opportunity to get to know each other without having to deal directly with such gates.

(c) Lack of other means to know each other

Another reason for the greater self-disclosure in online relationships is that this is the only way in which the correspondents can get to know each other. In offline relationships, people know a lot about each other from their actual meetings and interaction, as well as possibly from their circle of acquaintances, family, neighbors, or friends. This information is absent in online relationships. Moreover, since conversations are at the heart of online affairs, it is essential that they be frequent and cover a large range of topics – some of them profoundly personal, such as the correspondents' feelings about themselves and each other, and some of them more trivial, such as describing the writers' neighborhoods, families, jobs, travels, and day-to-day activities. Both personal and trivial topics serve to increase intimacy. Knowing about each other is essential for intimate relationships, but, in online relationships, this information can be provided only through self-disclosure. Although Miss Manners (Judith Martin) tells us that it is far more impressive when others discover your good qualities without your help, such help is necessary in online relationships. It may make the relationship less polite, but far more sincere.

In an online relationship, it is not merely permitted to articulate personal and intimate issues, it is an expected norm. Indeed, most people testify that they are more direct when flirting online than in person.[27] Accordingly, many people claim that they know their online partner better than they know some of their oldest and best friends. Thus, Wendy, who has had a few online affairs, says: "I don't think people can 'hide' [in online relationships] the real self for very long at all. I know a lot of people online better than I've known almost anybody offline. I know more about their inner lives and their thoughts and dreams and fears."[28] It is also worth noting that, despite the anonymity offered by the Web, people often tend to reveal intimate details about themselves on home Web pages.[29]

(d) *Greater ease in finding similar others*

People who share similar backgrounds, attitudes, and interests are more likely to establish romantic relationships and to remain together.[30] Finding similar others is not easy in offline circumstances where the availability of such people is limited to your local arena. Even within this arena, detecting such people is difficult. Finding others similar to oneself in cyberspace is much easier as they are more available and one is able to detect such similarity, as well as other desirable characteristics, more rapidly than in offline circumstances. Since we feel closer to similar others, it is easier and more natural to disclose intimate information about ourselves when we engage with such people.

The above considerations indicate why many people are more comfortable about revealing whatever is on their mind when their exchange is typed than when it is spoken. In this sense, online conversations involve the art of seeing things that are invisible. It is no wonder, therefore, that a 42-year-old woman writes: "What I dislike about online dating is the lack of mystery."[31] It is interesting to note that a newly developed software program can extrapolate the underlying emotional feel of a piece of text as it passes through a mail server. Individual words are tagged such as "happy," "sad," "nice," or "nasty," and it searches for telltale punctuation, such as exclamation marks. When it has decided on the overall mood of the message being sent, it will insert what it feels as the definitive icon.[32] As the process of self-disclosure is significant online, such software is not so useful in this domain – and, of course, it can be fooled.

The greater opportunities for self-disclosure in cyberspace are part of the so-called "disinhibition effect," which makes people online feel more uninhibited and express themselves more openly. Accordingly, people say and do things in cyberspace that they would not ordinarily say and do in offline circumstances. John Suler indicates that this is a double-edged sword. On the one hand, people reveal intimate information and show unusual acts of kindness. On the other hand, the disinhibition effect may lead people to use rude language and openly express anger, hatred, even threats; they may also explore places that they would never visit in the actual world, such as online sites offering pornography or violence. Accordingly to Suler, the characteristics responsible for this effect are anonymity ("you don't know me"), invisibility ("you can't see me"), asynchronicity ("see you later"), solipsistic introjection ("it's all in my head"), dissociation ("it's just a game"), and neutralizing of status ("we're equals"). All these characteristics enable people to protect themselves better from the possible harmful consequences of being more open than usual. Anonymity and invisibility provide a hiding place. Asynchronicity helps one to avoid dealing with one's correspondent's immediate reaction and hence enables one to formulate a careful response, to be delivered when one wants. Solipsistic introjection, in which people assume that the whole event is merely in their heads, decreases the reality of the interaction and hence its emotional intensity. Considering the interaction to be merely a game has a similar effect of decreasing the degree of reality. Neutralizing status enhances people's ability to cope with other people.[33]

Intimacy. The disinhibition effect, and in particular the greater tendency toward self-disclosure online, can lead to a profound sense of intimacy online. Consider, for instance, the following message, which was sent by a woman to her online lover after just a few email exchanges: "I just LOVE talking to you. You are so funny, and you always seem to know exactly what I am thinking. It is as though your words were happening inside my HEART, and they ring so true, they make me feel like you and I are SOULMATES." A similar attitude is expressed by Sara, a married woman in Toronto, who is conducting an online affair with Edward in Australia: "I feel so close to you. I feel as though we have reached an intimacy that can only increase as time goes by. This relationship has made me feel more alive than I ever thought possible. When we're together, we are alone, safe, and excited! I love it!" Another person writes: "It is embarrassing how easily and quickly you can start dealing with very intimate matters. People start writing about things which couldn't be handled even within a year if they communicated all the time face-to-face."[34] Profound online intimacy seems to compensate for the physical distance; people report that they feel as if the great emotional heat between them melts the physical distance.

It has been claimed that the faster and more profound nature of online self-disclosure leads to faster and more profound intimacy. Profound intimacy that might take months or years to appear in offline relationships may only take days or weeks online. In online relationships, people usually get to know each other more quickly and more intimately. In online relationships, the information may arrive at a slower pace – although sometimes it may even arrive faster – but it has a potential to reach a greater variety and deeper aspects of the partner's life and to do it at a faster pace.[35]

Profound intimacy is not easy to achieve, as it may increase the vulnerability of the agent, and hence people are cautious about becoming too intimate when the risk of being hurt is significant. This is a major reason why in cyberspace, where vulnerability is low, intimacy may be more quickly achieved. The need for such quick intimacy is due to the more dynamic nature of cyberspace: it is easier to find an alternative partner and hence people can signoff or change their screenname at any time. The greater intimacy online is also due to the ability to lose track of current time and space and to be drawn into an alternative, imaginary world where only the two lovers exist and where they may feel very close to each other.

The increased level of intimacy often leads to extraordinarily intense emotional experiences. Thus, a woman whose handle name is Lady Shelby writes that "I didn't realize that you could fall so deep and so quickly to someone who was just a name and typed sentences on a computer." Another woman describes her feelings for her online lover: "I know that I care far more than I have been able to confess to him. It scares me to let someone have that much of me in so short a period of time."[36]

The initial development of relations in offline interactions is characterized by uncertainty reduction behavior. The more information one gets about the other person, the less uncertainty one experiences. Even greater uncertainty prevails in online relationships as the written medium precludes the exchange of nonverbal cues typical of face-to-face interaction. Furthermore, many offline strategies for reducing uncertainty are not available in online relationships. For example, one is unable to observe the partner while he or she interacts with other people, and one cannot garner information about the partner from mutual acquaintances.[37]

Self-disclosure is the major means for reducing uncertainty in online relationships. Such a reduction can be done directly, when the partner offers details about herself, or indirectly, by using strategies such as verbal interrogation, deception detection, and analysis of the style and content of the written messages. Many studies indicate the value of self-disclosure for the development of personal relationships – one reason being that people who disclose more intimately are often viewed by others as more trusting, friendly, and warm. However, self-disclosure may also be viewed as inappropriate. Thus, disclosing personal information in the earliest stages of a relationship may be too much, too soon. There appear to be fairly strict social rules governing what information is appropriate to reveal and in what contexts.[38] It seems that these rules are being altered in cyberspace, where revealing information at early stages of the relationship is regarded as more appropriate.

Different types of information about the partner are revealed in the initial stages of online and offline romantic affairs. In online affairs, much intimate information about the partner is revealed, but the partner's real identity and certain external characteristics may remain hidden. When people are certain that they are anonymous, they can reveal everything else without becoming vulnerable. In face-to-face affairs, the identity is evident, but intimate information is withheld – it is not revealed until further trust is established and vulnerability is considerably reduced. However, since self-disclosure facilitates the development of personal relationships, its slower pace in offline relationships will result in a slower pace in the development of the whole relationship.

Sincerity and deception

> Q. – Dr. CyberLove, I met a great woman online and I'm crazy about her. I'm wondering though – she sent me a picture of herself, and she looks just like Cindy Crawford. Do you think she sent me a fake picture?
> A. – Of course not! You'd be surprised how many people look just like Cindy Crawford. In fact, that's why she's so successful. She has that familiar, girl-next-door look.[39]

Romantic relationships have traditionally involved deceptive elements; these are supposed to increase the romantic attraction and to decrease the risk of ending the relationship. Cyberspace provides more means to improve the deception. The more voluntary nature of online self-presentation involves the risk of being more susceptible to manipulations; in such controlled exposure, there is much room for deception and misrepresentation. As one woman remarked: "It's harder to lie when you live 3 blocks away than 500 miles away."[40]

Netizens are often dishonest about their identifying features, such as age, race, height, weight, gender, or employment. When it comes to interests and background, there are no significant differences between offline and online relationships. In the latter, false claims concerning age and external appearance are difficult to detect; false claims concerning interests, occupation, education, and other background characteristics are easier to refute, as those issues become the topic of conversations between the two online partners. Indeed, in one survey, 48% of users reported that they changed their age "occasionally," and 23% reported they did so "often." Furthermore, 38% changed their race while online, and 5% admitted to changing their gender occasionally. In both offline and online relationships, when the level of commitment is high, misrepresentation is low.[41]

It is interesting to note that, in chat rooms, men are more likely to lie than women. Men are more likely to lie about their socio economic status; women are more likely to lie for safety reasons. Both often believe that by disguising their identity, they can be more emotionally honest and open. Lying in this case signifies a desire to reveal a deeper level of truth about the self, while avoiding the risk involved in reducing privacy.[42]

Online relationships, however, encourage many people to present a more accurate picture of their true self, which is characterized as that version of self that a person believes she actually is, but is unable to present, or is prevented from presenting, to others in most situations. This is especially true for people whose immediate apparent characteristics are not perceived in the most favorable light. These people are motivated to deepen their new relationships further by transforming them into offline relationships as well. Indeed, a sizeable proportion of such relationships leads to engagement or marriage. The stability of these online relationships compares quite favorably to that of offline relationships.[43]

Greater control over the aspects people are ready to conceal or reveal puts less strain on online relationships and reduces the conflict between emotional disclosure and privacy. Although cyberspace provides opportunities for individuals to present themselves as someone else, many people present themselves honestly online. This is especially true if the relationship continues and develops further. The more time people spend in chatting with each other, the more open they are about themselves and the less likely they are to lie.

At the beginning of online relationships, people may lie about external identifying features, such as age, race, marital status, number of children, or employment; however, they cannot lie about constitutive personal features, such as kindness, a sense of humor, wittiness, and personal interests, all of which emerge during lengthy online conversations. While external identifying features may prevent the formation of an offline relationship, constitutive features are crucial for maintaining an enduring loving relationship. One married woman, who had an online affair with a married man, reports that she lied to him about her real name, age (instead of thirty-eight, she claimed to be twenty-eight), and the number of children she has. They both admitted to being married. After six months of online romance and "being madly in love with him," she came out with the truth. To her surprise, "he said that he understood why I lied and that he loved my inner me." She also notes: "when people lie online it isn't always because they are vicious or mean to hurt anyone."[44] As in offline circumstances, the development of trust in online relationships is a gradual process.

Sincerity is a great asset to successful personal relationships as it is correlated with a higher degree of intimacy. In a study of regular personal advertisements, sincerity was the single most frequently listed characteristic sought by women – male advertisers also seek sincerity in women but this characteristic is far less important to them.[45] Accordingly, someone who wants to be emotionally close to another person will attempt to be sincere – or at least need to fake sincerity. By sharing intimate information, you are flattering the other person with your trust. Accordingly, if you are seeking to flatter someone, one of the best ways of doing this is to reveal a secret.[46] Someone once said: "The secret of success is sincerity. Once you can fake that, you've got it made." In online relationships, it may be easier to fake sincerity but, nevertheless, profound sincerity is common as well.

The more sincere and open nature of cyberspace induces people to behave in ways that do not accord with their stereotypic figure. Thus, women may be more sexually expressive than they are in offline relationships and men may be more emotionally sensitive. A 40-year-old married woman whose husband has no sexual interest in her notes:

> I have always had a very high rate of sexual interest. We've had several discussions about his lack of interest in recent years. I've always been forthright with him and recently told him that if he is not willing to be an active participant in regards to an active sex life between the two of us, that I would seek an alternative solution for "my problem," as he has called it. My alternative solution is cybersex. I can remain anonymous, act upon my wildest fantasies, and talk as dirty as I want.[47]

Indeed, cyberspace has been characterized by disinhibition, including phenomena such as flaming and excessive self-disclosure that are untypical of people's behavior offline. The reduced weight of ordinary constraints, such as social norms and harmful practical implications, enables online behavior to be less constrained. This may be expressed in more violent behavior or in more intense love and sexual desire.[48]

The opposing aspects of online relationships are also expressed in the issue of sincerity and anonymity. On the one hand, a typical feature of online relationships is the relative anonymity of the participants. On the other hand, the greater tendency toward sincerity and self-disclosure online makes the participants less anonymous. It seems that in cyberspace, everybody knows your thoughts. This is so since people more easily express their intimate thoughts about themselves and others, and since, once they have said something, it is not forgotten; it is out there in writing and can be quoted.[49]

A related conflict in cyberspace is that between sincerity and imagination. On the one hand, online relationships involve more sincere communication, which more accurately expresses the real attitudes of the correspondents. On the other hand, imagination and fantasies, which ignore offline reality, play a central role in online relationships. These accurate and inaccurate descriptions of reality actually refer to different aspects. Online relationships typically involve more accurate descriptions of people's own personal attitudes, but less accurate descriptions of the reality beyond them. When someone writes to her online friend that she would like to have sexual intercourse with him, she typically describes her present emotions in an accurate manner; in face-to-face relationships, such sincere expression of one's desires is less frequent. But when this woman writing to her online friend describes how she is taking his clothes off and kissing his lips, she is describing an illusory reality, which exists in her fantasy. Sincerity about emotional desires is not at odds with a fantasy concerning the fulfillment of these desires.

A high degree of concealment along with a high degree of self-disclosure and sincerity are both common in online relationships. In such relationships, we often either do not know anything real about our online partner or know more about her than her most intimate friends do. Such extreme levels of familiarity are not common in offline circumstances. Having no true information at all about our offline friend is impossible, since our activities together will reveal some of her characteristics. It is also rare, however, to know our actual friend's most profound secrets; she is likely to keep such secrets private since they may make her extremely vulnerable.

Like self-disclosure, sincerity can also be painful. Sometimes we do not want to know all the other person's secrets. When we are more sincere, though, the less vulnerable nature of cyberspace reduces the risks of hurting other people.

In light of the above considerations, I would say that dreams, rather than deception, characterize online relationships. Such dreams are often accompanied by a profound knowledge of reality.

Continuity and discontinuity

Let there be spaces in your togetherness.

Khalil Gibran

In an important sense, offline romantic relationships can be regarded as continuous. The two lovers may not be together all the time, but they typically have an idea of each other's whereabouts. This idea may be wrong in some of its details, but the general picture is usually accurate. In offline relationships, people typically do not suddenly disappear from each other's view. They gradually leave the room, they often say good-bye, and they usually return. In offline relationships, discontinuity – such as sudden disappearance or sudden return – requires an explanation.

Such continuity is often absent in online romantic relationships where people can simply disappear, not because they have died, but because they have suddenly decided not to communicate (temporarily or permanently) or because matters in their offline environment have become more important to them. Sudden disappearance in cyberspace is easy – it merely requires not pressing a certain button; hence, it is common and needs no explanation. As one person puts it: "The cool thing about cybersex is you never have to talk to the other person again if you don't want to. It is a lot harder to do that in real life."[50] Indeed, the tactic of avoidance and escape is likely to prevail in online relationships more than in offline relationships.[51] Accordingly, the termination of online affairs can be of a more unexpected and sudden nature. The termination can be unexpected since people are not aware of most of their partners' actual circumstances. It may also be sudden since it is easy to terminate online relationships – there are almost no practical matters one needs to take care of. The great online spiritual match between the two partners does not mean that the partners have similar expectations of pursuing that match offline; this discrepancy may lead to a sudden termination of the online relationship. Such a sudden termination is clearly expressed in the following description: "I knew we were too different, but things didn't even GRADUALLY get worse. They just stopped."[52]

In another way, however, online romantic relationships can be regarded as more continuous than offline relationships. They are continuous in the sense that they can be conducted at any time; accordingly, people anticipate them and think about them all the time. Online relationships have scarcely any barriers: they can take place twenty-four hours, seven days a week, in the comfort of your house or office – regardless of bad weather, having "nothing" to wear, the children playing around you, catching a cold, or having a plain bad hair day! Having an online affair is like going to a party whenever you want to, without having to leave your home.

The following are a few authentic descriptions of this continuous aspect of online affairs. Heidi is a married woman having an online affair with Todd, who has a girlfriend; she writes: "I can't seem to be away from him for a minute! He is in my EVERY thought! Everything I say, everything I do, it's all him!" Another married woman describes her online affair: "We could not stop thinking about each other every moment of the day and night." Another woman says: "I missed not talking to him throughout the day." A 27-year-old woman having an online affair with an 18-year-old man writes: "I spend every waking hour thinking about him. I can't get him out of my mind and it's driving me crazy. I can't wait to get home everyday just to see if he has mailed me any letters." Another woman testifies: "I couldn't eat, sleep, or think about anything but him. No man had ever made me feel this way." A married woman who is conducting a cyberaffair with a married man – even though she testifies that she loves her husband – notes: "If I don't see him online or we miss a scheduled chat, I feel depressed for days. I just can't stop looking for him online."[53]

We can say that online romantic relationships may be discontinuous in a physical, temporal sense because online communication is not continuous; nevertheless, these relationships are continuous in an emotional sense, in that the online lovers are always on each other's mind. This continuous, yet distanced, aspect of online relationships can be problematic, as it creates expectations that are not always fulfilled. Email exchange can occur many times a day, and since people are constantly waiting for these messages to arrive, the relationship and the beloved is always on the mind of the lover. As Belle, a married woman for twelve years, reports: "When I would shut my eyes, read a book or poem, listen to music, watch a movie, drive my car, anything, he was there with me, inside my mind leading my life on, like a dog leading a blind man."[54]

A related cause of this type of online continuity is the lack of minimum time limitations upon online "meeting": email messages can be very brief, consisting of one sentence or even one word. This enables sending and receiving messages many times a day. Take, for example, the following description by Karl: "I usually picked up her messages in the morning, and when I didn't get mail from her, I really felt let down. I worried about her and wondered if she was safe. I'd log on every hour to see if she was just sending me mail late that day." One woman writes: "For me cybering caused me numerous sleepless nights, tons of tears, day after day of 'will he be online.' Do I advise it for others??????? NOOOOOOOOOOOOOOOOOOO."[55]

In offline relationships, practical constraints, such as one's work, determine to a large extent people's schedule and hence their separation from their intimates. In such relationships, you cannot meet a person for thirty seconds, say that you love her, and then go about your business. You can, of course, call your lover twenty times a day and tell her that you love her, but this may ruin her schedule since the call may come at an inconvenient time for her. In online communication, sending twenty messages is common and not intrusive since people are sending and receiving these messages at their own convenience. There is no need to coordinate schedules and venues.

The continuous aspect of online romantic relationships indicates the continuous emotional effect on the participants. Take, for example, an unfriendly dispute stemming from a misunderstanding or insult. In offline relationships, the two people have to face the dispute and solve it one way or another. In online relationships, one person can just disappear for a while without any explanation. This sudden discontinuity does not prevent each of them from ruminating about the relationship and experiencing various emotions toward the other person. However, significant discontinuity reduces, and sometimes even eliminates, the extent of concentration on the other person.

In both offline and online romantic relationships, external factors influence the continuity, or lack of it, of the relationship. In online relationships, it is the actual, different physical environment of each participant that underlies the discontinuous aspect: each is living in a different environment – including sometimes having a different partner – and the separation is overcome by a sophisticated type of communication. In offline relationships, the physical environment of the two lovers is essentially similar, but there are practical constraints upon their communication, such as busy schedules or too much familiarity.

Physical and mental investment

He must have made that before he died.
Yogi Berra, referring to Steve McQueen while watching one of his movies

Face-to-face romantic relationships are characterized by significant investment in the relationship by both partners. The investment can be physical – involving, for example, money, time, and obligations to do various activities that one does not typically want to do – or mental, which can include intense emotions and mental effort.

Cyberspace seems to be a perfect world – by investing minimum physical resources, people can do almost anything they wish to do. Finding the right online partner and maintaining the relationship with this partner often require fewer resources than finding a suitable offline partner. Paying attention to incoming emails costs much less than paying for a dinner or a movie. No one is so poor that he is unable even to pay attention. Jackie Kennedy once said that sex is a bad thing because it rumples the clothes. Well, cybersex, which some people may consider as not much more than one-hand typing, overcomes this problem, as it never rumples clothes.

People often justify their online sexual affairs by mentioning that they had very little time in their busy schedules to pursue sexual contacts on a face-to-face basis. In contrast to enduring romantic relationships online, cybersex does not necessarily require a lot of preparatory, nonsexual small talk; it can skip this stage. As one woman wrote: "During my separation and into my divorce, I found cyber and phone sex to be relatively satisfying. I had a non-cyber relationship for a year, but found the demands on my time to be excessive and the payback too small. I work in the type of job that sucks a hundred percent out of you."[56] Using imagination requires fewer resources – especially physical ones – than those required for real actions. Emotional imagination enables us to accrue various affective benefits, such as feeling better, without carrying out the relevant tasks required in offline relationships for obtaining such benefits. For example, in sexual fantasies one may simulate the pleasure of intercourse with an attractive person without finding such a willing person, without investing in building an actual relationship with this person, and without carrying the burden associated with it.

Online emotional experiences may be compared to receiving a salary without earning it by hard work. Needless to say, there is no free lunch and there is a price people must pay for their online, unearned emotional salary. The price is related to their actual partners, who suffer most from the occupation with online affairs. Based on her experience, a married woman writes: "cyber affairs create unhappiness in the home; even when the innocent spouse knows nothing of the affair. Women become emotionally detached from their husbands and depend more on the cyber lover to give them their fix."[57] The cost of the unearned emotional salary is also expressed in the agent's ability to function. Thus, one woman writes: "I get up every morning and I can't function till I check my email. I feel the rush each time I receive one. The times there is no mail, I walk around like the world has just ended."[58] Unlike with a one-night cyberstand, people invest a lot of mental energy and time in long-term romantic online relationships.

Modern society promotes the value of efficiency – and hence speed. Through the Internet, and other modern types of communication, we acquire needed information in a speedy and efficient manner, thereby saving a lot of resources. Time has become one of the precious commodities we most like to save. Indeed, by pressing a button, we can immediately know the weather in the country we are going to visit next week, or acquire personal information about someone whom we are going to meet or write about. Greater pace at a lower cost has become the hallmark of modern society.

The need to be efficient – that is, to save resources, and particularly time – is also evident in the realm of romantic relationships: we do not have enough resources to meet all available partners before deciding who would be our best soul mate. However, romantic relationships are also characterized by an opposing need: getting to know each other is a time-consuming activity that should not be done too quickly. Cyberspace is useful in dealing with these opposing trends. It provides a most efficient way to meet the maximum number of desirable people. Accordingly, not only "losers" take advantage of online dating, but also those who are searching for better choices in the limited time they have. Cyberspace, however, also fulfills the need to get to know the other person well – to have information not merely about external appearance, but also about basic characteristics, values, attitudes, and desires, which are so crucial for long-term relationships. The greater tendency toward self-disclosure online facilitates such knowledge. There is, of course, certain information that is missing from online communication and is significant for its future prospects. However, this information is easy to reveal in a subsequent face-to-face meeting.

The above considerations concerning the paradoxical nature of cyberlove clearly pertain to cybersex as well. In the same manner that cyberlove occupies a middle position between private fantasies and actual romance with another person – and hence it may have features of both – cybersex occupies a middle position between masturbation, which is a solo activity, and actual sex, which involves another person. Both kinds of online affairs are neither completely private, nor fully public – they are based upon private fantasies, but the interaction is with real people in a medium that can become public. The other person is both an imaginary actor in our private fantasies and a real partner in actual interactions. The virtual reality that is constructed is built upon actual raw materials. It is like play and art, both of which comprise a blend of fact and fiction.[59]

Distant relationships

> Relationship at a distance can do things for the heart that a closer, day-to-day companionship cannot.
>
> Thomas Moore

Closeness is a crucial element determining emotional significance and hence emotional intensity. Because emotions are highly personal, they are usually elicited by those who are relevant or close to us. When someone is too detached from us, we are unlikely to have any emotional attitude toward her.

Distance typically decreases emotional intensity, as it is contrary to the involved and intimate perspective typical of emotions. Love, which incorporates a profoundly positive evaluation of the other person, includes the wish to become as close as possible to that person. The intensity of hate can often be decreased by increasing the subject–object distance. Hate is not directed at those who are completely strangers to us and who have no contact with us whatsoever. When the object of hate is no longer close or relevant, hatred is very likely to diminish or fade completely. In marital relationships, hate is usually expressed by evading the situation and acting coldly, as if the close relationship that is supposed to prevail in marriage no longer existed. Hate is then directed at people whom we perceive to be too close to us. Laughing at ourselves serves to distance us from the shameful situation, as we join others in taking a fresh view of our circumstances. This humorous perspective also helps to reduce the significance of the shaming situation. Temporal distance, like other types of distance, decreases emotional intensity. Thus, in hope and fear a temporal distance between the agent and the emotional object will reduce emotional intensity. At a distance, events often seem less significant than they are when they are nearer. Accordingly, as the saying goes, sometimes time can heal a wounded heart.

Physical proximity is usually emotionally significant because it is often relevant to our well-being. Emotions are often directed at our neighbors. Envy is notorious in this regard: our neighbor's grass seems greener than ours. As one proverb puts it: "The envious man thinks that he will be able to walk better if his neighbor breaks a leg." However, not everyone who lives in our neighborhood is of great emotional significance to us. Some people may be sadder when their favorite football team loses than when they hear that a person in their neighborhood has died. Physical proximity does not always lead to emotional significance.

Although distance typically decreases emotional intensity, there are circumstances in which distance increases it. Diderot argued that "distance is a great promoter of admiration." Indeed, a typical difference between envy and admiration is that, in envy, the subject–object gap is much smaller. Admiration is different from love in that it implies distance and hence a lack of reciprocity. There are also circumstances in which temporal distance may amplify the event. In these cases, the time that separates us from the event is used for incessant rumination upon it; this makes the event more central for us and hence our emotions intensify.

Contemporary personal relationships among primary groups, such as friends, family, and partners, are different from such classical relationships in the sense that the physical distance among individuals has increased – thus, individuals no longer live together from birth to death.[60] Whereas the Internet offers a vital way to bridge that distance, online relationships create a type of personal relationship in which such distance is further increased.

Physical proximity has long been considered a positive factor in both initiating and maintaining romantic bonds. Indeed, romantic relationships are partially differentiated from mere friendships by involving behaviors (such as fondling, caressing, kissing, and making love) that necessitate physical proximity.[61] The chances were good that the seeker's "one and only" would be found not far from where the seeker lived.[62] The resources and effort required in this case are considerably less than in the case of distant relationships. Accordingly, distance is often considered a negative factor in maintaining romantic bonds, because, at great distances, it is much more difficult to carry on the activities typical of such bonds. In the absence of physical proximity and the activities that it allows, it is doubtful whether romantic relationships can flourish. Distant relationships often rely on either imagining physical proximity or expecting that proximity to be achieved in the future.

Online personal relationships are characterized by physical distance and emotional closeness. Other relationships may involve physical closeness and emotional distance. An example of the latter is a forced relationship with a disliked partner. Although personal relationships are typically characterized by voluntary choice associated with affection and respect, many intimate relationships are not voluntary; people may dislike their partner, but feel that they must maintain the relationships whether or not they wish to. Such relationships can be maintained by increasing the emotional distance between the two partners.[63] This type of situation is rare in online relationships, which involve less commitment and fewer practical limitations on terminating the relationship.

The increasing number of distant relationships is associated with the fact that more women are pursuing goals independent of their male partners. This increases the mobility of women and hence the prevalence of distant relationships. However, whereas offline distant relationships cost money to maintain, online relationships are cheap to maintain. Moreover, cyberspace offers the chance of distant relationships not merely to mobile people, but to everyone. Another commonly reported difficulty in distant relationships, such as commuter marriages, is that couples miss the luxury of daily discussions of "trivial" matters with their spouses – the sharing of little things.[64] This difficulty, too, does not appear in online relationships, which entirely consist of conversations about everything, be it large or small.

The Buddhist state of neutral feeling, which is an attitude of even-mindedness and impartiality toward all people, is a radical state of physical closeness and emotional distance. In such a state, emotions are eliminated – even toward those who are physically close to us – by eliminating sensitivity to our surroundings. Whereas online relationships have been characterized as "detached attachment" – that is, physically remote, but emotionally close – the relationship associated with this Buddhist state may be characterized as "attached detachment" – that is, physically close, but emotionally detached.

Distance is important for gaining an adequate perspective. Thus, when we look at something from very close up, our vision is fragmented and often distorted. In the extreme case where there is no distance at all, that is, when we place the object right next to the eye itself, we do not see it for what it actually is. We need some distance in order to achieve a perspective that encompasses multiple aspects of the object and thereby makes the perspective less fragmented.

In a similar manner, some kind of distance is important for personal relationships. Significant and temporally extended physical distance may harm them, but more limited distance may be beneficial. As the saying goes: "Absence makes the heart grow fonder." Several studies indicate that long-distance couples are more satisfied with their relationships and with their communication and more in love than are geographically close couples; accordingly, the former relationships enjoy a higher rate of survival.[65] It seems that the distance may focus the partners' attention on profound aspects of their relationships and help them to disregard the superficial ones. These people are likely to value their relationships even more, and, at the same time, the distance enhances the likelihood that they will idealize their partners.

In itself, distance is not necessarily harmful to romantic relationships. Finding the right measure and nature of physical and emotional distance is crucial for a satisfactory romantic relationship. Distance may have its own costs, but an appropriate distance can minimize the impact of those costs.

Online relationships are a unique type of distant relationship that seems to overcome some of the main problems of other types of distant relationships. The Internet enables a constant flow of communication that can become profound and intimate. Love becomes intense, and the participants feel close to each other. Nevertheless, online relationships cannot overcome the desire for physical closeness. Accordingly, online romantic relationships can typically complement, but not completely substitute for, offline relationships. Consider the following confession of a married woman about her online romance with a married man:

> It started out with very innocent conversation. As time went on, we discussed our families and how happily married we were with our spouses. Before we knew it, we had fallen deeply in love with each other. Even though we both knew in our hearts that we loved our spouses, we cannot resist these feelings we have for each other. We are closer with each other than with our spouses. I have never loved a man as I do this one. I feel more for him than I ever have for my husband. This may sound odd, but we believe you can love two people at one time.[66]

Online distant relationships are often associated with nostalgia. Nostalgia is a longing for circumstances that no longer exist or have never existed. Nostalgia has a utopian dimension stemming from the considerable role imagination plays in it. Hence, nostalgia is often about virtual reality that cannot be actualized. In this sense, nostalgia is not always about the past; it can also be directed toward the future or the present.[67] Like nostalgia, online romantic relationships often involve yearning for virtual circumstances that cannot exist. In both cases, the moment we try to actualize longing by transferring it to belonging, longing often disappears. In this sense, by actualizing nostalgia or actualizing an online affair, we may kill the thing we love.

Summary

> Letter writing is the only device for combining solitude with good company.
>
> Lord Byron

Online communication involves a new type of romantic relationship in which features of close and remote relationships are combined. In online relationships, people are neither close, intimate friends nor complete strangers. Online relationships constitute a unique kind of relationship – termed "detached attachment," or, in short, "detattachment" – that includes opposing features whose presence in offline relationships would be paradoxical. The major opposing aspects of online romantic relationships are as follows: (1) distance and immediacy; (2) lean and rich communication; (3) anonymity and self-disclosure; (4) sincerity and deception; (5) continuity and discontinuity; (6) marginal physical investment and considerable mental investment.

Online romantic relationships are distant in a spatial sense, but are immediate in a temporal sense – the two lovers can communicate with no significant time delay and there is no human third party that mediates the conversation. Online communication relies on fewer sources of information and is often based merely on written messages. However, this communication provides richer and more intimate information than that typical of offline romantic communication. Online relationships are characterized by both greater anonymity and greater self-disclosure. Anonymity is associated with concealment, which runs counter to self-disclosure. However, greater anonymity typically facilitates greater self-disclosure, and in turn increases intimacy.

Online relationships involve a greater degree of both deception and sincerity. It is easier to present deceptive information in cyberspace, as it is more difficult to check the accuracy of such information. However, the greater online self-disclosure is associated with more profound sincerity. The development of online relationships is characterized by the urge to dream or fantasize, rather than to deceive. Unlike offline relationships, an online communication can become sporadic when matters in people's offline environment become more important to them. Online romantic relationships are continuous in the sense that they can be conducted at any time; accordingly, people may anticipate the next contact and think about it more frequently than in offline affairs. Online relationships involve less investment of physical resources, but greater investment of mental resources, as these relationships are emotionally highly intense.

People participating in online relationships may be strangers to each other in the sense that they have never actually met. However, they are also close to each other since they share intimate information and common desires.

In online relationships, people try to enjoy the benefits of both close and remote relationships, while avoiding their flaws. People enjoy the highly valued products of close relationships while paying the low cost of remote relationships. Thus, they are able to get away from people when they want to, and be instantly close to them, if they so desire. In this sense, online relationships help promote social relationships as they reduce the price of such relationships.

Online relationships are a type of distant relationship characterized by physical separation and emotional closeness. Like other types of distant relationships, online relationships can be quite satisfactory, although they do have their own particular shortcomings. Appropriate distance, which is combined with a type of closeness, may be useful for romantic purposes.

A distant online relationship seems to be paradoxical in a few related senses: (a) it involves detached attachment – physical distance with emotional closeness; (b) it is a social activity that is done alone – interacting with another person from the privacy of your personal computer; (c) it is a form of personal communication that uses features of mass communication – being able to communicate personally with many people at the same time. The unique nature of cyberspace, which can sustain such paradoxical features, has facilitated the development of a new type of romantic relationship not so far known.

People know what to expect from a close relationship; they know what to expect from remote relationships. They do not know what to expect from relationships characterized as detached attachment. Our emotional system is not (yet?) structured to deal with such opposing features. It seems that the new technology has not been accompanied by a corresponding mental change. In particular, we may not be ready to face living with seemingly highly available and desired romantic alternatives that cannot be actualized. The contradictions and uncertainty associated with online romantic relationships make them less stable and more intense. Emotions play a much greater role in these relationships.

3 *Emotions on the Net*

For it was not into my ear you whispered, but into my heart. It was not my lips you kissed, but my soul.

Judy Garland

After describing in the last chapter the nature of online relationships, this chapter describes the nature of emotions.[1] It examines whether characteristics typical of emotions prevail in online relationships, and hence whether such relationships are likely to involve intense emotions. Although online relationships involve some virtual aspects, the emotions they generate are quite real.

Emotions are highly complex and subtle phenomena whose explanation requires careful and systematic analysis of their multiple characteristics and components. The major reason for the complexity of emotions is their great sensitivity to personal and contextual circumstances. Cyberspace also involves a complex psychological reality: it includes many forms of relating that are highly available because of the imaginary nature of cyberspace. In light of this complexity, it is hard to generalize about the emotional realm in cyberspace.

The typical cause of emotion: A perceived significant change

Better make it four; I don't think I can eat eight.

Yogi Berra's reply when asked if he wanted his pizza cut into four or eight slices.

Emotions typically occur when we perceive positive or negative *significant changes in our personal situation*, or in the situation of those related to us. A major positive or negative change significantly improves or interrupts a stable situation relevant to our concerns. Like burglar alarms going off when an intruder appears, emotions signal that something needs attention. When no attention is needed, the signaling system can be switched off. We respond to the unusual by paying attention to it. A change cannot persist for a very long time; after a while, the system construes the change as a normal state and it excites us no more. Accordingly, sexual response to a familiar partner is less intense than to a novel partner. Indeed, the frequency of sexual activity with one's partner declines steadily as the relationship lengthens, reaching roughly half the frequency after one year of marriage compared to the first month of marriage, and declining more gradually thereafter. Decline has also been found in cohabiting, heterosexual couples and in gay and lesbian couples.[2]

Cyberspace is full of changes and new opportunities – in this sense it is indeed an exciting place. This is particularly true of cybersex. As one man testifies: **"The possibility of sex outside usual norms seems a kind of new frontier, which awakens the spirit of pioneers."**[3] The online changes are of less personal significance since the available opportunities are not designed for a specific person, and if you miss one opportunity, many others are still available. The presence of so many changes and the active role that imagination plays in cyberspace can somewhat compensate for the habituation effect in which a change becomes normal and hence unexciting. The physical absence of the partner removes certain constraints upon our imagination, which makes the habituation effect weaker.[4]

Our psychological reality consists of both stable and unstable events. The successful combination of the two gives us both emotional excitement and a sense of calmness and security – both are crucial for a happy and healthy mental life. Cyberspace is more unstable, dynamic, and transitory than our actual environment is. Thus we would expect to find that transitory emotions are more dominant in cyberspace while enduring affective attitudes are more rare. If in offline circumstances we often look for changes in order to make our life more exciting, in cyberspace we look for stability in order to facilitate calmer and enduring online relationships.

The lack of stability in cyberspace often generates more intense and transitory emotions. This is true of both positive emotions and negative ones. In cyberspace we find intense love and sexual desire, but also intense fear and despair. As one man testifies: **"It was a turbulent relationship. It ran the gamut between the top and the bottom as far as feelings go. We knew joy and pain."**[5] A married woman, who is having an affair with a married man, says that despite the unbelievable depth of their emotions, the man had at one stage stopped the relationship because of guilt feelings, but now they are back together in cyberspace. She adds: "Now I carry the fear that he will regress again, back to the guilt and leave me again with the heartache and longing I felt. But this is the chance I must take. The moments we share together now are far too precious than any heartache could ever hurt."[6]

The price of having a world full of exciting, positive emotions is that many intense, negative emotions are also generated. We have to take the bitter with the sweet, as love is a bittersweet experience. This is particularly true in cyberspace where changes and instability are prevalent and where the conflict with reality, which may shatter romantic dreams, is more evident. Accordingly, people may be afraid to get involved in this exciting world: a broken heart is a load that is not easy to carry. To fear cyberspace, though, is to fear one of the most exciting parts of our contemporary life style.

In spite of the dynamic and unstable nature of cyberspace, online relationships can also become stable and repetitive. Take, for example, cybersex. Given the ability to be (virtually) engaged in more daring and uncommon sexual activities, cybersex is often more intense and wild than offline sex. However, after a while cybersex becomes repetitive for many people, and the excitement begins to fade. Thus, a married woman notes: "At the time, cybersex was new to me and extremely exciting; however, I no longer have an interest in it."[7] People in an online relationship may become frustrated and bored and search for some kind of change, either by transforming the online affair into an offline affair or by beginning a new online affair in which fantasies may be even more extreme.[8]

The typical emotional concern: A comparative personal concern

> It's been a rough day. I got up this morning, put on a shirt, and a button fell off. I picked up my briefcase and the handle came off. I'm afraid to go to the bathroom.
>
> Rodney Dangerfield

Emotions occur when a change is evaluated as relevant to our personal concerns. Concerns are our short- or long-term disposition toward a preference for particular states of the world or of the self. Emotions serve to monitor and safeguard our personal concerns; they give the eliciting event its significance.[9]

An important difference between general and emotional changes is that the latter are of great personal significance. Our attention may be directed to any type of change, but in order for the change to generate emotions, it must be perceived as having significant implications for us or for those related to us. An emotional change is always related to a certain personal frame of reference against which its significance is evaluated.

Emotional meaning is mainly comparative. The emotional environment contains not only what is and what will be experienced, but also all that could be or that one wishes will be experienced. For the emotional system, all such possibilities are posited as simultaneously available and are compared to each other. The importance of the comparative concern in emotions is also connected with the central role of changes in generating emotions. An event can be perceived as a significant change only when compared against a certain background framework.

The emotional meaning of online relationships is also comparative by nature: it relates, first of all, to our offline environment. The belief that cyberspace provides us with better alternatives is crucial in generating intense emotions. This may somewhat compensate for the less personal nature of cyberspace.

The comparison underlying emotional significance encompasses the mental construction of the *availability of an alternative situation*. The more available the alternative – that is, the closer the imagined alternative is to reality – the more intense the emotion. Thus, the fate of someone who dies in an airplane crash after switching flights evokes a stronger emotion than that of a fellow traveler who was booked on the flight all along. Greater availability indicates greater instability and the presence of significant changes. In fact, a crucial element in intense emotions is the imagined condition of "it could have been otherwise."

Cyberspace does not merely significantly increase the availability of desired alternatives, but it is in fact an alternative, available world, which runs parallel to the actual one. Sophisticated technology allows a rapid shift from one world to another. For many people, cyberspace is even better than the world they actually live in.[10]

Great availability of desired circumstances is particularly significant in the romantic realm, as cyberspace is the largest gathering in human history. A woman, who has been married for twenty years, writes: "In the fall I bought a computer. A whole new world opened up for me. I was amazed. I didn't understand the term cyber but I was soon educated. I had many cyber experiences that were very exciting. I have a vivid imagination and I am good with words so I never lacked for partners. I was having cyber daily."[11] Although finding a suitable mate in cyberspace requires the investment of some resources – mainly time – the ease of locating an exciting and suitable person is perhaps one of the most salient features of cyberspace. Moreover, multiconversing – the ability to conduct conversations simultaneously, but nevertheless privately, with a few people at the same time – enables a further reduction in the time devoted to each partner. One person even compared finding an online romantic partner to ordering a pizza: you state the type, size, toppings, and mode of delivery, and it will be available in thirty minutes or less. On Internet dating sites, you can list everything you want in a partner, including age, hair color, religious background, occupation, and interest, and you can then choose to date only those people who meet your criteria. Clearly, this is also true of offline dating services, but for those you have to submit a list of your preferences to the dating agency and such lists cannot go into great detail. Cyberspace, however, allows a huge array of highly specific sites aimed at very particular groups; thus there is a dating site for Jewish vegetarian singles and another for people with back and neck injuries. It is also possible to define one's sexual preferences precisely: consider the following personal ad that a 25-year-old woman from Sedalia, Missouri, posted on a dating site: "Need a good massage? I'll give you one if you let my hubby watch. He's straight, laid back, and enjoys seeing me have fun. We're swingers, but I only play if he's involved. If this is something you think you would enjoy, email me. I'm 38D, busty, curvy, full smooth hips, and attractive. I'm also your housewife next door."[12]

The vast availability of online contacts is particularly valuable for people who feel that, as life goes on, their desired options are gradually vanishing. The presence of many highly available alternatives is exciting, as many significant changes appear to be just around the corner. However, this great availability reduces the degree of commitment in such relationships. When the availability of a desired alternative is great, the incentive to invest substantial resources in the present situation is considerably reduced, and hence commitment is low as well.[13]

The greater number of alternatives is related to the sophisticated nature of online communication. One's message can be delivered to many people at the same time, and one is aware of the presence of many interested people as soon as the computer is switched on. Online alternatives are not only greater in number, but also more available, since people openly and rapidly indicate their willingness to develop a personal relationship. Hence, the statement, "I've been trying to meet a person like you for weeks," which would sound peculiar in offline circumstances, is not so strange in cyberspace.

The greater flexibility of online group membership contributes to the more positive nature of online relationships: cyberspace offers a wider range of available people and hence gives us the opportunity to choose the more suitable among them. We can choose people who do not threaten our self-image and may even help us stabilize and enhance it. In such circumstances, we are also more able to become aware of our unique personal characteristics.

Typical characteristics and components

> No matter how happily a woman may be married, it always pleases her to discover that there is a nice man who wishes she were not.
>
> H. L. Mencken

Instability, great intensity, a partial perspective, and relative brevity can be considered as the basic characteristics of typical emotions. This characterization refers to "hot emotions," which are the typical intense emotions. The more moderate emotions lack some of the characteristics associated with typical emotions.

In light of the crucial role that changes play in generating emotions, *instability* of the mental (as well as the physiological) system is a basic characteristic of emotions. Emotions indicate a transition in which the preceding context has changed, but no new context has yet stabilized. Emotions are like storms – they are unstable states that signify some agitation; they are intense, occasional, and limited in duration.

Instability is even more evident in cyberspace. Making a change in one's online circumstances is relatively easy and depends more on one's voluntary imagination than on practical concerns. It is easy to leave a particular online partner and find others; similarly, there is a good likelihood that your partner will terminate the relationship. Cyberspace has created upheavals in personal, social, and moral norms and circumstances. The relative stability of offline circumstances is threatened by the instability of cyberspace.

One of the typical characteristics of emotions is their *great intensity*. Emotions are intense reactions. In emotions, the mental system has not yet adapted to the given change, and, due to its significance, the change requires the mobilization of many resources. No wonder that emotions are associated with urgency and heat. In emotions there is no such thing as a minor concern; if the concern is minor, it is not emotional. A typical characteristic of emotions is their magnifying nature: everything looms larger when we are emotional.

The great instability associated with online relationships intensifies emotions in cyberspace. Although there are features that reduce emotional intensity – for instance, the virtual and non-personal nature of cyberspace – other aspects such as its novel and unstable nature generate intense emotions. Thus, Mark writes: "My love and I are feeling this incredible feeling that neither of us thought it was possible to feel. Impractical? Yes! Unlikely? Yes! For real? TOTALLY 100% MINDBLOWINGLY HEARTSTOPPINGLY BUTTERFLY GIVINGLY SMITTEN!!!"[14] Likewise, a 32-year-old married woman, who has many online sexual affairs, reports: "I have never had such a sexual experience in real life. I have never had multiple orgasms. Without the net this would never have happened."[15]

Emotions are *partial* in two basic senses: they are focused on a *narrow* target, such as one person or very few people, and they express a *personal* and interested perspective. Emotions direct and color our attention by selecting what attracts and holds it; in this sense, emotions are similar to heat-seeking missiles, having no other concern but to find the heat-generating target. Emotions address practical concerns from a personal perspective. We cannot assume an emotional state toward everyone or toward those with whom we have no relation whatsoever. Focusing upon fewer objects increases the resources available for each and hence increases emotional intensity, just as a laser beam focuses upon a very narrow area and consequently achieves high intensity at that point. Emotions express our values and preferences; hence, they cannot be indiscriminate.

In offline circumstances, we cannot be indiscriminate in whom we love. We cannot love everyone; our romantic love must be directed at a few people only. Since romantic love, like other emotions, necessitates limiting parameters such as time and attention, the number of its objects must be limited as well. We have greater resources to offer when we limit the number of emotional objects to which we are committed.

In online relationships, people's perspective is more partial than that typical of offline relationships: they do not have comprehensive knowledge about their cybermates. All they know is what their mate wants to tell them – and this typically focuses on positive information. The types of activities and resources required for maintaining online relationships are also more partial, as the relationships are limited to electronic correspondence; hence, their intensity is greater. A married woman who has begun to practice cybersex remarks: "Good grief – my sex life has improved tenfold! Probably because now I think about sex so much. In fact, these days I am the aggressor more often than my husband. He is a happy man since I discovered cybersex."[16] Focusing her attention on sex intensifies her sexual desire.

The limited cognitive and behavioral resources needed in order to conduct an online affair make it possible to direct emotions at more objects. Accordingly, online affairs with several people at the same time are common practice. When the affair merely consists of typing on a keyboard, having a few online romantic partners at the same time is both feasible and increasingly acceptable. Moreover, new technology enables a person to carry on many private conversations at the same time; hence, each relationship is less personal.

Typical emotions are essentially states with *relative brevity*. The mobilization of all resources to focus on one event cannot last forever. If emotions were to endure for a long time regardless of what was occurring in our environment, they would not have an adaptive value. The exact duration of an emotion is a matter for dispute: depending on the type of emotion and the circumstances, it can last from a few seconds to a few hours and sometimes even longer.

In light of the more unstable and transient nature of online events, intense, brief emotions may be more frequent in online affairs, while enduring emotions (sentiments) may be less characteristic. This difference is significant: it emphasizes the transitory nature of online emotional attitudes and the difficulties of maintaining long-term emotional relationships in cyberspace. It is not surprising, therefore, that participants in online affairs frequently wish to make their relationship more stable and enduring, and often seek to do so by continuing the affair offline. Difficulties in maintaining long-term personal relationships have become characteristic of contemporary society in which changes are rapid and significant; in cyberspace, however, they are even more evident.

In addition to the typical characteristics of emotions mentioned above, I may specify four basic components, that is, cognition, evaluation, motivation, and feeling. The cognitive component consists of information about the given circumstances; the evaluative component assesses the personal significance of this information; the motivational component addresses our desires, or readiness to act, in these circumstances; the feeling component is a mode of consciousness expressing our own state. When John envies Adam for having better grades, John has some information about Adam's grades, evaluates his own inferior position negatively, wishes to eliminate this inferiority, and has a certain unpleasant feeling. All four components of emotions are also evident in cyberspace emotions. In this sense, emotions generated by online communication are similar to those generated in our everyday life. The major difference in this regard is expressed in the connection of the motivational component to actual behavior: this connection is less evident in cyberspace.

Emotional intensity

> The first sign of maturity is the discovery that the volume knob also turns to the left.
>
> "Smile" zingers

The concept of "emotional intensity" is complex; it applies to different phenomena, not all of which are correlated. Despite this complexity, emotional intensity is often measured and compared in everyday life as well as in scientific experiments. The diverse features of emotional intensity are expressed in two basic aspects: magnitude (peak intensity) and temporal structure (mainly, duration). Duration can vary dramatically with comparable levels of peak intensity. In one study, participants rated the positive emotion associated with having "someone you find attractive suggest you meet for coffee" as almost as high as the emotion experienced after "saving your neighbor's child from a car accident." However, the average estimated duration associated with the former was twenty minutes, whereas for the latter it was more than five hours. Similarly, respondents estimated that they would stop ruminating about the coffee suggestion after about two hours, whereas the experience of the car accident would lead to rumination for about a week.[17]

High levels of peak intensity characterize online relationships. Many online relationships are relatively short and run their course in no more than three months, after which they either fade away or turn into an offline relationship.[18] However, as in offline circumstances, in online relationships there is also great variability. Some people engage in months (or even a year) of online communication before they actually meet and have offline or have online sex for the first time. One woman writes: "I'm a 33 year old female who's been married now to a wonderful man for 9 years. I started chatting on line about a year ago and I met this guy on line. We talked for about 6 months and he asked me if I wanted to cyber, so of course I tried. I started having feelings for him."[19] Other people may meet online and have cybersex within five minutes. Moreover, it is plausible that where the geographical distance between the two lovers is less, the relationship that is conducted only online will be briefer, as the first face-to-face meeting will typically be sooner. Hence, in small countries, affairs conducted only online between people within the country will typically be briefer than affairs where the participants live in a large country or in different countries.

Emotional intensity is determined by several variables that may be divided into two major groups, one referring to the perceived *impact of the event* eliciting the emotional state and the other to *background circumstances of the agents* involved in the emotional state. The major variables constituting the event's impact are the strength, reality, and relevance of the event; the major variables constituting the background circumstances are accountability, readiness, and deservingness.

The event's strength is a major variable in determining the intensity of the emotional encounter. It refers, for example, to the extent of our perception of the misfortune in pity and the extent of our perception of inferiority in envy. A positive correlation usually exists between the strength of the perceived event and emotional intensity: the stronger the event is, the more intense the emotion.

In online relationships, the event's strength is often depicted as stronger than in actual reality – this is also the case in works of art. One woman notes about her online lover: "He is my every fantasy come true." Another woman writes to her online friend: "When I look at the movies, I see strong men who can make decisions and take care of their women, but when I meet men in real life, they seem – well, dependent. Maybe I'll meet a guy like you, eh? Someone strong and capable and stalwart." The woman compares her online lover, who she has never seen, to the strong men she sees in movies and not to those men she sees around her. Imagination makes the online events stronger. A woman who is looking for an online affair voiced the same desire: "I love my husband very much and want to stay with him. But I want to be accepted and loved by someone who will be my hero."[20]

There is no doubt that the online partner is idealized, and hence the emotions toward this person are intense. We should, however, also take into account that the event's strength depends upon its personal bearing. As suggested, online events are less personal than actual events and this weakens their emotional intensity.

The more we perceive the event as *real*, the more intense the emotion. The notion of "emotional reality" has an ontological sense referring to whether the event actually exists, and an epistemological sense, referring to its vividness. Emotional intensity is greatest when an event is real in both senses. Referring to the ontological sense of reality, we may say that when we know that the danger actually exists, we are more frightened than when we suspect that the danger is illusory. Concerning the epistemological sense, we may say that the more vivid the image is, the more intense the emotion it generates.

Cyberspace is less real in the ontological sense – since it is a virtual place – but it can be real in the epistemological sense as it facilitates vivid fantasies. These fantasies are even more real since they do not merely involve passive images, but actual interactions. A 52-year-old married man writes: "Each time I had cybersex, I was really acting out some of my more common fantasies. With the help of some unknown and unseen people on the Internet, these experiences were very rewarding."[21] Moreover, in light of the greater sincerity of online communication, the conveyed information is sometimes more adequate. Indeed, some people testify that their online lovers are more real to them than their offline spouses are. Thus, a woman may feel that even when her husband is at home, he is less real to her than her unseen online friend is. In addition, the freedom to behave more openly can make an individual feel more of a real person while in cyberspace.

We often treat imaginary people as real people – this is true even when we realize the imaginary nature of the given circumstances. People's response to computers, movies, television, and new media are similar to the reactions they have to real people. Thus, people are as flattered and become as emotionally excited by computer messages as they are by real people, and they are polite to a computer asking a user about himself.[22] In online communication, the correspondent is not merely a computer, but a person using the computer; hence, emotional excitement is even more intense.

The variable of *relevance* restricts the emotional impact to areas that are particularly significant for us. As indicated, the intensity of emotions is achieved by their focus upon a limited group of objects. Emotional relevance is related to emotional *closeness*. Events close to us in time, space, or effect are usually emotionally relevant and significant. Greater closeness typically implies greater emotional intensity.

The variable of relevance is usually less significant in cyberspace since most people determine their self-image and significant goals in their actual environment. Online relationships involve physical distance, which is sometimes an obstacle to emotional closeness. Sometimes, however, the great tendency for online self-disclosure and extended conversations generate significant emotional closeness and hence intense emotions.

Responsibility (or accountability) refers to the nature of the agency generating the emotional encounter. Major issues relevant here are: (a) degree of *controllability*, (b) invested *effort*, and (c) *intent*. The greater the degree of controllability there was, the more effort we invested, and the more intended the result was, the more significant the event usually is and the greater the emotional intensity it generates. Thus, frustration is intensified if we attribute a failure to ourselves and if we have invested a lot of effort in trying to succeed.

The issue of responsibility is of greater impact in offline circumstances. In cyberspace, although we have greater control over the choice of the person to whom we relate, the consequences of such control are of less significance since mistakes can be easily corrected. Moreover, we scarcely need to invest any effort in cyberspace – on the contrary, we just go with the flow. This indicates that being in that space is in accordance with our emotional tendencies. As a result of all this, the impact of the variable of responsibility is weaker in cyberspace. Indeed, online lovers often confess that they are carried away by an intense love that they cannot control.

Readiness refers to the cognitive change in our mind; major factors in this regard are *unexpectedness* (or anticipation) and *uncertainty*. Since emotions are generated at the time of sudden change, unexpectedness is typical of emotions and is usually positively correlated with their intensity, at least up to a certain point. A factor related to, but not identical with, unexpectedness is uncertainty. We might expect some event to happen but not be certain of its actual likelihood. Uncertainty is also positively correlated with emotional intensity: the more uncertain we are that the eliciting event will occur, the more surprised we are at its actual occurrence and the more intense the emotion is.

The variable of the agent's preparedness, which is expressed in the agent's surprise and uncertainty, is typically stronger in cyberspace, where instability and changes are more dominant. The great availability of other attractive alternatives increases the uncertainty in cyberspace. The novel nature of cyberspace makes people do things they would not expect to do in offline circumstances. A 47-year-old married woman, who has an online affair, notes: "Never in my 23 years of marriage did I ever expect to have an affair."[23] Uncertainty is particularly high before date zero (the first face-to-face meeting of two online correspondents). Accordingly, before such a meeting, fear, and even anxiety, about being inadequate or rejected are high.[24]

The perceived *deservingness* (equity, fairness) of our situation or that of others is of great importance in determining the emotional significance of a certain event. People do not want to be unjustly treated, or to receive what is contrary to their wishes. Accordingly, the feeling of injustice is hard to bear – sometimes even more so than the actual hardship caused.

The variable of deservingness is of less impact in cyberspace. The fact that there are fewer practical implications and more positive alternatives weakens the impact of a negative event perceived as undeserved. Nevertheless, when online love is intense, participants may feel that the practical constraints preventing this love from being fulfilled are highly undeserved. The issue of deservingness is clearly expressed in the following confession:

> I was no longer in love with my husband and he deserved much more than I could ever offer him, so I left to give him a chance to love again. My lover is refusing to leave his wife for me, because of the kids, and I continue to love him with all of my heart, mind, body and soul, and yet he cannot make the choice. I too have a daughter, and she was hurt and angry. My life is ruined because of my deep love for this other man. I know what his wife is feeling and I don't hate her, but if she knew how much her husband loved me and how much I love him, wouldn't she rather give him up than keep him?[25]

As situations like this will become more and more common in cyberspace, the issue of deservingness will gain greater prominence as well.

The above regularities determining the relationship between an emotional variable and emotional intensity are also valid in cyberspace, just as they are valid in offline circumstances. The difference between cyberspace and offline circumstances is in the value of each variable.

It should be obvious by now that there is no simple answer to the question of whether online relationships involve more or less intense emotions than offline relationships. Although some general considerations relevant to this issue have been indicated, the answer depends on many circumstantial and personal factors. It should be clear, however, that online affairs involve intense emotions. People really do fall in love in cyberspace, and their love is often quite intense.

Emotions and intelligence

> I have noted that persons with bad judgment are most insistent that we do what they think best.
>
> Lionel Abel

There is a long tradition separating emotional experiences from intellectual considerations and accordingly criticizing the rationality and functionality of emotions. In this tradition, which pervades much of current culture, emotions are regarded as an impediment to rational reasoning and hence as an obstacle to normal functioning. I believe that this criticism is unfounded as emotions are highly functional and are rational in the sense of being the optimal response in many circumstances. Emotions are not functional in all circumstances, but they are tremendously important when facing urgent situations involving a significant change.

Emotional excess may have harmful consequences, but so can all types of excess. We should neither suppress our emotions nor allow them to overwhelm us excessively; we should aim at emotional balance.

In light of the novel nature of cyberspace and the fewer practical constraints associated with it, online emotions are typically of less functional value. The novelty of an online affair and the ease of inducing pleasant emotions may cause its participants to become addicted to it. This may have serious and harmful consequences. Future developments of online relationships may help people cope with online emotions and increase their functional value. In this regard, a major contribution will be made when we learn to combine, in a beneficial manner, online and offline relationships.

An emotion is a general mental mode of the mental system expressing a certain functioning arrangement of that system. Other possible modes are the perceptual and the intellectual modes. A given mental mode is not necessarily the complete opposite of another mode; they may differ in a few, but not all, features. For example, perception is found in the intellectual and emotional modes. Similarly, while feelings are intense in the emotional mode, they are not essential for the perceptual and intellectual modes. Thinking dominates the intellectual mode, but not the perceptual and emotional modes. Since the features constituting a mental mode admit degrees, the borderlines between various modes are not clear-cut.[26]

It seems implausible to assume that cyberspace has created a new type of mental mode. A mental mode, which has developed during many years of evolution and which expresses a general functioning arrangement of the whole mental system, is too profound to be altered by the introduction of a new type of communication. This may be changed in the future, but, for the time being, it seems that cyberspace has only caused various modifications in the emotional mode itself. Some of these changes have been indicated already: the online emotional mode is more dynamic, unstable, and transient; it is more partial and offers a greater role for the imagination. Accordingly, the online emotional mode is less structured than the offline mode.

The emotional mode in online relationships seems to incorporate more elements from the intellectual mode. Thus, the weight of conversation – which is essentially an intellectual activity – is by far greater in online relationships than in offline relationships. A woman who has participated in cybersex writes: "The best sex, obviously, is with someone literate enough to 'paint a picture' describing activities or thoughts. I suppose that in face-to-face activities, someone stupid could still be extraordinarily sexy. But stupid doesn't work online, at least not for me." Another woman described how, after a very intense online love affair, she married her online lover and discovered that their love deepened even more after their marriage: "I think being able to get to know someone deeply on an intellectual level makes a huge difference in how a relationship grows. (As long as Honesty is always observed.)"[27]

Philip Barry wryly characterized love as "Two minds without a single thought." Such an ironic characterization applies much less to online romantic relationships, which are based upon thoughts. As one man remarks: "I would argue that cybersex is good for the brain."[28] Accordingly, if typical offline communication can be described as face-to-face communication, online romantic communication might be described as brain-to-brain communication. Intellectual means play a greater role in achieving emotional intimacy in online relationships. Accordingly, it is easier to gauge a person's intellectual abilities in such relationships – so it is not surprising that many perceive their online partner to be more intelligent than their offline spouse. Indeed, a married woman recounts the pain she felt when her husband said that, although he loves her (the wife) and would never leave her, his online partner is "the most intelligent woman he's ever talked to."[29] The greater role played by intelligence in online relationships makes the online partner appear more attractive, since intelligence, as well as a sense of humor, are among the most engaging features of the opposite sex.[30] This may be an illusion, reflecting a greater use of intelligence, rather than a better quality.

From another perspective, online relationships may be considered to be more emotional than offline relationships. The great availability of exciting alternatives and the lack of practical considerations enable people to go with their emotional drives and instincts when visiting cyberspace. Rational considerations concerning the costs involved in ending an unsuccessful personal relationship carry considerably less weight in cyberspace, where people can more easily follow their hearts.

In online relationships, then, intellectual means are used for generating intense emotions. The other direction of influence is evident as well: emotional features influence intellectual attitudes. Thus, most sober and intellectual people experience intense emotions in cyberspace. As one person testifies: "I'm a rational woman whose heart has never been touched until now."[31]

Emotional intelligence is the optimal integration of the emotional and intellectual modes; it entails recognizing and regulating emotions in an optimal manner. In light of the differences between the two modes, we may consider emotional reasoning as different to intellectual reasoning. Neither type violates the rules of formal logic, such as the rules of contradiction and identity, but they do follow different principles from the point of view of their content.[32]

The conflict between emotional and intellectual perspectives is less significant in cyberspace as practical implications, which are calculated through intellectual deliberations, are less important. Since the integration of the two perspectives is easier to achieve online, it is easier to make more extensive use of both the emotional and intellectual capacities. In this sense, it often seems more comfortable to express emotional intelligence in cyberspace. Indeed, many online romantic relationships successfully combine emotional and intellectual aspects. Such a combination, which is at the heart of emotional intelligence, is indeed of great value in the romantic realm.

Netiquette

> A Code of Honor: Never approach a friend's girlfriend or wife with mischief as your goal. There are just too many women in the world to justify that sort of dishonorable behavior. Unless she's really attractive.
>
> Bruce Friedman

The spontaneous, profound, and sincere nature of emotions is to a certain extent contrary to the somewhat superficial, and insincere nature of polite behavior. Although good manners often have moral value, profound moral attitudes go far beyond politeness.[33] Murder is not considered impolite; it is a grave moral crime. Similarly, falling asleep during intercourse is not merely impolite; it is emotionally offensive. The borderline between immoral and impolite actions is not always clear – it depends upon the given context. Thus, in some circumstances ignoring a person may be just impolite, in others morally offensive. The importance of context is illustrated by the stripper who said that she does not find the show she performs degrading: "What I find degrading is when you're not being watched – if guys turn their back to you or keep talking or talk on the phone while you're dancing."[34]

Emotions can often hurt other people, whereas the main function of good manners is to prevent such harm. Accordingly, good manners are a useful means of hiding genuine emotions. Teaching children good manners is teaching them, among other things, to hide their real emotional attitudes. Indeed, because children's behavior is based more on spontaneous emotional attitudes, they tend to be more sincere than adults are. Over time, we learn to hide our emotions. Unlike emotions, good manners often express superficial attitudes that are more typical of our behavior toward strangers. In light of their superficial nature, good manners can be deceptive insofar as they do not necessarily express our genuine attitudes.

Good manners are focused upon actions – thereby concealing the underlying intentions and attitudes – whereas emotions express these intentions and attitudes. Translating emotions into actions is often limited by the practical and moral constraints of our present circumstances. Such constraints are less significant in online relationships where the practical aspect is marginal. This is another reason why good manners are of lesser importance in online relationships and sincerity is more dominant.

In intense emotions, terms like "proper" or "improper" become meaningless, as emotions are the only beacon leading our way. In intense online affairs, it is easier to be drawn into the emotional ocean and not to pay attention to practical constraints or superficial good manners. Moreover, the informal nature of online communication, in contrast to the formal nature of good manners, further reduces the role of good manners in cyberspace.

Although good manners are less significant in online relationships, they still have a role, since it is not a monitor you correspond with, but a real person who has values and emotions and who can be offended. Thus, although it is easy and common in cyberspace to end an unwanted romantic affair by ceasing all further correspondence, this impolite behavior may hurt the other person.

While communication connects people, it is also a form of intrusion. Good manners attempt to reduce the damage caused by this intrusion. An extreme form of such etiquette is that prevailing in Victorian England when speaking was considered a breach of privacy; hence, the (paradoxical) instruction "Do not speak unless spoken to," and the rule that no gentleman should address a lady until she had first spoken to him.[35] Because of the intrusive character of communication, the early appearances of modern means of communication, such as the telephone, radio, television, and the Internet were accompanied by concerns about what code of politeness was most appropriate to each form.[36] A new technology often generates a new social environment in which the appropriate behavior has not yet been determined. It is thus hardly surprising that several manuals detailing online etiquette have been published.

Here are a few examples of "netiquette."

- Do not type your message in capital letters – it is considered tantamount to yelling.
- Do not abandon a conversational partner without saying good-bye.

- Keep it clean – vulgarity is never impressive.
- Write a new and relevant subject line for your message.
- Acknowledge that you received the message (even if the message only says, "I'm not interested").
- Do not try to force a woman to reveal her telephone number or agree to a face-to-face meeting.
- Do not complain about the opposite gender or make generalized remarks about men or women.
- Once both cyberpartners have been satisfied, or faked satisfaction, at least say thank you.

Moreover, familiar deceptive compliments – such as telling the other person that she certainly does not look her age in her photo – are recommended as well.[37]

Some of the rules constituting netiquette run counter to the direct, sincere, and emotionally loaded nature of online communications. Thus, Miss Manners even forbids the use of email for love letters; she approves of email for neutral or positive business communication, but not for bad news or for emotionally charged good news. Another etiquette expert argues that you should never mail or post anything you would not say to your reader's face. Such advice identifies online and offline relationships and tries to apply similar rules to both. This is inappropriate, however, as the two types of relationships are different, each having its own advantages and flaws. This is not to deny the presence of some rules that are common to both relationships. But when two people spend hours writing back and forth to each other, there is little value in being formal or dishonest.

Indeed, flattery, which is a kind of insincere, purposive praise, is more common in offline relationships, where telling the truth can often hurt you and your relationships with those around you. Concerning flattery, Richard Stengel gives the following advice: "Never ever be candid when a person asks you to be candid." He explains that people "are seeking compliments, not candor; support, not frankness – so anything even mildly negative is interpreted as a harsh criticism."[38]

In online relationships, flattery is less common since people are less vulnerable and there are fewer practical benefits to gain by flattering the other person. Moreover, since cyberspace is a more egalitarian environment, hierarchies are less significant there; thus, there is less incentive to use flattery. In online relationships, people are not seeking to be flattered, but really want you to be candid. Hence, genuine compliments are more frequent. This may somewhat compensate for the imaginary nature of cyberspace. In a dream you can be candid, as you are less accountable and less likely to hurt others. Dreams often express our genuine emotions and needs.

Summary

> I told you I was sick.
>
> Inscription on a tombstone in Ashland,
> New Hampshire

This chapter has described the nature of the emotional mode of the mental system. Typical emotions are generated by perceived significant changes and their focus of concern is personal and comparative. Typical emotional characteristics are: instability, great intensity, partiality, and brief duration. Basic components are cognition, evaluation, motivation, and feelings.

Although the emotional mode in cyberspace in many respects resembles that of offline circumstances, there are some differences. Thus, change, instability, and transition are more noticeable in cyberspace. Another crucial feature in generating emotions, that is, the availability of an alternative, is far more dominant in cyberspace, where the number of available alternatives is almost unlimited. This has profound implications for the nature of online romantic relationships. As cyberspace is an unstable environment, enduring emotions are less dominant there.

Emotions are functional and rational in many offline circumstances. Their functionality and rationality is less evident in cyberspace because of its novel nature and the fact that people have not yet learned how to cope with it. That may change as this medium evolves and as we become more able to combine online and offline relationships.

Cyberspace facilitates greater use of both the emotional and the intellectual capacities of participants in romantic relationships, as the conflict between these two capacities is reduced. The greater involvement of intellectual capacities in our emotional world may decrease the spontaneity of emotional responses, but may facilitate the communication of more complex emotional messages.

Online relationships have a profound impact upon our emotional experiences. It is not clear yet whether online relationships will constitute such significant changes in our emotional life as to generate new types of emotions.

Unlike the spontaneous, profound, and sincere nature of emotions, good manners often express superficial and insincere attitudes. The main function of good manners is to avoid hurting other people, especially strangers. Since online relationships are to a large extent sincere and their potential harm is lower, the role of good manners is reduced in such relationships. Nevertheless, since online relationships are conducted between real people, some rules of polite behavior should be kept in order to avoid hurting other people.

4 *Online imagination*

The Internet is the brave new world of the imagination.
Deb Levine

Imagination is the stuff that cyberspace in general and online relationships in particular are made of. Nevertheless, people take their online relationships seriously and experience real intense emotions. The advantage of online imagination in improving reality is also its drawback: people may have difficulties distinguishing between imaginary and actual circumstances. This chapter examines the nature and consequences of online imagination.[1]

Emotions and imagination

You may say I'm a dreamer, but I'm not the only one.
John Lennon

Imagination may be broadly characterized as a capacity to consider possibilities that are not actually present to the senses. In this broad characterization, which is epistemological in nature, memory and thought are types of imagination, since in both we consider such possibilities. A narrower characterization of imagination, which facilitates distinctions between imagination and capacities such as memory and thought, adds an ontological criterion to imagination: imagination is an intentional capacity referring to nonexistent events – or at least those believed by us to be such events.

In the narrow sense, imagination refers to an object that is not present to the senses and that has never existed (or that, on the basis of our current knowledge, has a very low probability of existing). This type of imagination can be further divided into two kinds: (a) the subject does not know about the falsity of the imagined content, and (b) the subject does know about the falsity of the imagined content. The first type includes cases of hallucinations, illusions, and simple mistakes. In the second type, which may be termed "counterfactual imagination," the imaginary content is false and is known to be so. This type involves fantasies and reference to alternatives that could have occurred. The significance in our life of the second type of imagination can be gauged from the impact of various forms of art upon our life. Art often describes events that do not actually exist, but are vividly presented.

Imagination has a crucial role in generating emotions. This role has to do with the comparative nature of emotions: emotional comparison involves reference to a situation that is different from the present one. Emotional imagination does not merely refer to situations that are not present to our senses, but also to situations that do not exist at the moment – most of which will never exist at all.

Imagination has important cognitive and affective functions: (a) it helps us understand our environment and prepare ourselves for future situations, and (b) it improves our affective attitudes. Although emotional imagination is frequently connected with illusions and self-deception, it is often advantageous in helping us to cope with the harsh reality around us.

The ability to imagine situations that are different from those presented to the senses, and that may not exist, is an essential feature of human consciousness in general and of emotions in particular. Fear and hope entail imagining a future alternative to the present one, and regret involves the imagination of a past alternative that could have been but is no longer available to us. Jealousy also often involves fantasy – frequently, our jealousy does not vanish when we realize its imaginary nature and any pretext is sufficient to revive it. Indeed, the most frequent event eliciting jealousy among married people is not actual infidelity, but involves the partner paying attention, or giving time and support to, a member of the opposite sex.[2]

The important role of emotional imagination, and positive cognitive biases in particular, is clearly evident in the romantic realm. Contrary to the belief that lasting romantic satisfaction depends on accurate understanding of the partners' real strength and frailties, positive cognitive biases are quite valuable in making romantic relationships more satisfying and less distressing. Sustaining a sense of security often requires weaving an elaborate story – which is often fictional – that both embellishes a partner's virtues and overlooks, or at least minimizes, his or her faults. Accordingly, some happily married couples avoid unpleasant topics, lie about their feelings, and repudiate their own or their spouse's statements. Stable satisfied relationships reflect intimates' ability to see imperfect partners in idealized ways.[3]

The reality of online imagination

> The difference between fiction and reality? Fiction has to make sense.
>
> Tom Clancy

The role of imagination in generating emotions in cyberspace is even greater than in actual-space. The factual information we have about an online partner is usually more limited than our knowledge of an offline partner, and our imagination must fill in the gap. Particularly absent, or at least not verified, is information concerning negative features, which an online partner may have reason not to reveal. In such matters, our imagination typically enhances our image of the partner. Although people are aware of the illusory nature of this supplementation, online imagination still generates intense emotions.

In cyberspace, the identity of the partner is sometimes fictitious, and we are communicating with the received construct of a person who may not actually exist. When we are not sure of the real nature of our online partner, emotional intensity is typically reduced, as the degree of reality is small. The longer the online communication continues, the lesser the probability of maintaining a deceptive presentation. People who disguise themselves at the beginning of these relationships tend to reveal their true identity when they become closer to their online friend. In one such interesting case, two people fell in love with each other and only then did they reveal their secret: the one who had presented "himself" as a man was actually a woman, and the one who had presented "herself" as a woman was actually a man. Upon discovering their mutual deceit, they terminated the relationship, angrily accusing each other of dishonesty. Eventually they resumed their online relationship and even married, but this time the relationship was based upon phone conversations and face-to-face meetings. Even in such a case, where the true identity of the partner was not disclosed, the communication was nevertheless with a real existing person.

In many online relationships, most of the partner's characteristics are known. The imaginary aspect is mainly expressed in communicating fantasies, which cannot be fulfilled – not because the two people do not desire it, but because of spatial separation and other actual constraints, such as family obligations. The kind of imaginary reality in which these two partners interact may not actually exist, but it expresses what the two people really want. This imaginary reality is quite real and vivid to its participants.

The philosopher Immanuel Kant, who lived in the eighteenth century, argued that imagination should be cultivated and curbed in order to decrease its negative impact upon proper reasoning. He severely criticized the effect of reading novels, particularly – but not only – on children:

> Novel-reading is the worst thing for children, since they can make no further use of it, and it merely affords them entertainment for the moment . . . Therefore all novels should be taken away from children. Whilst reading them they weave, as it were, an inner romance of their own, rearranging the circumstances for themselves; their fancy is thus imprisoned, but there is no exercise of thought.

For Kant, children should be allowed to use their imagination only when it is not allowed to roam and when it is controlled by rules, as in the use of maps that confine the imagination to certain figures. Accordingly, Kant highly recommends the study of geography for children. With reference to adults, too, Kant believed that "*Reading novels* has the result, along with many other mental disorders, of making distraction habitual."[4] In comparison to activities such as cybersex, and in light of Kant's criteria, reading novels may today be regarded as an educational, and even virtuous, activity. Paraphrasing what President Gerald Ford said about Lincoln, we may say that if Kant were alive today, he'd roll over in his grave.

Although imagination describes events that do not obey all normal regularities and are not constrained by all laws of nature, cyberspace is different from free-form fantasy in that it is constrained by various factors. In order for online imagination to be most effective, it should largely emulate reality, while also improving upon it and making it more exciting. Similarly, works of art often provide us with imaginary situations, but their authors make us believe in their reality by referring to real everyday features.

The sense of reality in online relationships is enhanced by several factors. First, online relationships involve interactions with real people in real situations. Second, online relationships facilitate the adoption of the other's perspective. These relationships basically consist of the partners' self-descriptions of their situations; this exposes people to looking at events and circumstances from another's point of view. By seeing life through the eyes of those directly involved, we adopt their perspective and feel emotionally close to them; consequently, intense emotions are easily generated. Third, cyberspace introduces many alternatives to our present situation. It does not necessarily describe how people behave in reality but how they could behave. This opens the door for alternatives we did not think existed. Encountering such new alternatives excites us.

When having an online affair, people are often aware of its imaginary aspects. However, they knowingly abandon the actual realm for an imaginary one in which they accept events as though they were real. This entails a suspension of disbelief. Indeed, sometimes people describe their online relationship as "dreaming while awake." And people delight in these dreams; as one woman writes: "If this is a dream, let me sleep forever."[5]

Despite the interactive nature of cyberspace, in offline circumstances people are more active. People do not merely write about their imagined activity; they actually perform it. However, in offline circumstances people do not act upon many of their fantasies and desires, whereas in cyberspace they write about them and share them with other people – thus giving them greater significance and reality. Accordingly, there is more likelihood of realizing fantasies with people you meet in cyberspace than with people you encounter offline. The higher degree of significance and reality and the fact that many inhibitions have already been broken down also facilitate this process.

In cyberspace people are more physically isolated – having fewer face-to-face human contacts – but they have more social connections with other human beings. This development does not make us less human; on the contrary, the development of complex imaginary capacities is unique to the human race. Indeed, imagination plays a far greater role in the generation of emotions in humans than it does in animals' emotions. Cyberspace does not diminish the sociability of our life; rather, social relations that are partially imaginary complement our actual social relations. It is still unclear whether this is for better or for worse in the majority of cases.

Although online communication is a kind of detached communication, it arouses real emotions in its participants. Kurt, a married man having an online affair, describes emotions toward his online lover: "I was falling in love with this woman and I had no idea what she looked like. I thought about her all the time. The next night, I told her, 'I think I'm falling in love with you.' We both fell hard, fast and deep. I was miserable when I couldn't talk to her all the time."[6] The great sense of reality is also evident in the fact that women often complain that clicking into a chat room is like walking into a room full of men standing with their pants down screaming, "Hey, look at mine."[7]

The reality of an online relationship may be a useful preparatory tool for a good interpersonal relationship. Consider the following advice from Deb Levine, a sex-educator: "Once you become comfortable with your flirting skills on-line, practice them with someone you know in real life but have been too timid to approach. This is the ultimate test, and a perfect way to use the medium to your advantage."[8] Sometimes when a person is involved in cybersex, it can increase the sexual satisfaction of this person and her offline partner. Thus, a married woman says: "I enjoy seeing my lover receive pleasure, and I would watch with delight! Then, while he was enjoying his conversation on-line, I could play with him, and do the actions that the person on the screen was doing to him." Another woman reports a similar experience: "Since my husband can't type, I do it for him when he's online. His first cyber experience was a blast for both of us. We had a great time online and an even better time afterward."[9]

Online interactions may be considered as a kind of virtual laboratory for exploring each other and experimenting with types of relationships. In this sense, they are similar to games that children play and that enable them to develop, in a relatively safe and benign way, social skills for adult life. Indeed, cyberspace has been characterized as an amazing sex toy.[10] Brenda Danet shows that cyberspace has many features of playful activity. It is free – participation is not obligatory; it is highly uncertain – its anonymity leaves space for many surprises; it is unproductive – creating neither goods, nor wealth; it is governed by rules, which are not the ordinary laws of society; it has the character of make-believe – because their identity is disguised, participants enjoy reduced accountability for their actions and can engage in "pretend" or "make-believe" behavior. People can reinvent themselves. As in games, in cyberspace the process is often more important than the outcome, and, as are many games, cyberspace is characterized by spontaneity, manifest joy, and a sense of humor.[11]

Exciting information

> I may not be a great actress but I've become the greatest at screen orgasms. Ten seconds of heavy breathing, roll your head from side to side, simulate a slight asthma attack and die a little.
>
> Candice Bergen

Cyberspace is an exciting place – because of this it is both seductive and compulsive. The excitement involved in online relationships does not merely stem from their closeness to reality, but also from the type of information communicated in them. Thus, information conveyed in online relationships, and in particular the disclosure of highly personal details, is often more candid than that conveyed in offline relationships.

In this sense, online information is more real and hence emotionally more exciting.

Online communication, when it is mainly based upon written messages and not on visual information, may be considered less real in the sense of being less vivid, since vision provides more vivid information than the other senses do. A picture or, better still, a film-clip, of one wounded child usually has more emotional impact than reports about thousands killed. A picture is worth a thousand words. This is true, but this deficiency may be compensated for in cyberspace by the act of sincere self-disclosure. Moreover, many people now exchange pictures before cybersex; in fact, for many people that is a prerequisite if they are to take the relationship any further than the initial greeting.

Another important consideration in this regard concerns the fact that sometimes less information is more exciting than detailed information, since imagination fills in the missing data, and, in the process, enhances and romanticizes the object. A half-naked body may in some cases be more exciting than a fully dressed or a stark-naked body, since a half-naked body offers visual excitement while leaving enough room for fantasy, which is also significant in sexual desire. Nakedness increases arousal level, while its partiality leaves the imagination room to fantasize and embroider upon reality. Likewise, in online relationships, less information can be more exciting than more information. The informational gaps are filled with titillating details supplied by our imagination or by the partner's enhanced self-description. Imagination involves abstraction or selective attention more than ordinary perception does; this selection can improve the overall picture and make it more exciting.

The lack of information in general, and negative information in particular, further contributes to the intensification of positive emotions. It has been found that the more you think about your romantic partner, the greater your love is for that person. Moreover, in the absence of any new information, thoughts intensify romantic emotional attitudes toward one's partner.[12] These phenomena are particularly evident in online relationships, where information about the partner is limited, and its only source is what the partner chooses to tell.

Online sexual affairs are often wilder and more passionate than those in real life. There are no constraints or limitations upon the imaginary content or the types of activity involved. The combination of the wildest fantasies with actual, verbal interaction is extremely arousing. Thus, a 32-year-old woman, married for the second time, claims: "The sexual release from cybering has been a great experience and the arousal factor is just magnificent."[13]

The excitement created by the imaginative reality is further intensified by knowing what your partner is thinking while making love to you – and it is typically the case that the description of such thinking is easier to produce and quite sincere: "Many of us have never been with anyone who says or does the sexy, exciting things we crave. Cybersex allows us to retreat into our imaginations and experience some of the wild sexual adventures we don't dare do in real life."[14] Sharing sexual fantasies with your partner – which is more rare in offline sex – further intensifies the excitement of online affairs. The printed form of the message, which is yours to examine and read as often as you wish, increases the degree of reality of the fantasies and hence the excitement they generate.

I have suggested that partial information is sometimes more exciting than full information. This phenomenon exists when a large portion of the relevant information is available and only a small portion of it is not revealed. However, when most of the information is not available and must be supplemented by imagination, detailed descriptions, which give the impression of vivid and real events, generate more excitement. Cybersex is an example of this. Since cybersex is essentially an imaginative activity consisting of verbal interaction, the verbal dimension needs to be very detailed in order to be exciting and to compensate for the lack of physical interaction. Consider the following excerpts from a cybersex encounter between Andrew, a 30-year-old married man, and Bree, a 45-year-old divorced woman:

> *Andrew:* as you lean over me . . . your nipple so close . . . my tongue . . . finds one – it's hard . . . I roughly lick it – I am admiring your body as I worship its beauty with my mouth, paying close attention to every detail. I take your left breast slowly into my mouth, slowly swirling my tongue around your erect nipple. I place my leg between your legs and you respond by thrusting your hips forward and rubbing your scalding pussy against it, slowly, then faster. I push your breasts close together and take turns pleasing each nipple; they are so hard. My cock is fully erect and searching for a place to go.
> *Bree:* oh yes . . . honey . . . lips open . . . for your hard cock . . . want to feel you deep inside me. Make me cum . . . baby . . . now . . . I'm so ready.[15]

These vivid and detailed descriptions excite the imagination and go some way toward overcoming the lack of direct visual and tactual stimuli. Cybersex must be detailed and creative in order to be exciting – you cannot just say to the other person "I fuck you" and expect her to reach orgasm. Foreplays involving creative gestures and activities are quite important here. Michael Bader compares cybersex to musical improvisation: "the presence of a clearly defined overall structure or theme allowing tremendous room for creative and highly varied improvisation. Cybersex doesn't have to be a one-note song."[16]

The great excitement involved in cybersex generates for some people better online orgasms than the ones they experience offline. This may be frustrating to those who are also engaged in actual sex, and it may be particularly harmful for the primary offline relationships.

Cybersex sometimes has positive effects on people's sexual encounters with their offline partners. The online sexual freedom is often carried over into people's actual sexual behavior. Many relationship therapists indicate the importance of talking openly about intimate matters, including your sex life. This is exactly what is done in online sexual affairs, where sex and other intimate matters are discussed without being physically performed.[17]

Traditional norms of sexuality, which are quite restrictive, have been mainly designed for face-to-face relationships. Even if not everyone obeys these norms, the norms have a status of guiding normative principles, and hence deviations from them are not taken lightly. Although these norms are sometimes directed also at fantasies – in some cultures it is forbidden even to think about adultery – it is clear that fantasyland is not their main arena. Imaginative online relationships can more easily transgress traditional norms of sexuality. Accordingly, people are sexually freer in cyberspace than in offline circumstances. The kind of anonymity provided by the computer enables people to say things they would not think of saying face-to-face.

The reality of romantic and sexual imagination

> Cybersex can be a wonderful experience. It is the coming together of two minds – joined for the pleasure of mind-sex. (Of course, if done right, it can be VERY physically rewarding as well.) You describe your actions instead of doing them. Each partner tells the other(s) what you're doing, what you want to do, and how you feel. Using your imagination, you can set scenes that enhance the activities or otherwise play a role in your experience.
>
> Deb Levine[18]

Online affairs, and particularly cybersex, are often condemned. It has been claimed that these affairs show no regard for actual friends, that they are selfish, involve lust, rampant imagination, and immorality, and that they lack any sincere or affectionate attitudes toward others. Although these claims may be true in some online relationships, it is certainly not necessarily so. Levine's description of cybersex, referring to "the coming together of two minds," expresses the fundamental wish of profound love: fusion of the two lovers. Indeed, Erich Fromm describes romantic love as "the craving for complete fusion, for union with one other person."[19] Online imagination helps people fulfill this fusion, which is much harder to achieve in offline circumstances. As one woman writes: "It is hard to think of any differences that we have. Although there are differences they are such surface issues. I feel like he is the other side of the same coin. We are one."[20] The unlimited power of imagination makes online fusion easier.

While engaging in romantic affairs, many people behave as if they are real affairs. However, because of their offline obligations, people may want to play down the reality of their online affairs. Consider the following statement by Anne:

> I admit that I like to flirt and occasionally play out sexual fantasies on the Net with select partners. But I draw the line by never going beyond the keyboard even though I've been asked to. I'm certainly not having an affair but I am having fun. When I turn off the PC at night, it's my husband's bed I climb into, not my partner in cyberspace. I'd hardly call that an affair.[21]

The issue here is whether when Anne turns off her PC, she can turn off her imagination and emotions. Not going beyond the keyboard no doubt helps, but this physical limitation does not necessarily limit the mind's activities.

Most online affairs are too real to be considered as mere fantasies. In such affairs people bring more than a dash of reality into the imaginary environment. Thus, a married woman who frequently participates in bisexual cybersex and is currently conducting an offline affair with another woman, reports: "I always 'prepare myself' for cybering, showered, perfumed, comfortable with all my sex toys at hand and away I go."[22] Furthermore, this is greatly assisted when the other person is perceived as being real. Therefore questions like "What are you wearing right now?" are frequently asked in online affairs; the description of the clothes – or their absence – makes the other person more real. The more aspects of reality that are introduced, the more exciting the affair becomes – and accordingly the more morally problematic it becomes. One person said that innocent conversations about general matters actually became a romantic affair for him once he had told his online friend his real first name and had asked her to tell him her real name. She replied that although she normally does not do so, she nevertheless would tell him.[23] The real name should actually make no difference; after all, there are so many first names and they have no relevance to the person's characteristics. However, exchanging real names adds the dash of reality that is so crucial for the further development of the relationship. (It should be remembered that in most online communication, the abbreviated online names have more to do with drawing attention to the writer than with self-expression.[24])

After the name came phone calls, pictures, personal cards, written letters, gifts, and face-to-face meetings. Some people send personal items, such as clothing, a ring, or even a lock of their hair. All these items make the other person appear more real. The addition of written letters may appear to be odd, as it does not seem to furnish extra information or another form of interaction to the already existing online communication. In fact, certain information is added – that of the person's real address and his or her handwriting. Furthermore, writing letters, which is a more time-consuming activity than online communication, may also express the partner's readiness to invest greater effort in the relationship.

The anonymity of cyberspace sustains a greater degree of biases and even illusions: the hole beckons the burglar. Indeed, individuals are able to present more idealized versions of themselves through online communication than in face-to-face interaction. Accordingly, modesty is less frequent in cyberspace.

It may be argued that positive biases are not solely characteristic of online romantic relationships, but also of offline relationships. This is true, but such biases are more significant in cyberspace. Imagination is most prominent in the first stages of the offline affair, that is, when falling in love. At first we do not know much about the beloved person, and thus tend to idealize her; many relationships fall apart when it turns out that the person we fell in love with is not really quite like we imagined her to be. Such idealization is one woman's claim that: "I really felt that I've found a knight with a noble soul in cyberspace." Only in their first face-to-face meeting did she find that her "dearest cyber angel" had been married for just two months.[25]

Dangers of online imagination

> If you eat something, but no one else sees you eat it, it has no calories.
>
> Lewis Grizzard

Online relationships ignore actual circumstances much more than any face-to-face relationship can afford to do. This is their strength and their weakness. By ignoring sad circumstances, we may be happier, but since this positive attitude is to a certain degree unrealistic, it may increase our disappointment when we face reality. When cyberspace becomes the major source of our emotional nourishment, we increase the risk of distorting reality to the extent that coping with it becomes not easier, but harder. Since in online imagination we control the imagined content, we may lose the ability to distinguish the really trivial from the really important.[26] This may lead to harmful consequences.

The penalties attached to having an online affair are often similar to those of an offline affair; they include, for example, hurting the offline partner, endangering the successful maintenance of romantic relationships with offline partners, or disappointment stemming from the virtual nature of the online affair.

Discovering that your partner is engaged in an online affair can be as painful as discovering the existence of an offline affair. As a 50-year-old woman writes: "I had been happily remarried for two years when I found that my husband was on the computer having cyber-sex. I was shocked, horrified and felt like murdering him." A married man reports a similar experience upon finding his wife having cybersex:

> It hurt every bit as much if not more than when she had cheated on me physically. If a lover chooses to give their body to another, if it was not meaningful and just a cry for attention, then they can be forgiven, and the relationship can be strengthened by it. But if a lover gives their heart, their mind, then how can it be considered right?[27]

Sometimes, emotional infidelity can be more hurtful than sexual unfaithfulness, as it is a more profound expression of the partner's attitudes.

An online affair can be costly because it may reduce the ability of the agent to conduct a primary offline relationship successfully. Thus, people having online affairs may find it difficult to maintain positive emotional attitudes toward their offline partner. A 35-year-old married woman who visits sex sites and engages in cybersex remarks: "My husband could no longer satisfy me. I wanted what I saw in the videos and pictures, and was too embarrassed to ask him for it."[28] It is difficult, though not impossible, to integrate the excitement generated online into an offline relationship.

The illusory nature of cyberspace may lead to frustration. Thus, the diverse social connections available online may further increase the feeling of loneliness in actual everyday life, as online communication is a social activity done alone. This is clearly illustrated in the following statement by a woman: "I am often the most lonely after I've spent a day talking to people on the computer. I don't think I'm alone in feeling that way."[29] It is also the case that, when lonely, people are more likely to use their imagination – there are less actual people around them to constrain it.[30] The frustration stemming from the imaginary nature of an online affair may indeed be significant. Consider the following description:

> Mike, a 35 year old man, married unhappily for one year at the time he met in the cyberspace Wilma, a 17 year old girl who had, he thought, the charming freshness of a child but also the intelligence and depth of an older woman. They had much to say to each other, most of it sexual, most of it exciting. They conducted private email, telephone calls, and impassioned telephone sex. Sometimes when Mike called it was Wilma's mother, Judy, who answered. Sometimes he talked with Judy about his work and ambitions and Judy would talk about her life, her problems, and her abandoning husband. Mike liked Judy, but was in love with her daughter Wilma. After a few months – when his marriage was already over as he and his wife grew further apart – he made concrete plans to meet Wilma. At that time Judy confessed: there was no Wilma and never had been – Judy had made up Wilma by acting on her part. When Mike was asked how he felt he said that he is not angry with Judy, but rather: "I'm miserable. I've lost Wilma! I've lost the girl I love!"[31]

When I was a boy, I hung the following saying in my room: "The loss of our illusions is the only loss from which we never recover." The Internet allows people to escape from their everyday problems into an environment that can sometimes be fictional, but is consequently also much better. This environment may fulfill many of our dreams: it flatters us by enabling us to define ourselves in any way we wish; similarly it helps us invent other desirable people.[32] In this sense, the Internet may provide a lot of support to many people. When this support is found to be illusory, the pain is immense. Advance knowledge of the limitations and risks involved in online relationships may help people cope with such adverse circumstances.

The tendency to escape into emotional imagination appears to be more pronounced in modern society. Although computer-mediated communication has created the global village by generating many links between people, it has also separated us from actual experiences of the world by creating an environment in which images substitute for reality and communication substitutes for actual encounters. Cyberspace lacks many typical constraints of the actual world, and hence may be a safer and cleaner environment. However, it can also distort reality to the extent that it becomes more difficult for us to cope with the actual world.

Regret and online affairs

To err is human – but it feels divine.

Mae West

Regret is basically a sorrow over a past alternative that was available to us, but that we missed. Regret is an emotion that, by use of our vivid imagination, bridges the past and present with an eye to the future. In typical regret, we negatively evaluate in the present something we did or refrained from doing in the past; we do so in light of present and future considerations. Regret affects people's behavior not only after a decision is made but also before the decision is made, when they anticipate the regret they may feel later. Therefore, most people tend to make regret-minimizing choices – that is, they make choices to minimize their possible future regret. These choices are typically risk-avoiding.

We may distinguish between two types of regret – short- and long-term regret. As a short-term emotion, regret is concerned with a loss caused by a specific, recent action; the long term sentiment of regret is concerned with loss in the past, which has repercussions on the general course of life. In the short term, people regret their actions more than their inactions, but when people look back on their lives, those things that they have not done are the ones that produce the most regret. Accordingly, the fear of short-term regret encourages inaction, whereas the fear of long-term regret encourages actions. Long-run considerations are mainly concerned with lost opportunities, whereas short-term considerations are concerned more with actual gains.[33]

Romantic affairs are deeply connected with both types of regret. In the short term, people often regret their brief sexual affairs – this is "the-morning-after affect"; in the long term, people typically regret romantic and sexual affairs they did not have. Initiating romantic and sexual affairs involves various risks – especially if one of the partners is already within a committed relationship; such affairs are likely to generate regret in the short, and often also in the long, term. Avoiding such affairs is likely to produce regret in the long term and dissatisfaction in the short term.

Online affairs may make it easier to deal with the problem of regret, as it facilitates low-risk affairs. Such affairs provide the excitement associated with romantic affairs, hence avoiding romantic dissatisfaction in the short term and regret in the long term. The lesser degree of risk and moral criticism associated with such affairs also enables participants to avoid short-term regret and actual harm. Avoiding romantically exciting affairs may succeed in preventing short-term regret concerning the harmful consequences of our actions. As time goes by, however, regret over inaction is stronger, and avoiding pleasant actions becomes more and more difficult.

Accepting painful reality is easier if we can conceive of it as inevitable – that is, if we can persuade ourselves that there are no practical chances of changing the situation. When faced with disappointment, people may mentally reduce the estimated odds for a better outcome, thus making the actual outcome more palatable.[34] Adopting the belief that "nothing can be done," or "I do not have a chance," which is a useful tactic to mitigate disappointment, is difficult when cyberspace offers easy access to many attractive alternatives. The presence of many attractive online partners increases the pain of doing nothing about an unsatisfactory offline relationship.

In a way, cyberspace forces people to face reality – a reality that often contains one's actual, disappointing romantic relationship. One cannot avoid unpleasant reality by leading oneself to believe that better alternatives are not available. Cyberspace takes an intermediate position between reality and sheer fantasy. The escape into cyberspace is not essentially an escape into fantasy; it is often an escape to a semi-reality that presents our everyday life in a more realistic manner. Sometimes, offline relationships may benefit from such a presentation. Indeed, people testify that their online affair has been a beneficial, learning experience and has revealed many aspects of their offline relationship to them. Consider, for instance, the following account written by a married woman:

> A cybersexual affair was a real wake-up call in my life. I had been married for 20 years, happily I thought, but was lonely in my life. I made friends on the Net and rapidly found the sexual undercurrent to be intriguing. Within a year I was having some of the most exciting sex I'd ever experienced. It really is true what they say about the mind being the most powerful sex organ. I learned that there were things in my marriage that I needed badly and didn't know it till I experienced them elsewhere. All of this was learning and it helped my marriage in the long run.[35]

There are, of course, many other cases in which the excitement of an online affair resulted in the breakup of the offline relationship.

One way to prevent long-term regret is to encourage people to act on their impulses more often; people should focus less on the short-term consequences of their action and more often "just do it." However, acting on this advice may be dangerous as the status quo is usually safer than trying something new. Awarding greater significance to unwise actions may promote risky behavior and decrease chances of surviving. Cyberspace provides a kind of solution to this dilemma: it lets people act on their impulses, thus reducing long-term regret, and it significantly reduces the risks involved in such activity, thus reducing the prospects of short-term regret.

Summary

I'll let you be in my dream, if I can be in yours.

Bob Dylan

Cyberspace has managed to blur the borderlines of reality in many powerful ways. Fantasies, and in particular romantic fantasies, are much more accessible, cheaper, and real in cyberspace. The lure of such fantasies is greater and their consequences are more uncertain and dangerous.

A significant difference between offline and online personal relationships is the greater role of imagination in the latter. In online relationships, imagination substitutes for many actual activities. This has the advantage of enabling partners to participate in many experiences that actual circumstances would preclude; such virtual adventures are also cheaper and safer. Taking advantage of this aspect requires perceiving the imaginary environment as real to an important degree. This is indeed the prevailing attitude to online relationships, and it makes the imaginary content very exciting. Relying so much on imaginary information runs the risk of confusing the illusory environment with the actual one, and hence it may impede functioning within the actual environment.

Cyberspace removes our masks, but does not leave us naked. The soul has its own unique online colors, but these do not hide our personality; rather, they emphasize its essential features – warmth, sensitivity, and longing for intimacy. When we paint our online soul, we must use subtle brush strokes; no coarse or harsh elements belong in this enchanting world. When by mistake, or because of haste, such coarseness creeps in, its peculiarity is immediately obvious; it is apparent that it is an anomaly. It can make us as sick as if some microbe had aggressively entered our soul and tried to contaminate it. Cyberspace is sterilized from everyday worries, masks, and taboos. However, it is also quite fragile – many events can spoil it. Masks not only hide, but protect as well. The problematic nature of cyberspace has to do with its connection to the actual world. The risk of contamination is essentially an external risk. As long as we do not know how to connect the two worlds in a way that would immunize each of them from possible external harmful contamination, being in cyberspace can be hazardous.

For some people, the Internet is an imaginary replacement for various aspects of their actual world; for others, it is part of that world.[36] For the former group, the Internet presents a vivid and imaginary environment in which they can enjoy themselves. The latter perform many professional and social activities online – for example, checking their stocks, reading the news, and ordering their weekly supply of food or their airline tickets. These activities are not imaginary, and the Internet is a tool with which to perform them more efficiently.

The problem of the regret associated with romantic affairs is less severe in cyberspace as these are low-risk affairs. Online affairs provide romantic excitement at a lower degree of risk and moral criticism. Accordingly, short-term regret, which is often the unhappy consequence of a romantic affair, or long-term regret, which may arise from yearning for a past romance, occur less often in cyberspace. Regret in cyberspace is less prevalent, but it is not absent. Thus, people deeply regret the end of their cyber-relationships.

5 *Online privacy and emotional closeness*

It's so simple to be wise. Just think of something stupid to say and then don't say it.

Sam Levenson

Privacy is characterized as the right to be left alone, to be allowed to pursue one's activities without interference, scrutiny, or comment. Why is such a right important? Why do we want to be left alone without having the focus or attention of other people trained on us? The simple answer is that such scrutiny can harm us as it may conflict with some of the values that we, or those close to us, hold. However, while we wish to guard our privacy, we also want to be close and open with others by expressing our genuine emotional attitudes through which honesty is developed in a relationship. In personal relationships, privacy involves a process of boundary regulation, while openness implies boundary deregulation.

Emotions are typically associated with both closeness and openness. The desire for privacy seems to contradict these related features. Being emotionally close and open means losing some of our privacy, and maintaining a greater degree of privacy prevents us from being emotionally close and open.

The conflict between privacy and emotional closeness and openness is considerably weaker in cyberspace. The relative anonymity of cyberspace and the ability to control which matters we wish to reveal allow us to safeguard our privacy while increasing emotional closeness and openness. In fact, the nature of privacy itself has undergone a significant change in cyberspace, since many matters that are usually kept private tend to be discussed there.

The greater tendency toward closeness and openness online has led to a redefinition of the nature of shame, which like privacy is connected to fundamental values that we want to safeguard.

Privacy: Initial distinctions

> Nothing is quite as bad as being without privacy and lonely at the same time.
>
> Alexander Theroux

Understanding the concept of "private" requires distinguishing it from related and opposing concepts such as "personal," "secret," "solitude," "public," and "political."

Private is that which is confined to, or intended only for, a certain person. The realm of the private is whatever is not the legitimate concern of others.[1] *Personal* is that which is of or pertaining to a particular person's own affairs. Not everything that is personal is also private. The book I am writing is personal in the sense that it pertains to me: it expresses my own views; but the book is not private since it is not confined to me – at least, so I hope. Likewise, not everything that is private is also personal. My password for entering my Internet account is private since it is confined to me, but there is nothing personal about it: it consists of meaningless numbers. The distinction between personal and private is also kept in cyberspace. However, many personal details, which remain private in offline circumstances, become public in cyberspace. The need to guard privacy is less pronounced in a place where anonymity provides such protection.

What is private should also be distinguished from what is *secret* – although private information is often something we want to keep secret. Something secret is something that is withheld from the knowledge of others. Something can be private, that is, confined to a certain person, but not secret, as it may be known to others. George's love for his wife is not a secret: everyone knows about it; however, his loving attitude is private as it is confined to him. Something may be secret – for example, the nuclear weapons capability of a certain country – but not private: it is not confined to a certain person. In cyberspace, the overlap between privacy and secrecy is reduced. The relative anonymity of cyberspace decreases our vulnerability and so reduces the necessity for such secrecy in our private matters.

A distinction should also be drawn between privacy and *solitude* – that is, the wish to be completely alone, without the need for company. Privacy expresses a wish for a limited solitude: the wish to keep apart in terms of certain aspects but at the same time to be together in other aspects. Accordingly, privacy does not express the wish to retire, to withdraw, or go away, or be apart. One may like privacy, but still be gregarious. Ferdinand Schoeman rightly argues that privacy is important largely because of the way in which it facilitates associations between people, rather than the independence of people. Hence, the identification of the right to privacy with the right to be left alone is incomplete and misleading. The point of restricting access to our private actions is not generally in order to isolate us but to enable us to relate intimately.[2] Privacy expresses a wish to belong to a social group, to keep its principles (or at least its essential ones), but still have space for imagining and doing whatever one wants – even if this may sometimes conflict with certain prevailing norms. Privacy involves the wish to maintain some discretion over one's intimate affairs; it is not the wish for loneliness.[3]

Public is the opposite of private: it refers to something that is not confined to a certain person, but is open to all people. People often think in binary terms about the distinction between the private and the public: either something is seen as restricted to one person's access or it is available to everyone. In fact, the private–public distinction involves a more gradual differentiation. In order for my privacy to be violated, vital information about me does not have to appear on prime-time national television; if personal information that I want to keep private is revealed to a few other people, this also constitutes a violation of my privacy. Violation of privacy does not necessarily mean complete access to everyone; it can be any type of unwanted access.

Political is something of, or pertaining to, the state or its government. The issue of limited, or unlimited, access is not part of the definition of political; this definition refers to issues about which the government should take a stand. Political is the opposite of personal. Feminists have attacked the division between public and personal arguing that "the personal is political." The feminist position may be correct concerning certain relationships within the family; those should not always be considered personal, as it is the obligation of the state to prevent abuse within the family. However, this does not warrant the nullification of the distinction between the private and the public or that between the personal and the political. It also does not mean that all types of privacy are unjustified.

Types of privacy

> If privacy is outlawed, only outlaws will have privacy.
>
> Charles Wolf, Jr.

Various classifications of types of privacy are possible. As my main concern is the connection between privacy and emotions, my classification will relate to this concern. Any invasion of our privacy may invoke negative emotions if it poses a threat to our well-being. We can delineate three major types of circumstances in which an invasion of our privacy can harm us.

(a) Actions (real or imaginary) that are *in conflict with certain norms* of other people, and sometimes also with our own; here, an invasion of our privacy may provoke our *shame*. Examples of such actions are having, or even merely imagining, an extramarital affair, masturbating, having a homosexual relationship, sexual fantasies, and cybersex.

(b) Actions (real or imaginary) that are *normatively expected to be done when we are alone*, or at least in the presence of very few individuals; here, an invasion of our privacy may provoke our *humiliation*. Examples include performing ablutions in public, letting others see our intimate sexual organs or our intimate sexual activities, and having a domestic argument in public.

(c) *Information* about us that is harmless in one domain but *may become harmful* in another domain; here, an invasion of our privacy may provoke our *fear*. An example of such an invasion is providing information about our financial or medical situation to commercial companies or governmental agencies.

We may speak then about three types of privacy.

(a) Privacy intended to maintain individual norms that are in conflict with prevailing norms; this is basically *shame-preventing privacy*.
(b) Privacy intended to maintain our right to be in certain circumstances and to act in certain ways without the inspection of other people; this is basically *humiliation-preventing privacy*.
(c) Privacy intended to maintain our security; this is basically *fear-preventing privacy*.

Privacy guards our right not to be subjected to these negative emotions of shame, humiliation, and fear.

In the first group, which refers to actions that are considered as immoral by people who are significant to us, the normative aspect is most pronounced. Intrusion of our privacy in this regard may generate *shame in us* and *anger in other people*. The shame generated does not necessarily mean that we believe our actions to be morally wrong; however, we are aware that other significant people believe they are. This sense of privacy is typically associated with secrecy. Here, privacy protects us from revealing our immoral activities and may be characterized as *shame-preventing privacy*.

The second type of privacy, that is, *humiliation-preventing privacy*, does not involve the agent's immoral actions, but rather is a result of the fact that the agent's actions are not intended to be watched by others. There is nothing wrong in performing these activities: all of us, and often animals too, engage in them, but aesthetic and social norms require us not to do them in public. Individuals who are apprehended in such situations are liable to be viewed merely in terms of such activities.[4] This kind of privacy is typically associated with the search for limited solitude. Intrusion into our privacy here may generate humiliation in us and disgust or surprise in other people.

The new Webcams that provide total real-time surveillance of all the everyday activities of other people, including the most intimate and private ones, indicate the changes in norms of humiliation-preventing privacy. These activities performed in public do not generate humiliation or shame in the people engaging in them; on the contrary, they often generate pride. Some people get their thrills precisely from being watched.[5] The explanation of these phenomena is related to changes in the nature of privacy and shame in the Net. I will discuss this issue below.

The third type of threat to our privacy – when non-derogatory personal information is improperly used – involves a conflict between the individual and certain organizations within society. Our buying habits or medical problems do not express non-normative behavior, but the release of this information to governmental agencies or commercial companies may intrude upon our life and may harm us in the future. People do not want others to possess too detailed and complete a picture of them, in case it might be used against them at some time. Moreover, people want to be treated as autonomous individuals and not as statistical details. Invasion of this kind of privacy may generate our fear, and sometimes anger and humiliation. Hence, this privacy can be characterized as *fear-preventing privacy*.

Certain behaviors belong to more than one category of privacy. Thus, homosexual activity and masturbation belong to the first two types of privacy. Assigning each behavior to a specific category is of less importance than the realization that there are various types of privacy.

Privacy in modern society has become a matter of great concern, since many electronic tracing devices now exist that can reveal the most intimate information about each of us. This is particularly true concerning online relationships that are conducted through written messages, which can be kept by the respondent and can be retrieved by other people. The problem is especially evident at work, where many companies record all email messages automatically – these include, of course, any romantic messages that employees send and receive. Some employees have been fired because they were found to have conducted such a correspondence from work. Cyberspace has become an efficient place for storing and retrieving data, but it has increased the consequent risks when such data falls into the wrong hands.

Privacy, emotional closeness, and openness

Honesty has ruined more marriages than infidelity.
Charles McCabe

We often have to compromise our privacy with our wish to maintain significant personal and social relationships. We cannot be close to someone without revealing some personal, and often private, information about ourselves. Friendship means sharing, and sharing means relinquishing some privacy.

The need for privacy may be less pronounced in two extreme cases: (a) in a close, intimate relationship where two people feel themselves to be one augmented self; (b) in a relationship with a complete stranger. Privacy remains important in those relationships that fall between these two extremes: in relationships among people with some emotional ties.

Living in an isolated environment enables us to maintain almost complete privacy; living in a society and having close emotional ties implies losing some privacy. By letting emotions play a central role in our lives, we assent to being exposed to a certain extent; we relinquish some privacy in order to be able to live emotionally. Yet this is precisely what our friends may value in our relationships with them – that we show willingness to be emotionally drawn, to be vulnerable, to lose our privacy and reveal our secrets. Friendships entail having less privacy. Telling our secrets to someone may establish a friendship, but it also exposes our vulnerability. Those who are close to us can hurt us easily and we can easily hurt them – as the popular song puts it: "You always hurt the one you love." Some people actually avoid having friendships for this reason.

Having emotional ties may result in the loss of a certain degree of privacy, but there is no doubt that it has other advantages. It is hard to imagine a person living in complete social isolation. Social interactions enable us to promote our well-being and to avoid various types of danger. Being completely isolated is not a real option for a human being.

The choice we face is not that of having full or partial privacy, but rather to what extent we are ready to give up our privacy in return for close emotional ties. There is then an opposite correlation between emotional closeness and openness on the one hand and privacy on the other hand.

In intimate relationships people are often less careful about certain things they say and do. This opens the way for the other person to get hurt. The price of being able to behave freely without having to consider every consequence of each action we take is that we might hastily speak or act in ways that may hurt people who are close to us. Another relevant consideration in this context is that in a loving relationship, each partner usually has firsthand, intimate knowledge of the other's private aspects. Hasty use of this knowledge can cause considerable pain.

Concerns of privacy are also less significant when we are in the company of complete strangers who are not emotionally close to us, and in a sense do not care about us. As Garry Shandling said: "I'm too shy to express my sexual needs except over the phone to people I don't know." We can disclose intimate information to complete strangers, since they play an insignificant role in our life. Social pressure from a stranger typically counts less than pressure from people with whom we have some significant connections and who are vulnerable because of our disclosure.[6] With complete strangers, the issue of privacy is of little concern, since we are in a sense anonymous. Someone who likes to see pornographic movies may be ashamed to rent them at his neighborhood store, but is likely to feel more comfortable ordering them from a hotel room. To be sure, some people in the hotel will know that he ordered a pornographic movie, but that will not bother him because they are strangers having no bearing upon him. A society made up of complete strangers would not be a particularly attractive place, as it would be devoid of close psychological ties.[7] The likelihood of committing immoral actions would significantly increase in such a society.

Becoming closer to each other is typically associated with the process of decreasing the privacy zone around each of us. Both processes are gradual but not linear: there are points that are more significant than others, at which the emotional distance and the privacy zone decrease more rapidly.

There is then an interesting tradeoff between emotional closeness and openness on the one hand and privacy on the other hand: greater emotional closeness and openness imply lesser privacy, and greater privacy implies a decrease in emotional closeness and openness. The closer we are to a certain person, the more we want to be sincere and open by revealing intimate information; hence, our privacy zone is likely to contract. However, the closer we are to a certain person, the more stakes we have in the relationship, and intimate information is potentially more harmful for us; hence, we wish to expand our privacy zone. Accordingly, we need to find the right balance between emotional closeness, openness, and privacy.

Privacy is a context-dependent property: its boundaries depend upon the type of relationship and the kind of information revealed. Thus, we may reveal to a friend certain information that we may not want to share with our spouse. A woman may not tell her spouse about her extramarital affairs and sexual fantasies, while she may openly discuss such matters with her online friend. A young man may find it easy revealing his homosexuality to his friend but not to his family. But both the woman and the young man will be less careful about their privacy in front of their spouse or family in matters such as walking around half-naked or unshaven in their presence.

From the latter part of the twentieth century onwards, openness – and, in particular, self-disclosure – and the limitation of one's privacy have been regarded as the hallmark of a close relationship. The gradual exchange of intimate information is considered the major process through which relationships between people develop. Indeed, self-disclosure appears to decrease as relationships move through various stages of deterioration. Moreover, there is good evidence that some forms of self-disclosure help reduce negative effects and improve health in the long run.[8]

However, some people claim that self-disclosure and open communication are not all that important to couples in many stable marriages. They emphasize the importance of interdependence for close relationships. For such people, self-disclosure becomes merely one of many possible manifestations of the range and diversity of the links between partners. Self-disclosure is differentially important in various close relationships.[9]

There is no doubt that sharing intimate information is one aspect of close relationships. Becoming closer implies greater emotional openness and hence some limitations upon our privacy. This, however, does not mean that there is a linear relationship between closeness and the loss of privacy. The complete loss of emotional privacy may have harmful consequences. A close relationship does not entail becoming one entity: the relationship is between two individuals, each of whom has a unique identity. Maintaining that identity requires a certain degree of privacy and autonomy.

Online closeness

> Goldfish in the privacy of bowls do it.
>
> Cole Porter

Emotions typically express our profound values and attitudes – often, even better than words do. As such, they are crucial for sincere communication. However, because of their profound nature, revealing our emotional attitudes is in contrast to our wish to defend our privacy. Protecting our privacy seems to require hiding our emotions. Should we reveal our emotions, thereby becoming more sincere, or should we conceal them and thereby protect our privacy?

The conflict between privacy and sincerity is even deeper if we take into account that privacy not only protects our profound values, but also guarantees the depth of our life. Without the protection of privacy, there is the risk that our unique profound values, which may not be held by most people, will be attacked and that maintaining or asserting them will be difficult. Privacy may protect us from being tempted or coerced into surrendering to the more superficial values within the consensus. As Hannah Arendt comments: "A life spent entirely in public, in the presence of others, becomes . . . shallow." Moreover, there are "a great many things which cannot withstand the implacable, bright light of the constant presence of others."[10] Privacy is, no doubt, important, but so is sincere self-disclosure.

In the song "Me and Bobby McGee" (written by Kris Kristofferson), Janis Joplin reminds us that freedom is when you have "nothing left to lose"; in such a state, privacy is of no value. Privacy is required when we have something to lose and hope that, by keeping it private, the loss will be prevented. Our wish to keep something private indicates the presence of some conflict. Is such a conflict a necessary feature of our social life, or is it something we should aspire to overcome? Are there differences in this regard between offline and online circumstances?

In committed intimate relationships, such as marriage, one's personal freedom is limited as each partner is committed to the relationship as a whole and to those involved in the relationship. The limited freedom also involves limited self-disclosure, as unlimited self-disclosure will make us more vulnerable; hence privacy should not be nullified in such relationships. In light of the significant value of privacy in marriage, many married couples set boundaries to protect their privacy. Consider the following statement by a 27-year-old married female:

> I don't agree that you have to tell your partner EXACTLY what you're engaged in online. My husband and myself have agreed on previous boundary issues, and like most couples, we agree that some things are private. He doesn't listen in on my phone calls, read my letters, or ask me what I'm doing in the bathroom for so long. I don't ask him if he got a lap dance from the stripper. I don't particularly want to know that he may masturbate to thoughts of my sister. This is all about respecting your partner's right to have some things that are their own.

The problem of privacy is even more significant when one is engaging in online relationships – in addition to a face-to-face relationship. In this case, we are not speaking merely about (forbidden) thoughts, but about a (forbidden) relationship with a real person. In this regard, the woman cited above further claims:

> My partner knows I chat online and I'm sure he knows that not all of these conversations are about the weather (he's no dumb bunny). He does not want to know the details because he trusts me not to let the occasional cybersex session affect our relationship. 100% *disclosure* is neither attainable nor desirable; basic honesty, trust, and respect are different matters – they are necessary. Part of loving someone is acknowledging and accepting that they have "a life" outside of what you share together – even in the area of sexuality.[11]

This woman expresses a fundamental conflict between emotions and sincerity: in order to keep our emotional attitudes private, we must be insincere especially if social and moral rules oppose them. We should be ready to live with the occasional exception or with a society that is not totally pure but nevertheless allows us to maintain our privacy and remain authentic regarding our profound emotional attitudes. Society often turns a blind eye to adultery as a way of balancing social values with the need for privacy and tolerance.[12]

The tradeoff between privacy and emotional closeness is not so dominant in online relationships, mainly because of the greater ability to conceal private information and the decreased vulnerability of the participants. In face-to-face relationships, becoming closer to each other enables one to be aware of more intimate aspects of the other person's character and life, including those considered to be private. Becoming closer opens more doors through which one can see the other person. In online relationships, becoming closer also means having more information about the other person, but since one has greater control over the revealed information, this information may not include those aspects one would like to keep private. In this sense, getting emotionally closer in cyberspace does not necessarily mean revealing those private aspects that you want to keep private.

As long as the relationship is limited to cyberspace, emotional closeness can be increased without risking one's privacy. When the relationship begins to involve features such as revealing real names and addresses, phone calls, exchange of pictures, writing letters, and face-to-face meetings, the conflict between emotional closeness and privacy emerges once again.

Issues concerning privacy become more complex when the impact of the online relationship is not limited to cyberspace: for example, when an online relationship is conducted simultaneously with an offline relationship with a different person, or when the online relationship is intended to be transformed into an offline relationship. In such cases, the relative advantages of privacy in online affairs may be greatly reduced.

It is reasonable to assume that in online relationships, people typically share personal information that they do not share with their offline partners. The opposite claim is true as well: people share with their offline partners other information that they do not reveal to their online partners. Emotional self-disclosure – especially that which is at odds with accepted moral norms – is more likely to be revealed in online communication. Since emotional self-disclosure is more important to the experience of intimacy than factual self-disclosure,[13] online relationships often have a higher degree of intimacy than offline relationships.

We may conclude that, in cyberspace, the issue of privacy becomes central when an online relationship is intended to be transformed into an offline relationship; when the relationship is limited to cyberspace, privacy is less of a concern.

Cyberspace seems to offer both greater freedom and greater privacy. The freedom, however, is often imaginary as it is restricted to cyberspace. The enhanced sense of freedom to do whatever you would like to do in cyberspace is balanced by a greater need for actual privacy concerning your online activities. Once you are in cyberspace, you are free to do whatever you would like to without worrying too much about your privacy; however, your online intimate activities do often require considerable offline privacy. This kind of privacy is increasingly invaded in cyberspace by tools enabling people to know when you are online. However, new tools are constantly being developed that allow you to block this type of knowledge from other people.

In online relationships, emotional closeness is achieved without paying a significant price in terms of losing one's privacy. In this sense, these relationships appear to be an optimal solution to the problematic closeness–privacy tradeoff. We should remember, however, that these relationships are to a certain degree imaginary, as they lack some of the fundamental characteristics of face-to-face relationships.

The non-intrusive nature of online communication assures greater privacy than other types of remote communication, such as phone calls. Online communication enables people to continue with their regular schedule and engage in their online relationships only when it is least intrusive to do so. This is of particular importance for married people. Unlike spouses, children, and friends, who constantly interrupt our privacy and ongoing activities, online lovers are essentially non-intrusive – at least in a physical manner. They do not interrupt you when you are taking a bath or enjoying a good football game. An online lover is more patient, "always waiting for the convenient moment, never interrupting something else important or demanding attention that is already split five ways."[14] This is one area in which online lovers will always hold an advantage over offline partners.

In offline relationships, one's emotional attitudes and fantasies typically enjoy the right to privacy. This is so since they are usually not considered real actions that could break the law or have harmful consequences. The situation is more complex in online relationships, where people are not merely passively fantasizing about some desired action, but are involved in a dynamic and interactive relationship that could have significant implications.

The great anonymity of cyberspace gives individuals a higher degree of privacy. In cyberspace, the agent can choose which personal details to reveal, and consequently privacy is largely under the agent's control. Despite the high degree of privacy and control over the revealed information, it seems that the agent often voluntarily relinquishes much of her privacy and reveals many details that typically remain private in offline relationships. Such profound self-disclosure can be risked because there is less danger involved. The anonymity of cyberspace does not merely facilitate significant privacy, it also reduces vulnerability and hence allows people to forgo some of this privacy.

A different issue concerns the privacy of the offline spouse. Since online affairs consist of conversations and are characterized by candid self-disclosure, the participants' offline spouses are often the topic of these conversations. This violates the privacy of the spouses, and when they discover this, it can cause them considerable pain and anger.

Online openness

Pornographers subvert this last, vital privacy: they do our imagining for us.

George Steiner

The psychological revolution initiated by Freud has emphasized the importance of self-disclosure and the risks implicit in repressing our thoughts and emotions. Such self-disclosure is hard to achieve when greater openness implies greater vulnerability. Online relationships, which consist of prolonged conversations and in which vulnerability is significantly reduced, provide optimal circumstances for candid openness. A woman describes her online romance as follows: "Our relationship must be one of trust and honesty, because we have nothing physical yet, and the relationship is one solely of communication. As for that, we're both very open with the other. What else can we do but talk?"[15]

The greater tendency toward online openness is exemplified to an extreme in the many Webcams devoted to around-the-clock monitoring of the daily life of ordinary people. The cameras record ordinary activities, such as eating, reading, and talking on the phone, and the most private activities, such as having sex, being on the toilet, or shaving hair in intimate places. As Joshua Meyrowitz notes, our age "is fascinated by exposure. Indeed, the act of exposure itself now seems to excite us more than the content of the secrets exposed."[16]

A related perplexing phenomenon is the public confession of shameful actions. Many day-time television talk-shows share a confessional format that encourages participants to make public what in other times would have been kept private or else subjected to the sanction of shame.[17] People are willing to surrender their privacy and to endure any humiliation to gain some public fame. These people offer their privacy as the kindling for their moment of pseudo-celebrity.[18]

Do these phenomena indicate that our society is becoming more exhibitionist and voyeuristic, and, if so, will we consequently lose our sense of privacy and shame? Although I would agree that our society is much more exhibitionist than previous societies, I do not believe that this indicates any reduction in our sense of privacy and shame.

Until recent times, people had remarkably little privacy; many led their whole lives without ever really being alone. Every one of their actions was open to the scrutiny of other people. Over the past two centuries, with the increase of prosperity, the single-family home, the automobile, and the invention of television and computers, privacy has become more feasible and more valuable. Whereas, in the past, our neighbors knew how we dressed, how we shopped, whom we dated, as well as the meaning of the various noises and odors coming from our homes, today they may not even know our names.[19]

The advent of the Internet, which has meant that many of our activities can be carried out within the privacy of our own home, has significantly increased the degree of our privacy. It should also be mentioned that the same technologies that facilitate our increased privacy have made it possible to invade this privacy by monitoring and recording our behavior. However, whereas in the past it was our neighbors and associates who invaded our privacy, now it is mainly faceless strangers who are likely to do so.[20]

We desire different types of privacy in our relations with our friends and in our relations with strangers. In the case of close friends, we are careful not to reveal those aspects of our life that may make us vulnerable to future hurt. With strangers, we typically cannot reveal many personal details, as we are not with them for long enough. However, cyberspace, which has introduced a personal relationship of detached attachment, enables us to be in contact with specific strangers for a long time, and this creates the closeness required for revealing intimate private matters, as well as for engaging in discussions of our everyday activities.

The huge popularity of such an exposure of private matters, both in television "reality shows" and in cyberspace, is maybe a reaction to the greater role that imagination plays in television and cyberspace, which have become the central arena of modern social life.

It should be remembered that participants in television confessional shows or in cyberspace shows are rewarded with publicity or financial incentives. The participants' willingness to relinquish their privacy in return for such rewards has alarming implications. Revealing our private secrets typically involves intruding upon the privacy of other people as well – and they may not be ready for such intrusions. There are indeed a few reports of murders resulting from appearances on such shows. A few years ago, a Florida man beat his ex-wife to death shortly after they appeared on such a show, in which she openly revealed some of their private matters. Another murder occurred after a man declared his homosexual love to another man, who appeared together with him on such a show.

The popularity of "reality shows" is indicative of a more general phenomenon: the meaning of many private emotional matters is altered by public display. A private action that violates an accepted moral norm, but is not illegal, typically generates shame or humiliation when people associated with the agent learn of it. However, when the action is voluntarily and publicly revealed to the whole community, it may not be shameful anymore; on the contrary, it may become a matter of pride.[21]

Emotional pretense and sexual harassment

> Never miss a chance to keep your mouth shut.
>
> Robert Newton Peck

The right to privacy is of particular importance in romantic affairs, where people are obliged to reveal their emotional attitudes. Certainly, many people are unwilling to reveal their emotional attitudes at the beginning of a relationship. Romantic relationships are constant sources of threat to our self-esteem, as they are perceived to express the other's profound evaluation of us. Another's reluctance to enter a romantic relationship with us hurts our self-esteem. Emotional pretense in romantic relationships often increases uncertainty and mystery, which usually magnify emotional intensity. When a man proposes to a woman and she responds with "Maybe," rather than "Yes," it increases her mystique and hence her attractiveness; it also allows her to cope with any future disappointment should the man be unwilling to develop a genuine romantic relationship later on.[22]

Stephen Schulhofer reports that recent studies show that, even in the 1990s, most women indicate sexual interest by using subtle and extremely indirect cues. In one survey, women stated that they seldom used direct methods to express their sexual interest – for example, they did not talk directly about sex, guide their partner's hands to their genital area, or start undressing, signs which are considered to be the "most effective" way to signal sexual interest. Instead, they used more indirect means to express their interest in sex – for example, they dressed carefully, laughed easily, displayed interest in what the man said, or sat close to him. In another survey, less than 20 percent of women were willing to indicate their sexual interest directly. Almost 30 percent said they did nothing to indicate their sexual interest and relied entirely on male initiative or on the "natural" course of events.[23]

By using indirect rather than explicit cues, women can keep their emotional attitudes relatively private, and can thereby avoid being labeled as promiscuous. Moreover, women can more easily change their minds if, during the process of acquaintance, they discover that they are not as interested as they were when they first met the other person. Women may also not feel sure about or ready for the affair.[24] Indirect and subtle cues allow the woman greater control over the situation and may increase the man's desire toward her.

The wish to keep our emotional attitudes private may, however, cause emotional messages to be misinterpreted, with harmful consequences. This is obvious in the romantic realm, where confusing the real and the deceptive message may lead to charges of sexual harassment. Thus, it has been suggested that sexually aggressive men use a suspicion schema when interpreting the way women communicate their (lack of) sexual interest: such men assume that women do not tell the truth when it comes to sex.[25]

The uncertainty concerning the authenticity of emotional messages can be reduced by eliminating the use of deceptive tactics or, for that matter, any type of pretense. Such reduction, however, has its own shortcomings. Guarding our privacy, as well as avoiding hurting other people, requires the use of some deceptive measures. We should, however, limit their use in personal relationships.

Fulfilling the requirements of both privacy and openness may generate the accusation of "double standards." It would appear that relinquishing the privacy of our emotional attitudes is more dangerous – especially for women – in offline than in online relationships. The latter provide a safer environment for greater openness. The conflict between openness and privacy is lessened significantly in cyberspace. In cyberspace, the use of emotional pretense is of lesser value and generates less harmful consequences. The anonymity of cyberspace provides a certain security that does not require the protection of not being open. Moreover, since sincerity is common and positively evaluated in online personal relationships, emotional pretense has less justification. The manipulative reasons for not revealing one's emotional attitudes carry less weight in cyberspace.

So far I have discussed the conflict between the agent's privacy and the agent's openness. I have shown that this conflict is reduced in cyberspace. I now turn to discuss another type of conflict between privacy and openness, but this time between the agent's privacy and the other's openness. This conflict, which is related to the issue of sexual harassment, also seems to be reduced in cyberspace.

Part of the fundamental right underlying privacy – that is, the right to be left alone – is the right to an environment free from discrimination, intimidation, insult, and ridicule. One of the factors that can contaminate this environment is discrimination, which can be based on characteristics such as race, color, religion, and sex. This right to privacy limits the other's openness. If, for example, people have an extremely negative attitude toward a certain race or religion, they cannot openly express this attitude without violating another person's right to an environment free from insult and ridicule. When someone openly expresses his sexual interest in another person, this interest may be conceived as violating the other person's privacy and even as sexual harassment. Since emotions express our sincere attitudes, compelling us not to reveal these attitudes may lead to a significant reduction in the role of sincerity in personal relationships. Guarding other people's privacy, as well as avoiding hurting them, requires us to limit our openness. However, while privacy is valuable, so is openness; thus we should attempt to impose as few limitations as possible in order to safeguard both.

This problem is particularly evident in matters of sexual harassment, where one person's sexual conduct unreasonably interferes with another's privacy and performance. Such harassment significantly contaminates the other person's private environment by introducing into it unwanted sexual elements. This contamination can range from physical coercion to unwanted attention. Whereas physical sexual coercion clearly cannot be considered as part of an individual's legitimate right to openness, the issue of sexual attention is more complex. For example, in some places, male workers are not allowed to stare at women, since this is considered an unwanted sexual advance and, as such, constitutes an offensive act of sexual harassment. Someone even reports that a friend informed him that it was an infringement of her personal rights if he used her, without her permission, in his sexual fantasies, even if they were completely private.[26]

The conflict between the agent's privacy and the other's openness is lessened in cyberspace, as the actual harm that can be inflicted upon the agent's privacy and performance by the other's open sexual advances is significantly reduced. These advances are less threatening and easier to avoid. In the same way that in cyberspace one can be more open about oneself, thereby reducing one's privacy zone, in cyberspace one can be more open about one's attitudes toward another person, thereby reducing the other person's privacy zone. In both cases, the potential harm of being open is significantly reduced.

It is interesting to note that cyberspace cannot be described as having a more relaxed standard of sexual harassment; in some areas, the standard is even more stringent. Thus, it was found that the same misogynist comments were considered more harassing online than in traditional settings, as were using nicknames and making comments about dress. These findings can be explained by the great importance attached to written words and conversation in online relationships. The lack of face-to-face contact and a broader context can make online sexual comments appear even more inappropriate.[27]

The transparent society

> Honest criticism is hard to take, particularly from a relative, a friend, an acquaintance, or a stranger.
>
> Franklin P. Jones

The indiscretion involved in gossip is defended by Ronald De Sousa, who argues that the right to privacy, in the sense of the right to keep things to ourselves, has no moral ground. He says that people gossip when there is a strict distinction between the private and the public. If we abolished this distinction, gossip would no longer be necessary. De Sousa claims that to refrain from gossip is to be discreet, and, according to a common prejudice, discretion is a virtue; however, indiscretion, in his view, is a superior virtue, indeed a saintly one. He further argues that discretion is hypocrisy: if your friends had nothing worth keeping secret, discretion would be useless; accordingly, discretion is absent from Paradise. When petty crimes and mean thoughts can no longer be hidden, then the deception industries, private and public, will wither away. Personal relationships would be far less likely to be poisoned by misunderstandings, disappointments, and betrayals.[28]

In a similar manner, David Brin advocates the notion of a transparent society. He assumes that there is no way of hiding private information, and hence we should let everyone have access to it. In such an open transparent society, in which nothing is hidden and light would shine into nearly every corner of our lives, everyone could be held accountable. Rather than shutting down the flow of information, he argues that we should actually make the information flow even more freely. If we all lived in glass houses, no one would throw stones.[29] In a similar vein, nudists who sunbathed near the venue of an important NATO summit pleaded with Italian Prime Minister Berlusconi to allow their beach to remain open, pointing out: "A naked person has nowhere to hide any weapons."

At the root of the transparency view is the assumption that exposure can prevent many moral misdeeds. As Amitai Etzioni put it: "publicness reduces the need for public control, while excessive privacy often necessitates state-imposed limits on private choices."[30] While this may be so, there is a significant difference between the total eradication of privacy and a reduction in its scope. De Sousa's and Brin's transparent society, where the private–public distinction is abolished and discretion is no longer valued, is neither feasible nor morally commendable.

The value of privacy for both the individual and society is immense. As Carl Schneider argues:

> In private, one can relax, blow off steam, recoup after encounters with difficult and unbearable people. This release is a safety valve; it lessens personal tension and makes social relations endurable. Privacy also maintains the social system, allowing for backstage area and remissive spaces where it is not always incumbent upon individuals to maintain their proper role . . . When society does not provide for privacy, being apart can only take the form of hiding.[31]

Privacy is valuable for developing our interests and personalities in a way that is not always compatible with social norms or the wishes of powerful people. Accordingly, privacy is indispensable in a community that recognizes social freedom as good. Moreover, some actions lose their value when they are observed; quite often, external observation may kill the spontaneity and authenticity that are essential to intimacy. Many people dislike exposure of their private actions, not because they have acted irregularly, but because their psychological nature requires privacy.[32]

We should not merely act to secure our own unique individuality, but we should also be sensitive to such uniqueness in other people. This sensitivity enables the same person to be spontaneous and warm to some people and more calculated and detached toward other people. Each individual needs to have different emotional relationships with different people. People are not identical and should not be treated that way. Emotions are by their very nature exclusive: we do not have the same emotional attitudes toward all people. If other people had the ability to read you completely, there would be no inner self for you to call your own. No dissenting views and attitudes would be able to exist, and creativity and uniqueness would be suppressed. Humans would no longer be free. As Milan Kundera noted: "Any man who was the same in both public and intimate life would be a monster. He would be without spontaneity in his private life and without responsibility in his public life."[33]

The total loss of personal privacy is dangerous and inconceivable for human society. Similarly, total privacy is also dangerous and inconceivable for such a society – openness is a valuable human trait. We should be as open as we can, while keeping private those matters whose revelation might harm us. Privacy may have acquired too much importance in previous periods, but this is a reason to reduce its scope rather than abolish it.

Two major and seemingly opposing tendencies can be detected in today's society: a greater concern about the erosion of personal privacy and a greater openness concerning personal issues that were traditionally considered private. Openness is no doubt a worthy value, but so is privacy.

Modern technology has made it possible to monitor our actions in the most private places and situations. This has considerably increased concern about the erosion of privacy in everyday life. Thus, in 1998, 88 percent of Americans said they were concerned about their privacy.[34]

Together with increased concern over the erosion of privacy, our age is characterized by a greater desire for openness, which is considered to be an affirmation of honesty and authenticity. Our tendency to guard our privacy is considered a sign of distrust, while public openness is regarded as a sign of healing. The popular buzzword is "sharing" rather than "restraint," "reticence," or "discretion." This tendency is exemplified by TV tell-all shows and by Webcam sites. It is evident also in the behavior of public figures who are quick to detect fashionable trends. Many public figures now share their emotional personal affairs with a nationwide television audience. As Charles Sykes remarks, much of Princess Diana's popularity stemmed from her willingness to confess her unhappiness: "If Winston Churchill never had an unpublished thought, Diana never had an unreported cry."[35] Although emotions are by their nature personal, they are not always private, as they have important social and communicative functions. However, we do not feel comfortable expressing our emotions to everyone, as not everyone has the same emotional significance for us. Blurring the lines between various degrees of emotional intimacy endangers the uniqueness of such intimacy.

Cyberspace seems to provide an ideal place for the practice of a voluntary openness that reduces our privacy zone for those associated with us, without considerably increasing our vulnerability. Our private zone can contract around only those issues that we select, while we can expand the zone around issues that we wish to keep private. Online openness pertains to intimate issues, which we may not even discuss with our spouses. This kind of openness is accompanied by mutual self-disclosure that strengthens trust and affection.

Online relationships encourage great self-disclosure that makes participants almost mentally transparent. A woman who had an online affair says: "I wrote down all my feelings, my thoughts, my doubts and of course my joys and all the lovely things that happened." After they were together for a while in actual life and then separated, she wrote: "I've not only felt naked, but as though I've had no skin and he could see into my marrow. Compared to this, my dream, in which I walk among strangers on the street naked, was 'kinder.' I don't know if you can imagine what's it like to have someone see inside you."[36] The fact that cyberspace is inevitably connected to actual-space makes complete transparency dangerous even in cyberspace.

The great transparency that characterizes online communications is associated with significant privacy in those situations that people most want to keep private. Romantic affairs can be conducted in the privacy of one's home or office. The great availability and accessibility of such private affairs present the most significant challenge to actual, long-term romantic relationships.

Shame in cyberspace

> If God had meant for us to be naked, we'd have been born that way.
>
> Mark Twain

From a moral point of view, the degree of freedom to do whatever one wishes to do is much greater in cyberspace, as the moral norms in this space are less strict. The more lenient moral nature of cyberspace is the result of two major factors: (a) the central place of imagination in cyberspace makes online activity less real; (b) the anonymity available to both the sender and the receiver in cyberspace makes it easier to violate moral norms and much more difficult to reveal such violations and enforce these norms. In light of the greater moral freedom and anonymity of cyberspace, moral emotions such as shame and guilt are likely to be less prevalent and less intense in that space than in our actual environment. Conversely, emotions that are often considered immoral, such as hate and sexual desire, are likely to be more prevalent and more intense in cyberspace. Indeed, the number of sexual and hate sites in cyberspace is enormous.

Whereas guilt and regret involve a negative evaluation of a specific act that we have performed, shame involves a more global evaluation. In shame, one thinks of oneself as a flawed person, not simply as someone who has acted wrongly. When shame results from a particular action, this action is taken to be indisputable proof of one's own inferior character, rather than as an isolated incident that may be ascribed to negligence or weakness of will. Thus, people are often ashamed to seek help when they want to find a romantic partner, since their need for such help may not be interpreted as an isolated specific failure, but as a global flaw underlying their inferiority. This aspect of matching is less pronounced in cyberspace, where no other person or agency arranges a date for you – you do it by yourself. Accordingly, online matchmaking services are used much more than are those of offline agencies; furthermore, the former are far less expensive.

The global negative self-evaluation typical of shame creates the need to hide or cover oneself so as to avoid others seeing us. Indeed, hiding is a highly typical behavior pattern of shame that is often expressed in a shrinking of the body, as though in order to disappear from the eye of the self or the other.[37] The decreased role of vision and the ease of "hiding" in cyberspace reduce the intensity of shame there. The ease of finding others who are similar to you also reduces shame online.

Shame is closely connected with self-esteem and self-respect. Its emergence indicates that we have violated some of our most profound values. Shame prevents many people from behaving immorally, as they are fearful of losing their own self-respect. A preventive type of morality would educate people to realize their value as human beings and hence to enhance their self-respect; in such a system, shame would be likely to emerge when immoral actions were merely contemplated.

People will never be ashamed of their actions or behavior unless they have accepted a certain standard of rectitude. The feeling of shame, therefore, can bear witness to an uncorrupted conscience; and such a person is better than one who is shameless. Shame can be seen as a price we have to pay for our weaknesses and for the attempt to cope with them.

The importance of shame for moral behavior indicates the double moral aspect of shame: shame indicates that we have violated a certain profound norm, and in this sense we are morally wrong, but it also expresses the fact that we care about this norm, and this caring is commendable from a moral point of view. Indeed, we often praise people who are ashamed and condemn those who have lost their shame.

Shame is less common in cyberspace for several major reasons: (a) less strict moral norms pertain, (b) the agent is largely anonymous, and (c) there is more tolerance for unusual behavior. The first reason has bearing on the agent's actions, the second and the third on the way other people perceive the agent.

Shame is generated when the agent violates fundamental moral norms. The imaginary nature of cyberspace reduces the number and the significance of these norms. In a fantasyland, moral norms, if they exist at all, are much looser, and the agent does not perceive their violation as a reflection of the agent's character as a whole. A person may think: "I am not such a bad person if I have a fantasy affair with a married person in my dreams – at least I do not act that way in everyday life."

The second reason why shame is less prevalent in cyberspace is connected with the agent's anonymity. Shame is derived from, among other things, an interest in how others regard us. Shame seems to presuppose an audience, or others who are watching us. Shame involves a need to hide or cover oneself – to avoid others seeing us. When there is no way of avoiding others seeing us, the ultimate solution for some people is suicide. The need to hide or even disappear, which is so typical of shame, explains why shame is often connected with sight and being seen. In the biblical story of the Creation, we are told that, before Eve gave the apple to Adam, there was no shame. Shame emerged only after they had eaten the apple and "the eyes of both of them were opened, and they felt that they were naked." The crucial role of vision in shame, and the insignificant role of vision in cyberspace, make it unsurprising that shame does not play an important role in cyberspace. In cyberspace, when no one sees us, shame is less likely to be generated. Moreover, when people are publicly shamed in cyberspace, they can always leave, or change their screenname.

The third reason for the reduced intensity of shame online is that there is more tolerance for unusual behavior or desires. Hence, norms are less strict, and there are fewer conventions to break. Accordingly, when someone does infringe upon a norm, he or she is likely to feel less ashamed of this than in offline circumstances.

The reduced presence of shame in cyberspace can explain the more prevalent use of dirty talk in cybersex. In dirty talk people break taboos and other types of moral norms. The possibility of doing this without being ashamed or morally penalized in some manner can sexually excite some people. Consider the following message from a woman: "Online I felt safer and more daring. I even got myself a book about how to talk dirty to your partner; it has helped me talk about things and say things that I never ever thought would come out of my mouth, not filthy things, but things that sound pleasurable to me and my partner."[38] Dirty talk is also common in phone sex. Although people are not completely anonymous when participating in phone sex, it is acceptable to break – at least verbally – certain moral norms (which are typically kept in face-to-face sex). The lack of a face-to-face encounter helps in doing so as the situation is perceived to be more remote from ordinary circumstances, where ordinary norms prevail.

Does the popular tendency toward exposing private matters on television and cyberspace indicate a decline in shame in modern society? Not necessarily – it may rather indicate a change in the fundamental values that constitute our self-image and hence our sense of privacy. Certain actions that were once regarded as fundamentally negative are now more acceptable; consequently, these actions no longer generate shame. On the other hand, some of the above cases do indeed express loss of shame and not merely a change of values. It is arguable that we are more open concerning our private actions and our values today than we were in the past. It is amusing to note in this regard that when Monica Lewinsky was asked whether she would be voting for Hillary Clinton or for her opponent in the election to the Senate, Lewinsky refused to answer on the ground that one's vote is a private matter that should remain confidential. However, she described to the whole world the oral sex she had performed with Hillary's husband, Bill Clinton.

Although shame is less prevalent in cyberspace, it should not be considered as a useless emotion in this space. More than other emotions, shame expresses our deepest values and commitments; freeing ourselves from shame implies unloading these values and commitments. Shame is therefore a constitutive element in normative life. However, there is no doubt that some of our fundamental moral norms are perceived as invalid in cyberspace. The question is whether cyberspace lacks any such norms. A crucial issue in this regard is the reality of cyberspace.

If cyberspace were merely a fantasyland, shame would not play any role in it. We have seen, however, that people often confuse this imaginary land with the actual one, and consequently they attach a high degree of reality to their behavior in cyberspace. People do not completely separate their offline personality from their online personality. This is especially true when online relations develop further and anonymity is considerably reduced. It may be the case that online relationships include some different moral norms, but it is unlikely that a human relationship can lack any moral norms. Hence, shame is likely to play a role in online relationships. Indeed, people testify that they experienced shame and guilt as a result of their online sexual activities and their concealment of these activities from their offline partners.

Summary

> Tell me, George, if you had to do it all over would you fall in love with yourself again?
>
> Oscar Levant to George Gershwin

In face-to-face relationships, privacy conflicts with two major emotional features: closeness and openness. These conflicts are considerably weaker in cyberspace. The relative anonymity of cyberspace and the ability to reveal only those matters we would like to reveal provide an opportunity to guard privacy while increasing emotional closeness and openness.

The alternative world provided by cyberspace is essentially an ideal private world in which each person controls the information that is revealed. In this world, the full identity of the person is not revealed, and the two people are physically remote from each other. Hence, it is much easier to keep private whatever areas the participants so wish. These circumstances do not lead the participants to remain completely mysterious – on the contrary, in many cases it leads the participants to reveal much more about themselves than they would usually do. When we can keep private that which seems to threaten us, we can be more open concerning other matters. The greater degree of openness generates a greater degree of emotional closeness as well. Accordingly, in online relationships we can find both greater privacy and greater closeness and openness – this considerably reduces the common conflict between openness and privacy.

Shame, which is the most powerful moral emotion, is less common in cyberspace – although it is not completely absent from that space. In cyberspace, our ability not to disclose those aspects of ourselves that we would like to remain private means we are less exposed to shame-generating situations. Such situations are also less common since moral norms are less rigid in cyberspace – this decreased rigidity is explained in turn by the lesser amount of damage one can usually do. The decreased role of shame in cyberspace does not indicate its uselessness or the disappearance of our values – rather, it indicates a process in which we are restructuring our values.

From the point of view of the privacy–openness conflict, online relationships seem to be ideal relationships. However, as indicated in the following chapters, this relationship is perceived to be incomplete since it lacks the direct physical experience of being together. When an online relationship is satisfactory, the participants want to transform it into an offline relationship, at which point the conflict between privacy and openness emerges once again.

6 *Is it worth it?*

Happy people plan actions, they don't plan results.
Dennis Wholey

The nature of human activities is of great relevance in our quest to understand romantic relationships. This chapter distinguishes major types of activities and indicates their relevance to the characterization of love, sex, and happiness. The implications of these distinctions for online affairs are discussed. It is claimed that, from many aspects, online affairs are valuable, but they are not sufficiently complete to replace offline relationships.

Extrinsically and intrinsically valuable activities

Whatever women do they must do twice as well as men to be thought half as good. Luckily, this is not difficult.
Charlotte Whittond

Aristotle distinguishes between extrinsically and intrinsically valuable activities.[1] An extrinsically valuable activity is a means to an external goal; its value lies in achieving that goal. This goal-oriented activity is always incomplete: as long as the external goal has not been achieved, the activity is incomplete, and the moment the goal has been achieved, the activity is over. The major criterion for evaluating such activities is efficiency – that is, the ratio of benefits to costs. Time is one of the resources that we try to save when engaging in extrinsically valuable activities. Examples of such activities are building a house, paying bills, cleaning the house, attending job interviews, and so forth. We do not value these activities in themselves – in fact, we may even resent performing them, in the spirit of "Those who sow in tears will reap in pleasure."

The external goal is beneficial, but the means of achieving it are often costly and painful.

In an intrinsically valuable activity, our interest is focused upon the activity itself, not its results. Although such an activity has results, it is not performed in order to achieve these; rather, its value is in the activity itself. Listening to music is an example of an intrinsically valuable activity. We listen to music because we value doing so and not because of a certain external goal (such as developing our intellect or strengthening our peace of mind); accordingly, we do not try to finish listening as quickly as possible. Another example may be intellectual thinking whose basic motivation is creativity or intellectual curiosity, not the ensuing money or academic publications. Moral activity, which is accompanied by the pleasure of helping other people – without regard for cost–benefit calculations – is another example of an intrinsically valuable activity. All such activities are intrinsically rewarding. Despite the lack of external goals, these activities are valuable for the quality of our lives. As the Roman poet Ovid said: "Nothing is more useful to mankind than those arts which have no utility."

Most human activities have both intrinsic and extrinsic value. The factors underlying each type of value often conflict regarding how long activities should continue or how many resources should be invested in them.

Many human activities can become either intrinsically or extrinsically valuable activities. Take, for example, dancing. Dancing can be an intrinsically valuable activity, in which case our focus is upon the experience itself. Dancing, however, can also be an extrinsically valuable activity whose goal is to find a romantic partner. In this case, our attention is not focused on dancing but on the people who are in the dance hall – here, dancing is a means of achieving an external goal. In many cases, dancing can have elements of both types of activities: you may value dancing for itself, but also use dancing as a good opportunity to meet attractive people. Reading is another example of an activity that can be both intrinsically or extrinsically valuable: it can be done for its own sake, or for practical purposes. Touring may also be either an intrinsically or an extrinsically valuable activity. Those tourists who consider sightseeing an extrinsically valuable activity will want to visit as many possible sights in the shortest possible time: they want not to see, but to have seen.[2] Less hurried tourists will not worry about the number of sights they visit during their travels, but will rather value and enjoy the visit itself. In a similar manner, the Supreme Court of the United States made a distinction between gifts and bribes. A gift is something given for its own sake with no particular expectation of a return; a bribe is a gift intended to get something in return.[3]

In characterizing an intrinsically valuable activity, two main criteria may be used: (a) the *agent's attitude* is that of considering the activity to be valuable for its own sake; (b) the *activity* involves optimal functioning using and developing the agents' essential capacities and attitudes in a systematic manner over a sustained period of time. The first criterion is subjective, as it refers to the subject's attitude; the second criterion is more objective, as it refers to the nature of the given activity. A profound intrinsically valuable activity is one that fulfills both criteria. A superficial, but more prevalent, intrinsically valuable activity is one that fulfills the subjective criterion only. An activity that merely fulfills the objective criterion is not an intrinsically valuable activity at all.

A distinction can be drawn between superficial pleasure and profound satisfaction. Superficial pleasure is an immediately rewarding, relatively short-lived experience requiring few or no profound human capacities. Profound satisfaction involves optimal functioning, using and developing the agent's essential capacities and attitudes. Part of profound satisfaction is the ability to overcome problems and make some progress. The optimal functioning of human beings differs from the minimal functioning of animals, which involves mere contentment or relaxation. People suffering from advanced states of senility, and infants, often have pleasant moods, but those are not the profound satisfaction typically sought after by healthy adults, many of whom would rather be a dissatisfied Socrates than a satisfied pig. If we were satisfied with superficial pleasure, we would have no incentive to pursue our ambitions or to seek fulfilling activities. In the long run, this would make us miserable. Gorging ourselves on consumer goods may give us short-term pleasure, but it is unlikely to make us substantially happier; gluttony is not the same as nourishment.[4]

Intrinsically valuable activities characterized by merely the subjective criterion are typically pleasant. When we consider the activity to be valuable for its own sake, we can perform it in a pleasant enjoyable manner. Often the only value of such activities is simply that they are pleasant. Watching television typically has no other benefits except for the pleasure associated with it. However, intrinsically valuable activities are not necessarily pleasant. Thus, writing and painting are not necessarily pleasant at the time they occur – some writers and artists experience a lot of agony in the process of creating their work. In such cases, the value of the activity does not stem from its pleasant process but from its profoundness – it utilizes the agent's most distinctive human capacities.

Another criterion for an intrinsically valuable activity, according to Aristotle, is that it is complete, as there is no external goal that it has to achieve in order to be fulfilled. In this sense, it is an ongoing activity that does not have an inherent target: it is a never-ending process. External circumstances can impede the performance of such activities – hence, their vulnerable nature. Such circumstances cannot, however, define their completion.[5] Thus, if the painter considers painting as essential to her life – as part of her individual identity – she cannot "finish" painting. She can merely stop painting from time to time, or can finish painting a particular picture. Similarly, if we consider thinking intellectually or moral behavior as essential to our human identity, we cannot say that at a certain point of our life we "finish" these activities; we can say that, from time to time, we stop performing them. These activities are profound in the sense that they are essential to what we characterize as flourishing human life. Accordingly, they cannot be considered "finished" at a certain point in our life.

A profound intrinsically valuable activity is complete in another aspect: while engaging in such activity, the person's attention is completely absorbed by it. Accordingly, they can, for example, continue the activity for many hours without feeling hungry. In such circumstances, people can stop being aware of themselves as separate from their activities.[6] This is because such activities have great significance for the agent's self-identity.

Love and sex

> I always thought music was more important than sex – then I thought if I don't hear a concert for a year-and-a-half it doesn't bother me.
>
> Jackie Mason

In personal relationships, such as love and sex, the optimal functioning associated with intrinsically valuable activities refers not merely to one agent, but to all agents involved in the relationship. The consideration of the other person is intrinsically valuable in such relationships. Accordingly, the issue of egoism and altruism is highly relevant in these interactions.

The value of love is not determined by its practical value as a means to achieve ends that are external to the relationship. "Loving," as a means to satisfy one's sexual desire or to become rich, is a partial and transient activity: the moment the end is achieved, or a better means is found, this "love" disappears. Because of its intrinsic value, it has been claimed that, unlike other emotions, genuine love cannot be criticized. Love has been described as involving disinterested care for the beloved – care that does not contain considerations of our own benefit.[7]

As with other intrinsically valuable activities romantic love also involves goal-oriented activities. Since love is frequently expressed in a certain social relationship, such as marriage, cohabitation, or online communication, it often requires performing valuable external activities, such as cleaning the house, paying bills, or fixing the computer. Doing these unpleasant chores is one sign of the importance one attributes to the relationship. However, a more significant measure of the intensity of love is the extent to which two people share intrinsically valuable activities, such as dancing or walking together. The enjoyable and valuable nature of such activities provides the circumstances that can generate happiness. Indeed, love and happiness are closely related.

A sexual activity can be an extrinsically or an intrinsically valuable activity. It is an extrinsically valuable activity if the agent considers it to be a means for achieving an external goal such as money or social status. It is also an extrinsically valuable activity if the agent does not consider his or her partner as intrinsically valuable; as indicated, the intrinsic value of personal relationships refers to all those involved in the relationships. A sexual activity can be intrinsically valuable in the superficial sense of providing mere pleasure to the participants. It can be intrinsically valuable in the profound sense only when it is part of a more profound attitude, such as love.

In comparison with cybersex, which is an interactive masturbation, offline masturbation is much more goal-oriented: its aim is to reach orgasm, and the process is of no importance. Hence, masturbation may take less time than cybersex, but cybersex – and, more so, online romantic relationships – force you to interact with another person and thus involve some nonsexual aspects. In offline relationships, even more such aspects are involved, so the process becomes even less goal-oriented.

When sex is treated as an extrinsically valuable activity its value derives from attaining certain ends, such as money, social status, or revenge. Accordingly, when the end is social status, people who can provide us with this status, such as the rich, the famous, and the powerful, will generate more intense sexual desire and sexual satisfaction. Thus, a survey of hundreds of Italian women indicates that two-thirds found greater sexual satisfaction from "powerful men in socially respected positions" – bosses are perceived to be better in bed.[8]

A sexual relationship can have mere extrinsic value when the other person involved in the relationship is not considered to have an intrinsic value. Like other such goal-oriented activities, it is measured by its efficiency – namely, the ratio of costs to benefits. The aim is to achieve the goal with minimal investment. Time, for instance, is one type of cost that should be saved in a goal-oriented activity. People who hold such an attitude would try to shorten sexual activity as much as possible, to save time. They want to achieve their orgasm by investing as few mental (and other) resources as possible. Thus, a recent survey shows the average British man has sex twice a week, with each session lasting three minutes and one second.[9] Marilyn Monroe once complained to a friend that President John Kennedy's love-making was always very brief and hurried; her friend replied that since he had to run the country, he probably had no time for foreplay. Very religious people, who consider sexual relationships merely as a means for procreation, may also perceive sexual intercourse as a goal-oriented activity.

A sexual activity can have superficial intrinsic value when it provides pleasure to all participants. When viewed this way, the partners are in no rush to achieve satisfaction and thereby end the activity. Their satisfaction is found in the activity itself. This does not mean that sexual activity may not have certain side-benefits such as health or relaxation. Thus, an Italian professor who has been examining the exercise value of sexual activities has found that a 26-minute sex session that ends in orgasm works off the calories of half a pizza. Even undoing a bra can help lose fat. If you unclasp the bra with both hands, you will lose a mere eight calories; undoing it with only one hand burns up 18 calories; trying to unclasp a bra with one's mouth instead uses up an average of 87 calories.[10] Despite these supposed fitness benefits, most people engage in sexual activity because they enjoy it and not because of such side-benefits.

A Latin saying has it that every creature is sad after coitus. This may be true if sexual relationships are perceived as goal-oriented activities in which attaining the goal does not bring happiness. However, even when the sexual act is perceived as an intrinsically valuable activity, we may not be sad when we occasionally stop engaging in it.

The issue of whether a sexual activity can be intrinsically valuable in the profound sense is more complex. Love can be characterized as involving profound intrinsically valuable activities, since it satisfies both the subjective and the objective criterion. In genuine love, the agent considers love to be intrinsically rewarding and to involve optimal functioning, using and developing the agents' essential capacities and attitudes in a systematic manner over a sustained period of time.

Can we ascribe to sexual activities a profound intrinsic value? It has been claimed, for example, that cultivating sexual activities in a way that focuses on the development of physical and mental capacities and attitudes – as do, for example, the *Kama Sutra* and *The joy of sex* – may provide not merely superficial pleasure, but also the profound satisfaction associated with an intrinsically valuable activity in its fullest sense.[11]

I believe, however, that ascribing a profound intrinsic value to sexual activity is problematic, since, as compared with the comprehensive and profound nature of love, sexual activity is more partial and superficial. Sexual activities do not typically involve the use and development of essential capacities and attitudes in a systematic manner over a sustained period of time. Accordingly, sex is not an enduring emotion; it is an activity that ends and then begins again. In order to gain a profound intrinsic value, sexual activity must be part of the more comprehensive and profound attitude of love.

Because of the more partial and instrumental value of sex, its value for general happiness is less conclusive. Thus, some findings suggest that women who have sex frequently are less depressed and less likely to commit suicide.[12] Other findings indicate, however, that the number of sexual partners one has – as well as the frequency of sexual intercourse – matters very little in terms of happiness or even of sexual satisfaction. Although different sexual partners more easily evoke sexual desire, they do not necessarily increase happiness; happiness is more complex, and mere change or greater quantity cannot guarantee its presence.[13]

Happiness

My wife and I were happy for twenty years. Then we met!
Rodney Dangerfield

The distinction between the two types of intrinsically valuable activities is related to the distinction between the transitory emotion of joy and the more profound sentiment of happiness. An experience consisting of mere superficial joy includes immediately rewarding, relatively short-lived pleasure. Profound happiness is typically a byproduct of optimal functioning using and developing the agent's essential capacities and attitudes in a systematic manner over a sustained period of time. Profound happiness is to be found in complex activities that we value for their own sake.[14]

Profound happiness cannot be achieved by doing nothing or by involvement in extrinsically valuable activities. Even in highly goal-oriented activities, such as hunting, mine prospecting, gambling, or practicing law, the external goals are often not crucial for the happiness of the people engaged in them. Providing the huntsman with his prey or the gambler with the cash staked on the game may bring them momentary pleasure, but it will not make them happy; they must achieve these goals through their own activities. It is the activity itself that excites them.

Happiness cannot be achieved by merely repeating pleasant experiences. An enjoyable event is often progressively less enjoyable with repetition. A new acquisition, highly valued at first, comes to seem ordinary. Hence, acquisitions alone cannot provide us with profound, enduring satisfaction. Happiness is not an isolated achievement, but rather an ongoing dynamic process.

The minor and momentary significance of external goals in happiness is expressed in the fact that when the goal is obtained, it no longer continues to occupy our mind: now a new desire emerges and the imagination, as before, is directed at a distant goal. In love, it is only when the goal has been achieved – for example, I am finally dating Miss Colorado – that the intrinsically valuable activities typical of love can begin.

Attaining a specific goal may make us feel pleasure at a particular moment, but it may not lead to profound long-term happiness. The belief that it does, which many people hold, can lead to disappointment when the goal is attained. As we ascend the socio-economic ladder, we aspire to greater heights. We may satisfy more needs, but we constantly need and want more. Indeed, happiness depends little on the quantity of things we have attained; our attitude toward these things is of greater significance. Similarly, love depends less on the quantity of a person's so-called "good characteristics" or "good looks"; our attitude toward these features is of greater significance.[15]

It has been shown that the strongest predictor of life satisfaction found to date is a sense of satisfaction with the self. Satisfaction with the self consists of three major constituents: self-esteem, that is, a sense of worth or self-value; control, that is, a sense that one can change the environment in accordance with one's wishes; and a sense of optimism about the future.[16] Satisfaction with the self is closely related to the above notion of profound satisfaction or human flourishing.

There is no doubt that transitory types of joy or pleasure are easier to achieve in cyberspace. This is particularly obvious in the sexual domain: instant sexual gratification is available throughout cyberspace. It is hard to surf the Net without being offered instant sexual satisfaction. Other types of instant satisfaction are available as well. The virtual nature of cyberspace does not seem to be an obstacle in achieving superficial types of satisfaction.

The situation concerning profound satisfaction is more complex. As indicated, the major factor determining life satisfaction is satisfaction with the self. It is obvious that, in cyberspace, it is easier to obtain high dosages of the major constituents of self-satisfaction – that is, self-esteem, control, and optimism. Cyberspace significantly increases the degrees of all these components. Self-esteem is higher in cyberspace since people present themselves from a favorable perspective and the interaction is usually focused upon the positive aspects that are common to the two people. Even each person's flaws are presented favorably. Hence, one's sense of self-value is enhanced online. Our sense of control is clearly greater in cyberspace, since it affords us considerable ability to change the environment in accordance with our wishes. Given this greater self-esteem and control, as well as the more positive atmosphere in cyberspace, correspondents' sense of optimism about the future rises significantly as well.

It appears then that the strongest predictor of life satisfaction – that is, satisfaction with oneself – is considerably higher in cyberspace. Does this mean that life satisfaction, or long-term happiness, is also higher in cyberspace? Not necessarily so. In the long run, the virtual nature of cyberspace takes its toll. You can fool the mind about some aspects some of the time, but you cannot fool the mind about all aspects all of the time. Cyberspace is incomplete in the sense that it does not involve all types of activities; hence, profound flourishing is hard to achieve. Happiness is a kind of a comprehensive (or complete) attitude referring to all profound aspects of our life. When cyberspace is not our entire existence, but merely a part of it, it can be a place where satisfaction can be achieved. If other aspects of our life are fulfilling as well, cyberspace can be a significant factor in our happiness. A moderate use of cyberspace can therefore increase our happiness, while becoming addicted to this space will adversely influence our happiness.

An apparent advantage of cyberspace over real life is the huge number of available alternatives. Increasing our selective ability, and hence our control, is of great significance in increasing happiness.[17] However, the degree of selectivity or control that we have is relative to our circumstances. Thus, even very elderly people, whose only choice may be limited to which television program they watch, or which types of juice they have at breakfast, consider these choices as important, and they indeed do increase their life satisfaction.[18] Taking into account the somewhat imaginary nature of online alternatives, the relative advantage of cyberspace is of lesser importance. Nevertheless, the presence of so many alternatives may be significant, especially among certain groups, such as people who are old, disabled, or lonely.

It is important to note in this regard that most people are quite satisfied with their life, especially in affluent societies. On a scale from 0 to 100 the normative standard for life satisfaction in Western countries is about 75 (with a range between 70 and 80); when other countries are included as well, the value is about 70 (with a range between 60 and 80). This means that most people experience a level of satisfaction with their life that is moderately positive. This level is held under homeostatic control; that is, the mental system maintains a high level of satisfaction within a narrow range despite wide variations in positive and negative input.[19]

Two interesting features seem to arise from these findings: (a) most people are satisfied with their life, and (b) the range of differences in life satisfaction is relatively small. Various evolutionary and psychological reasons may be proposed for the high level and narrow range of life satisfaction. A major evolutionary reason for the high level has to do with the tendency of positive attitudes to motivate the agent – such an attitude is a kind of self-fulfilling prophecy. Feeling satisfied is also advantageous from a psychological point of view: it gives us the impression that our needs are gratified and prevents us from feeling inferior and depressed. The typical narrow range of life satisfaction gives people some mental stability. This is not an absolute stability, which is insensitive to the variability typical of human life: those who are currently happiest are not necessarily the happiest forever. The variability, though, is often transitory and remains within certain limits, thus enabling the agent to continue more or less normal functioning.[20]

As in other realms, cyberspace has both a positive and a negative impact on the level of our happiness. Our ability to keep the actual and the virtual worlds separate and to use the beneficial aspects of cyberspace may increase our happiness. However, since the changes in our level of happiness are typically not dramatic, the introduction of cyberspace may have no significant impact upon it.

Types of online intimate activities

Excuse me, but could you give me directions to your heart?

Bumper sticker

In accordance with the suggested distinction between extrinsically valuable activities, superficial intrinsically valuable activities, and profound intrinsically valuable activities, I would like to distinguish three types of online intimate activities:

(a) online relationships intended to find an offline sexual or romantic partner;
(b) superficial cyberflirting and cybersex;
(c) profound online-only romantic relationships.

The first type consists of extrinsically valuable activities intended to achieve the goal of finding an offline partner. The second and the third types are intrinsically valuable activities: their value is to be found in online-only activities. The second type involves superficial pleasure, whereas the third type generates profound satisfaction.

Many, and probably most, online relationships are goal-oriented activities intended to find an offline partner. The benefits of using the Internet as an efficient tool for finding an offline partner are evident in light of the large and accessible relevant information available on the Net. For those seeking a sexual affair this has many advantages: there are numerous sites and chat rooms devoted to finding a sexual partner. One such site, "Married And Lonely," which claims to be a non-profit organization exclusively managed by women, states that it features "real attached women looking for real SEX ON THE SIDE, because (they believe) they're not getting enough from their husbands or boyfriends!" The site promises to arrange a meeting with a married woman in your town.[21]

Online communication is also a beneficial tool for establishing romantic bonds. This is so not merely because of the many available alternatives present in cyberspace, but because written communication is often a more sincere and safer tool for initiating romantic relationships. Indeed, many people who had online affairs have moved on to face-to-face dates. In this regard, consider the following advice of Deb Levine:

> My suggestion to individuals who are looking for love online is to use the Internet to explore an intimate attraction, then take it offline within 1 month in order to get a concrete idea of the other person's attitudes, behaviors, and movement in the world. People who let attractions build online for long periods of time often have falsely raised expectations, leading to proportional disappointments.[22]

Many people adopt this attitude and consider an email correspondence to be primarily an efficient means with which to achieve a real romance. As one woman wrote: "I wasn't going to make the same mistake and get invested in this guy if he was the type to keep things strictly on a conversational level."[23]

The great efficiency of the Internet in locating potential mates for an offline affair may make the romantic search a degrading, mechanistic, and very goal-oriented activity that has little to do with romance or human dignity. Thus, people who use matching or dating sites report that they can sometimes "date" one or two different partners every day of the week. Their first contact is typically very brief – no more than five minutes – often consisting of no more than brief phrases, such as "next" or "you are not the person I expected." It is more like checking merchandise than meeting a human being. If the merchandise is flawed, there are many other products waiting to be examined. The frequent presence of such degrading attitudes and behavior may become deeply rooted in the personality of the agent in such a way that it may damage his or her future romantic relationships.

Using the Internet as an efficient tool for finding offline partners may reduce illusions and unrealistic expectations and hence lessen some of the risks involved in online affairs. However, it eliminates any intrinsic value from online relationships. Such an intrinsic value can be found in superficial cyberflirting and cybersex and in profound online-only romantic relationships. I discuss in detail flirting and profound online romantic relationships in the next two chapters. Here, I will illustrate the nature of such activities by briefly describing types of activities involved in cybersex.

Types of activities involved in cybersex

> Let me make this much clear: I don't fish in the desert, I don't sunbathe in the shower, and I do not have cybersex with my husband.
>
> Unknown

An offline sexual activity is an extrinsically valuable activity if the agent considers it to be a means for achieving an external goal such as money or social status or when the agent does not consider his or her partner as intrinsically valuable. A sexual activity can be intrinsically valuable in the superficial sense of providing mere pleasure to the participants or in the profound sense when it is part of a more profound attitude, such as love.

These types of activities can also be found in cybersex. Cybersex may be an extrinsically valuable activity if the agent uses it as a means to attract the other person into a different type of relationship – either an offline relationship or a more profound online relationship. It can also have a mere extrinsic value if there is no consideration of the partner's attitude.

The absence of the physical dimension in online sexual affairs may make these affairs less goal oriented. Orgasm is not always achieved, and people do not always gear their encounters toward achieving it. Much more weight is bestowed on the sexual activities preceding it. The value of these activities is more intrinsic and people enjoy them. The lack of practical implications and the disassociation from everyday practical concerns, which is typical of online affairs, may facilitate erotic enjoyment. A married man, who has an online affair, remarks: "I loved hearing that she loved me, that she couldn't wait to be with me. She reminded me of my early relationship with my wife when things were not hampered by bills, problems at school, and leaky faucets."[24] The more enjoyable nature of online affairs is one reason why cybersex, which is mainly imaginative and verbal, is often more passionate and wild than offline sex.

The limitation of online sexual activities – that is, the lack of physical contact – is advantageous from a different perspective: it forces participants to compensate for this absence by being more sensitive to other aspects that constitute an enjoyable sexual activity. In cybersex, where sexual activity is based on communication, the two people must respond to each other and be verbally sensitive to each other in order to keep the fantasy going. A blank screen cannot do that. In this sense, cybersex should be highly reciprocal and hence it often involves consideration of the other person as having an intrinsic value. In contrast, in offline sex one of the partners can be relatively passive.

As in offline sexual relationships, so online the participants do not necessarily have the same attitude toward the relationship and hence their expectations of it are different. This may cause disappointment. Thus, while one partner may consider cybersex to be a prelude to an extended meaningful (offline or online) relationship, the other partner may consider it to be a mere one-night cyberstand. Discrepancies in attitudes and expectations are common to both offline and online sexual affairs. It seems, however, that these are more frequent in online affairs, as deception is easier in cyberspace. Accordingly, people who wish to minimize the chance of being hurt should limit their expectations when they embark on an online affair.

Cybersex can, of course, have a superficial intrinsic value in the sense that it provides pleasure to all participants. Indeed, cybersex can be as exciting as offline sex and sometimes even more so.

Long-term offline personal relationships are often criticized for being composed of mainly goal-oriented activities that have only extrinsic value. Thus, it can be argued that many parents live together because it is more convenient to raise children this way and cheaper to live in one household.

Online romantic relationships intended to be limited to cyberspace are by and large of a different nature: they are based upon scarcely any goal-oriented activity – and are typically composed of activities that the participants want to do for their own sake. As one woman wrote: "He constantly told me that he can not provide me with what I would want, and I would always respond with 'I'm not asking for anything from you, but simply enjoy your company.'"[25] People want to communicate online with a stranger, because they enjoy such conversations and find them of value. This communication may be beneficial or harmful from other perspectives, but these are not the reasons why people engage in such activities. When people enjoy the communication, they do not worry much about attaining external goals. In cyberspace, people can pay a compliment without expecting a receipt or worrying about an overdraft.

An online-only romantic relationship can then be intrinsically valuable in the profound sense. In such a relationship, there are no face-to-face meetings – although those are not excluded in the long term – and no practical purposes are evident. Such a relationship is undertaken purely for the sake of romantic communication with each other. This explains the long hours that people spend in online romantic conversations; in intrinsically valuable activities, we do not want to save resources such as time. As a woman called Tracy writes: **"When we talk, we do not want to go. We always meet here at our special time, and talk for hours about what we need."**[26] Since we value the activity itself, we want it to keep going for as long as possible. Accordingly, the risk of addiction is high.

Online intimate communication often consists of a mixture of kinds of the above types of activities. A particular online relationship may begin as one of the above types and develop into a different one. Thus, some people initially enter cyberspace for the purpose of finding an offline romantic partner, but then agree to participate in cybersex in order to deepen the relationship.

The distinction between online relationships that are used as a way of finding an offline partner and online-only relationships is related to the more general distinction between considering the Internet as a cultural artifact – that is, a means of communication within an offline social world – and considering it as a culture of its own – that is, regarding cyberspace as a social space in its own right. Since the Internet is not a unified phenomenon, both types of uses of the Net coexist.[27]

The incomplete nature of online affairs

> A man is incomplete until he is married. After that, he is finished.
>
> Zsa Zsa Gabor

I have suggested that many online affairs are intrinsically valuable: some in the superficial sense of providing pleasure to their participants and some in the profound sense including also the use and development of essential capacities and attitudes. Accordingly, online affairs may seem to be an ideal kind of activity. Nevertheless, online affairs are not satisfactory in a profound aspect: they are incomplete in the sense that people typically want to transform them into an offline affair. In offline relationships, profound intrinsically valuable activities are complete. Online relationships violate this connection (assumed by Aristotle) between the intrinsically valuable nature of the activity and its completeness. In such relationships, the activity is incomplete not because the goal has not been achieved – for example, orgasm has not been reached – or because the relationship is not profound in the sense that it does not develop essential capacities and attitudes. It is incomplete because it is largely imaginary rather than actual. Being actual seems to be part of the profoundness associated with the optimal functioning typical of an intrinsically valuable activity in its fullest sense.

The wish to transform an online romantic relationship into an actual one is an indication of its incompleteness. Online romantic relationships are incomplete in the sense that they cannot be fulfilled by actual actions, such as physical interactions that typify romantic behavior. As Christina describes her online affair: "Everything with him was great. But it wasn't enough to sustain me. I needed more, I needed a real flesh and blood person who wasn't 800 miles away." Another woman describes her online love as "a love that at the moment cannot be allowed to live and breathe as it rightfully deserves."[28] This feeling of incompleteness is a major obstacle to being satisfied with online-only relationships. Indeed, when people reflect on when they feel most positive, they often report that positive feelings arise when they confront tasks that they have a chance of completing.[29]

In offline affairs, a sense of incompletion is sometimes due to a past that has not been fully actualized – for instance, it may refer to affairs where profound love was terminated (for practical or other reasons) despite its intensity. Hence, people often miss these affairs and idealize them. In online affairs, a sense of incompletion is often due to a future that has not yet been actualized and accordingly is greatly idealized. In the wonderful song, "Me and Bobby McGee," Janis Joplin says: "I'd trade all my tomorrows for just one yesterday – of holding Bobby's body close to mine." Should Ms. Joplin have had an online affair, she would probably have said: "I'd trade all my todays for just one tomorrow – of holding Bobby's body close to mine." As one woman engaged in an online affair writes: "We want to meet each other SO BADLY, we NEED to be in each other's arms, we NEED to look into each other's eyes, and we NEED that first kiss!!"[30]

It is easier to have an online-only friendship than an online-only romance, as the role of physical closeness and physical attractiveness is less central in friendship. Indeed, in one survey, 26 percent of Internet users said they have online friends whom they have not met in person.[31]

The decision to transform an online affair into an offline one is not easy, as it involves significant emotional risks and benefits. If an online affair is so good and so pure, why should people risk destroying it? Various psychological tendencies are involved in taking that risk and deciding to initiate the face-to-face meeting.

It is more difficult to bear the loss of something you have than not to gain something you never had. Given the choice, people usually prefer to win $40 when the odds are certain, rather than take a 50 percent chance of winning $100. One possible explanation for this is that the displeasure associated with losing a sum of money is generally greater than the pleasure associated with winning the same or even a greater sum. In most instances, losses loom larger than gains. Success, if not achieved in too strong a dose, usually makes for a less intense emotion than failure. The greater pain involved in a loss is one reason why jealousy is often more painful than envy.[32]

In accordance with such considerations, most people tend to make regret-minimizing choices – that is, they make choices to minimize their possible short-term regret. These choices are typically risk-avoiding – people are ready to sacrifice monetary gain to ensure that they will not experience subsequent short-term regret. The worry associated with attempting to actualize an online affair comes from our tendency to minimize short-term regret by taking the risk-avoiding route. We simply do not want to lose something we love so much. The tendency to minimize short-term regret may have negative consequences as it may paralyze people and prevent them from undergoing enjoyable experiences – thereby increasing the likelihood of long-term regret, which is concerned with lost opportunities.

The tendency to minimize short-term regret prevails among most, but not all people; some people are motivated to minimize long-term regret while others seek to maximize joy. Despite the powerful nature of the risk-avoiding tendency, most people who fall in love with their online partner want actually to meet the other person. When love is profound, the perceived opportunities are exciting and people do not want to miss such opportunities and regret them for the rest of their life. People are often tormented by what they imagine to be the consequences of the road not taken. Indeed, a survey of forty-eight women found that only one regretted having pursued a life dream, while almost all the women who had not pursued their life dream regretted it.[33] Cyberspace offers exciting dreams, and people are likely to pursue these dreams even while recognizing that this may ruin the dream.

The wish to actualize online relationships is not accidental: an emotion is not a disinterested state – it is not a theoretical state having no relevance to our life. As the online relationship becomes more intense and more intimate, it also becomes more seductive and the partners increasingly want to meet each other. If the transformation of an online relationship to an offline one is smooth, emotions may grow even stronger. As Vince describes the offline meeting with his online friend: "The online chat now seemed so pale in comparison with holding the woman I loved in my arms."[34] The inability to actualize the partners' emotional desires leaves these emotions incomplete. Indeed, most people believe that their commitment to an online relationship means not only that it should continue, but that this continuation should take an increasingly intimate form, with the ultimate aim of face-to-face encounters.[35]

Actualizing an existing online relationship is particularly desirable for those who have difficulties in forming significant offline relationships because of shyness or other social difficulties. For these people, a successful online relationship is of great significance for their self-image and hence they wish to transform it into existence in their actual life. Those who are already successful in establishing face-to-face romantic relationships are less motivated to transform a successful monitor-to-monitor affair into such a relationship.[36] Nevertheless, the wish to actualize the online relationship is present in all such successful affairs.

The wish to have an offline relationship could be fulfilled simply by initiating such a relationship in the first place – thereby preventing the difficult task of transforming an online affair into an offline one. However, in doing so, we would lose those romantic advantages, such as profound self-disclosure and intimacy, which are associated with online affairs. A 27-year-old woman having an online affair with an 18-year-old man writes:

> All my friends think I am crazy and they don't understand why I would spend all of my time on a computer talking to this guy when I could be out on real dates. I don't know either. We have never met or spoken. I don't even know what he looks like. All I know is that I am falling like a fool for someone I may never be able to have.[37]

It is easy to have either an offline affair or an online affair; it is more difficult to retain the advantages of both.

Some kinds of children's games – mainly those with a significant imaginative aspect – are similar to online interactions: they are both enjoyable and have an intrinsic value, but are incomplete in the sense that they typically involve the implicit wish to actualize them. Both children's games and online interactions are, to some extent, virtual in nature, a sort of game-playing with reality. This illusory aspect enables the participants to ignore some harsh facets of reality and to play in a relatively safe and benign environment. Like the environment of children, cyberspace is also not self-contained, as it is closely connected with the actual world and must obey some of its regularities and constraints. Accordingly, the enjoyable games played by children and cyberspace users cannot last forever: maturation and actual constraints require their dues.

In both children's games and cyberspace, the wish to actualize the interaction is not merely the result of external constraints, but is an inherent feature of the interaction. Actualization of relationships is perceived as deepening and increasing the satisfaction we derive from them. This perception may be incorrect – and indeed many people would prefer to return to their childhood – but it is certainly present and is responsible for the incomplete nature of these interactions.

Elvis Presley sang: "Love me tender, love me sweet, never let me go; you have made my life complete." This song, which so nicely describes the ideal of face-to-face romantic relationships, does not apply to an online romantic relationship: an online partner always lets you go (to your offline reality) and never makes your life complete.

The incompleteness of online romantic affairs typically generates great emotional intensity. This is so since incompleteness is related to instability and changes. Our attention is focused much more on an incomplete matter than on a complete one, since the former is a kind of change to which our system has not yet adapted. We have no reason to dwell upon something that is complete, but we have every reason to dwell upon something we strongly desire but that is yet to be achieved. Mystery and anticipation, which are part of romantic and sexual excitement, are greater in this case. A 29-year-old married woman, who often engages in cybersex, indicates: "I have been chatting and also cybering and it does give me pleasure. Maybe it is the unknown person behind the screen. Maybe it is the fantasy of him. Sometimes it's just the mystery of it."[38]

Online relationships usually have the characteristic of "unfinished business" since, as long as they are not transformed into offline relationships, there is something missing from them. In this sense, they are similar to an extended period of courtship, and accordingly emotional intensity remains high – in the words of one woman, "passion at an unbelievable peak" – even for a long period. A paradoxical aspect in this regard is that although online relationships are intense because of, among other factors, their incompleteness, such incompleteness involves the wish to transform the relationship into a more complete one – something that usually decreases the intensity and may lead to the termination of the relationship.

Numerous novels and movies deal with romantic relationships that are not complete, and this aspect helps to maintain the intense excitement of the affair. In one such circumstance, the two lovers meet every month (or year) for an intense sexual encounter while knowing virtually nothing about the life of their partners outside of their meetings. In other circumstances, the relationship is conducted solely via letters (written either before or after a passionate sexual encounter). Another type of incomplete romantic relation involves close emotional ties, but no sexual intercourse. In all these examples, the intensity of the romantic relationship is due to its incomplete nature – to the implicit desire by the participants to reach a more fulfilled interaction.

In this regard, online affairs resemble the courtly love espoused by the twelfth-century troubadours. The troubadours sang about "a new kind of tender, extramarital flirtation which (ideally) was sexually unconsummated and which, therefore, made the chaste lovers more noble and virtuous."[39] Thus, the two non-sexual lovers were supposed to sleep naked beside each other for the whole night without engaging in any sexual activity. This was supposed to test whether their love was strong enough to sustain the introduction of this new element into their relationship. Although cyberlove is a less painful means for examining the depth of participants' attitudes, it also consists of passionate emotional attitudes together with a lack of physical contact. In both cases, when the relationship can endure passion without any physical contact, it can be allowed to develop to the point where physical, sexual activities are a natural addition to it. Cyberlove is similar to ideal courtly love in another aspect: in both cases the relationship often involves a married person who cannot leave her or his primary relationship. This prevents the two lovers from sharing their daily, public life with each other, which further exacerbates the incomplete nature of the relationship.

When the online communication is satisfying, people naturally want to deepen it by adding ordinary types of communication, such as exchange of pictures, phone conversations, written letters, and face-to-face meetings, all of which make the relationship more real. Indeed, most online lovers use the above ordinary types of communication to supplement their online communication and hence to increase the reality of the other person.

Online relationships are overwhelmed with imaginary content, which may be an obstacle when people attempt to actualize the relationship or when there is a discrepancy between the imagined partner and the actual one. After meeting her online lover for the first time and discovering that he had pretended to be much younger and more handsome than he actually was, one woman expressed her dismay: "The reality of meeting him shattered my dream. I felt horrible guilt and disgust at myself for being so blind."[40] Another woman, who decided to meet her online lover after spending much time exchanging emails and talking to him on the phone, said: "He walked off the plane looking like he hadn't washed his clothes in a month and had never even looked at a toothbrush."[41]

Sometimes the unpleasant characteristics of a person are revealed not in the first face-to-face meeting, but even earlier, when the exchange moves from a public chat room and becomes private. The attempt to appear courteous and playful in the public room – in order to attract the attention of at least some of the many people visiting the chat room – may degenerate into rude and inconsiderate behavior once a more private relationship begins.

Even in cases where the partner's real characteristics are disclosed, and where they are not considered a significant problem in the online relationships, they can become so when the relationship is transformed into actual reality. Take, for example, age. An older man, who had an intense online affair with a young college student who was aware of his age, described her attitude after their first face-to-face meeting and just before she dropped him, in the following manner: "It began to occur to her that she would have to explain to her friends what she was doing with a guy so older than her."[42] A friend of mine, Dan, had a similar experience. After he had delivered a lecture, Dan, who is in his late fifties, was approached by a young woman in her early twenties who told him how much he had impressed her. Dan was immediately attracted to her. They began an online relationship during which she told him that she had a boyfriend, but that her affair with Dan was the most intense and profound love of her life. After a few weeks Dan suggested that they meet, with the intention of transforming their online relationship into an offline one. Then the correspondence began to be infrequent, and finally she completely broke off contact with him. Again, the quest to transform the relationship into an offline one brought with it all the difficulties associated with offline relationships – in this case, their significant age difference.

The negative impact of actual reality may be evident as a result of the mere decision to meet. Such a decision may increase excitement, but it may also have a negative impact on the relationship. One man describes such a change as dramatic: the relationship "became more reserved and dwelt a lot on the planning for her trip. Gradually our conversations dwindled."[43] Merely thinking about actual reality may have damaged the online affair.

A similar negative impact of actual reality may be found in offline relationships as well. A friend of mine told me that he once flirted with a married woman. On one occasion, she showed him a picture of her husband, after which he told her that he wanted to abandon his intentions of turning the flirtation into a sexual affair. The picture provided a dash of reality to the imaginary affair – the husband became much more real and vivid – and this emphasized the moral difficulty of pursuing such an affair. Despite what he told her, and indeed what he intended, the wish to materialize the flirtation was too strong, and a few days later the flirtation turned into an actual, passionate (though brief) sexual affair. The woman told him that his announcement, after seeing the picture, that he wished to refrain from the sexual affair had an opposite effect: it increased her motivation to have the affair. (This illustrates the impact of the "hard-to-get" strategy.) Such surprising mental twists are even more common in cyberspace, where imagination plays a more central role and it is easier to modify the circumstances.

Physical attractiveness is usually the stumbling block for transforming online relationships into offline ones. A person's character attributes are usually revealed in online communication, but physical attributes can be a source of disappointment. A man who after a face-to-face meeting does not feel physical attraction toward his online mate may end the relationship, although he may still love her character and behavior. However, the attraction and closeness created by the online affair could mitigate the reduced level of physical attraction and may enable the formation of a romantic relationship in situations where it would not usually begin. When there is no significant discrepancy between the imagined partner and the one revealed in the first face-to-face meeting, there is a good chance that the relationship will develop further, as each person already has a positive attitude toward the other.

Transforming a successful online relationship into an offline relationship may fail not because of some kind of deception, but because personal attraction involves activating a structured schema consisting of various elements. Even if all these elements are present, their combination may not be the one underlying the generation of attraction. Consider the following message sent after a first face-to-face meeting: "I thought we were in love. But I went to meet him this week, and even though he's a pretty good-looking guy, seeing him in person was weird. It wasn't like he was ugly or smelled bad or anything, but when we held hands, I just wanted to pull away."[44] The disappointment arising from the face-to-face meeting may generate longing for the relationship that existed prior to that meeting. In Bruno Kampel's words: "I feel nostalgic about the day on which we never met for the first time."[45]

Many people testify that their first face-to-face meeting was wonderful and that they thought their relationship would intensify further. However, they found that, shortly after that meeting, the great romance began to fade away. It was not that something in particular went wrong – it was just that a different dimension had been added to the enchanting environment of online communication, and that dimension had somehow shattered the dream. Even the mere transformation from online communication to phone calls may sometimes shatter the illusion. Since, in many respects, phone calls are more similar to actual reality than online communication is, this step toward reality may destabilize virtual reality. Sometimes only a dash of reality can ruin our dreams; sometimes a huge dose of reality cannot affect them.

There is one significant disadvantage in transforming online relationships into offline relationships: the crucial activity by which participants have fallen in love with each other – that is, exchanging electronic messages – is absent from their new relationships. They are still able to write to each other, but since they are able to talk or meet – or even live together – the value of such communication is reduced, and indeed in these situations most people stop exchanging emails.[46]

Another common reason for the failure to transform an online relationship into an offline one concerns the difficulties associated with such a move. Some of these difficulties are material, while others are mental. It is often the case that difficulties that have already been broached by the partners loom larger when they are actually faced. In some cases, meeting the family (including the spouse of the online partner) generates guilt feelings that prevent the continuation of the relationship. Thus, a married woman recounts how, after a long online affair with a married man, she met him and they spent a wonderful week together. Subsequently, when she next visited his town, their relationship had changed: "I got to meet his family and that changed things for me. His wife is a beautiful person and knowing how I felt about him, it suddenly didn't feel right anymore. They have a wonderful life and I have him to thank for giving me back the wonderful marriage I almost threw away."[47]

The more features of actual reality that are added, the greater the likelihood of shattering the dream. It is clear that photographs can do this. Phone conversations, however, may also reduce emotional intensity (in other cases, they may increase it), as information is less selective and responses are more spontaneous. Inserting pieces of actual reality often removes the magic of the virtual reality. The addition of other features of actual reality to online relationships is not without a cost: it decreases some of the advantages of online relationships. Such a process involves, for example, lesser anonymity, greater risk, and lower personal control. If the online relationship is good and a high degree of trust has been developed, losing these advantages and taking some risks may be worthwhile and beneficial. However, it should be realized that actualizing an online relationship might result in its termination.

In some cases, failing offline affairs turn into online affairs. In these cases, imagination is given a greater role and accordingly the participants can overlook or improve some negative aspects of their previous offline affair. Idealization of the past, selective memory, and positive biases, which are typical of such circumstances, can turn a problematic offline relationship into an enjoyable online one.

Online relationships gain their emotional intensity by referring to an imaginary world that is better than the actual one; by ignoring various aspects of actual reality and focusing upon the exciting ones, they increase emotional intensity. However, an important variable of emotional intensity is the degree of reality: the more we believe the situation to be real, the more intense is the emotion.[48] This explains the wish to actualize the relationship and thereby to increase its reality.

A face-to-face meeting usually terminates the online relationship – either because the meeting was so disappointing that the two cannot continue their communication or because the meeting was so enjoyable that the relationship is transferred offline. Ironically, the successful goal of an online romantic relationship is its termination. That is the sad aspect of online relationships. Since we cannot be content with our own limited online lot, we want to improve the relationship by extending it offline. The extension may prove to be suicidal. As Oscar Wilde said, "Each man kills the thing he loves."

This phenomenon is not limited to cyberspace – it is related to the general psychological problem of not being satisfied with our lot. A great obstacle to happiness is our inability to be satisfied with what we have: even when we are happy, we still wish to be happier; we want more and more, wishing to expand our lot. However, this wish may ruin our present happiness.

Advertisers, who know that new demands can be created constantly because people are never fully satisfied with their present lot, regularly offer new and improved products that promise a better and happier life. However, the remedy is not to reach for more, but to be able to be satisfied with our current situation. The natural wish to improve our condition should not be accompanied by deep dissatisfaction with our current circumstances. It should be seen as a tendency that may be beneficial, but that cannot justify the ruin of our present situation.

A somewhat similar case is expressed in the Peter Principle, which states that most people are promoted to positions for which they are not fit. When someone is successful in her current position, she is promoted to a higher one, and if she is successful in that position as well, she will continue to be promoted until she reaches a position in which she does not perform well – at which point, she will remain stuck in that unsuitable position. The wish to upgrade personal relationships may have a similar fate. When relationships that are good and enjoyable are upgraded, they may become complete failures.

The desire to deepen an online romantic relationship by adding face-to-face meetings is similar to a desire to deepen an enjoyable, non-sexual friendship by adding the sexual dimension. This addition may in some circumstances strengthen the relationship – especially when the addition is a natural result of a previous lengthy relationship. In other circumstances, such an addition may ruin the relationship – as it introduces a new central dimension that changes the nature of the whole relationship, and there is no guarantee that the new type of relationship will be as enjoyable as the former one. This is particularly true when prevailing moral norms criticize the very presence of sexual relationships between the two people – for instance, when both are married to other people. This is another example of the Peter Principle: participants in a good, enjoyable relationship want to deepen the relationship further by adding new dimensions to it; they continue to do so until the relationship is no longer enjoyable and there is no incentive to improve it.

Summary

Anything worth doing is worth doing slowly.

Mae West

Two types of activities have been discerned: an extrinsically valuable activity, which is a means to a certain goal, and an intrinsically valuable activity, whose value lies in the activity itself. I have distinguished two major types of intrinsically valuable activities: those promoting superficial pleasure and those promoting profound satisfaction. The second type is of particular significance for human flourishing, as it involves optimal functioning using and developing the agents' essential capacities and attitudes in a systematic manner over a sustained period of time.

The role of these types of activities in love, sex, and happiness has been shown. Intrinsically valuable activities involving optimal functioning are of particular importance for promoting happiness and for making life more worthwhile. Although all types of activities are present in both offline and online romantic affairs, a greater percentage of intrinsically valuable activities seems to characterize online-only affairs.

It is easier to achieve the transitory types of joy in cyberspace. This is particularly obvious in the sexual domain. The situation concerning profound satisfaction is less clear. Cyberspace has both a positive and a negative impact in this regard. Here, a crucial consideration is whether we are able to integrate the actual and the virtual worlds, but at the same time maintain a separation between them. Such an ability may increase our happiness, even if only slightly.

In the classic distinction between extrinsically and intrinsically valuable activities, the latter are complete in the sense that their value does not rest upon an external goal. However, although online affairs involve many profound intrinsically valuable activities, they are incomplete in another sense: they involve the wish to upgrade the relationship by transforming it into an offline, actual relationship. This feature of online affairs prevents them from continuing beyond a certain timeframe.

There are certain difficulties inherent in the transformation of an online romantic relationship into an offline one. A few of the main difficulties are: (a) the incompleteness of online affairs; (b) the discrepancy between the virtual and actual partner; (c) the introduction into the relationship of a new dimension – mainly, external appearance, and hence external attraction; (d) the abandoning of a successful communicative medium; and (e) various practical difficulties that arise from such a transformation. It is impossible to predict whether a given relationship will be powerful enough to overcome these difficulties.

Although online communication may connect us to a better world, it is by no means a perfect world. In light of the human tendency to improve one's lot, it is not surprising that a central wish in this imaginary, improved world is to be connected once again to the actual world.

7 *Flirting on- and offline*

All really great lovers are articulate, and verbal seduction is the surest road to actual seduction.

Marya Mannes

After analyzing in the previous chapter various types of activities, I turn now to examine a major activity in cyberspace, that is, cyberflirting. This activity is valuable in the sense that it provides great pleasure to its participants. I begin the discussion by examining the crucial element of both flirting and cyberlove, that is, conversation.

Online conversations

I can do anything you want me to do, as long as I don't have to speak.

Linda Evangelista

Online affairs consist of conversations having elements common to both gossip and profound types of non-purposive conversations.

Typical gossip is an intrinsically valuable activity whose value lies in the activity itself. Gossip is idle, relaxing, and enjoyable talk; it involves being playful and attaching little importance to the given subject. Gossip is typically relaxing and effortless and, like games, often relieves people's daily tensions. One reason for the relaxing nature of gossip is that it enables us to talk about what is really on our minds. People indulging in gossip do not want to ponder deeply on the content or consequences of what they say. Sometimes gossip seems to be talk for the sake of talking. When people are involved in serious, practical, and purposive talk, they are not gossiping, since gossip is idle frivolous talk. This does not imply that gossip has no consequences, but these are mostly byproducts, not ends in themselves.[1]

Idle conversations, engaged in for the sake of conversation alone, are more typical of online than offline relationships. In offline relationships, gossip fulfills the need for small talk. Online communication sometimes has the characteristics of gossip: it is conversation for the sake of conversation. The rapid pace of modern society leaves fewer opportunities for idle chat. Online communication supplies such opportunities. The fact that the person you are corresponding with has no practical connections with you that can influence your life enhances the necessary atmosphere in which to engage in such enjoyable, non-purposive conversations. Since the value of these conversations is in the conversation itself, there is no need to be efficient and brief; on the contrary, we want the conversations to continue for long as possible. No wonder that some online couples spend many hours a day writing to each other. When participating in such communication, people report that they feel as if they are immersed in an enjoyable ocean. They often testify that each hour seems like minutes because time passes so quickly when you are with the one you love.[2]

One difference between gossip and online conversations is that gossip often consists of negative information about other people, while online conversations often involve positive information about oneself. Online conversations are also more profound and include a greater variety of topics.

Another function of gossip is that of gaining access to intimate information that is of great interest to us. Since candid self-disclosure is rare among people who may influence each other's lives, in offline circumstances gossip is an enjoyable way to gather intimate information that is otherwise difficult to obtain. The sharing of such information and the manner of conveying it contribute to the formation of a personal relationship. In online communication, intimate information is divulged more readily because profound self-disclosure is more common. The profound sharing of intimate information facilitates the formation of an online friendship and later of online love. People gossip for pleasure, not in order to hurt someone; nevertheless, because we know the people about whom we are gossiping, gossip can sometimes cause harm. In online relationships, the likelihood of such harm is considerably reduced.

Online conversations fulfill some of the functions of gossip – that is, engaging in enjoyable and relaxing conversation and gaining access to interesting intimate information – without incurring some of the negative byproducts associated with it. Online conversations also fulfill the need to be able to discuss freely the profound aspects of our individual lives.

No wonder that conversation is of great value in online relationships. The following email message, posted on a message board, exemplifies this:

> *Subject: The art of the spoken word*
>
> Looking for ladies who enjoy being pampered with good conversation and the sensuality of the spoken word. Well-thought conversation is an art, and its appreciation is an extraordinary gift! I love to talk about anything and everything, so if you're interested in avoiding the immature, crass babble online and having a great talk, please e-mail me or look for me on-line.[3]

It is difficult to imagine the value of conversation being elevated to such heights in an offline relationship. It is refreshing to discover that neither physical contact nor visual content, but rather conversation, is at the heart of online affairs. As one woman comments: "A relationship based solely on communication is rare and too valuable to be dismissed."[4]

Conversations are indeed important in forming a good base for a strong romantic relationship. Thus, a woman who has a wonderful marriage with a man she had an online relationship with describes her current situation: "The only complaint I have is that I miss the relationship we used to have online. There was no routine, no garbage to take out and most of all, uninterrupted, deep conversations. I think there is no better way to meet someone and get to know them from the inside." The role of profound conversations in forming a romantic relationship has positive effects upon the subsequent stages of the relationship. As a woman who married her online lover indicates: "We are truly, truly, happy and very much in love. Just like every other couple, we have our moments, but we had such a strong friendship based on communication, we talk through any problems that come up."[5]

The American President, Calvin Coolidge, once said: "I have noticed that nothing I never said ever did me any harm." This claim cannot be true of cyberspace, where verbal communication is of crucial importance. The art of conversation should be distinguished from the power of speech. The latter can impress at first meeting; after this, an absorbing and genuine conversation should take place if the relationship is based merely upon verbal communication, as is the case in cyberspace.

The new means of communication available in current society have increased the value of verbal skills in some fields, such as politics. The introduction of television has also increased the value placed upon the individual's pleasant external appearance in politics and in many other fields. However, the value of verbal communication is constantly decreasing in personal relationships. In our current society, we scarcely have the time for genuine and prolonged conversations with those dear to us.

In cyberspace, conversations are more important, as this is the only means with which to make intimate connections with other people. Words are once again becoming essential in human interaction. In cyberspace, confidence in personal relationships is acquired by genuine conversations and not by expensive makeup. Conversation, rather than name and title, makes the difference. The emphasis upon verbal communication in online relationships can be perceived as a reaction to the excessive role given to visual content in modern society.[6]

The value of online conversations in romantic relationships is also evident from the fact that, after meeting face-to-face, couples tend to retain the online conversation for its unique value. Sometimes it is easier to write down what you feel than to describe it in the presence of someone. Writing enables you to focus upon those feelings and to express them in a more precise and less vulnerable manner.

A relationship with the same person that is conducted both offline and online may have distinct qualities in each domain. In some cases, the offline relationship may be more physical and sexual, whereas the online one may be more intellectual. In other cases, the two relationships may be of different types. In any case, having access to various ways of communicating may enhance the connection between partners.

Given the greater value placed on conversations in cyberspace, skills involving words are becoming more important than skills connected with appearance. In a site offering tips for online seduction, the authors advise people to spend some time honing their writing and spelling skills by reading more books, to practice by writing letters to friends and family, and to increase their vocabulary by thumbing through a dictionary or thesaurus.[7] People often allude to writing styles when they explain their attraction to their online partners. Thus, one woman explains in the following manner why she replied to an email from a man after being disappointed with online meetings and blind dates: "He seemed nice from the letter, spelled most things correctly and I figured I would write back to him."[8]

Online relationships are sometimes criticized on the grounds that participants invest many hours a day simply chatting with people who are almost strangers to them. While it is clear that too much of a good thing can be harmful, in comparison to prevailing alternatives in modern society – such as watching television, or playing computer games – chatting with strangers about everything that is on one's mind is at least of equal value, and may be the better alternative.

Online affairs as flirting

Angels fly because they take themselves lightly.
G. K. Chesterton

The enjoyable, idle aspect of online romantic affairs illustrates the affinity of these affairs to flirting. Flirting adds spice to our life and supports positive attitudes toward other people. It may involve flattery, but it is a subtle and enjoyable flattery that is closer to praise than to a lie. Flirting creates a relaxing, calm, and enjoyable atmosphere. It involves curiosity, humor, imagination, and empathy. Flirting is subtle: it is typically not an explicit sexual activity, but rather an enjoyable, gentle prelude or substitute for it. Flirting has elements of intellectual teasing flavored by emotional play. During flirting, each partner's soul is stirred, thereby enabling the two souls to respond to each other.[9] In her discussion on flirting, Miss Etiquette indicates that the meaning of flirting is to be playfully romantic; something of little value or importance; to speak or act in a playful or flirting way; to toy with. Indeed, her colleague, Miss Manners, considers flirtation "a gentle amusement," an activity that should be harmless and not lead to anything.[10] In a chat room entitled "Married and Flirting," people are advised to treat flirting as pure fun, as a good way to practice social skills and to make yourself and your targets feel good. This site, whose motto is "Married Not Dead," offers the following rules of flirting: **F** is for Flattery; **L** is for Listen; **I** is for Interest; **R** is for being Responsible; **T** is for Trusting yourself; **S** is for winning a Smile.[11]

Flirting encompasses seemingly contradictory aspects: honesty together with an element of innocence, as well as a mild level of deception (expressed in flattery); caring for others – by listening to and showing interest in them – while not taking them too seriously; being confident and feeling good about yourself while not attaching too much importance to yourself; intelligence flavored by emotional tone. All these characteristics are evident in online affairs.

Flirting is conducted within a tacit borderline; it is a kind of game, or rather a dance, in which participants move closer to the borderline – and sometimes even step across it – and then move back to a comfortable distance from it. Cyberflirting is a type of verbal dance in which the boundaries of sexuality are not clearly drawn. Flirting is like an inactive volcano that can become active any moment. In online affairs, crossing the line between innocent flirting and overt sexual interaction, and hence activating the sexual volcano, is greatly facilitated as the stimulation is high and the typical warning signals that alert people of infidelity – e.g., nonverbal signs of discomfort or shame – are not apparent in cyberspace.[12] The gradual manner in which people become involved in overt sexual interaction online is expressed in the following description:

> I am a single woman who has formed a relationship with a much younger married man. In real life there is no way I would have formed this relationship. I do not go out with married men. I met him in a chat room and at first it was just a nice friendly chat. This of course progressed until we eventually went into a private room. I was intrigued by what would happen but could not believe the feelings this man evoked in me.[13]

No wonder that many people are astonished upon finding out about their partner's online affair. One such woman, married for twenty-four years, describes her husband: **"He has always been a loving, honorable, honest man, so this broke my heart."** Another woman notes: **"I never thought in a million years that my husband would even learn how to type."**[14]

Flirting enables you to be yourself and express all types of personal characteristics. Typical flirting in general, and cyberflirting in particular, offer participants an enjoyable, frivolous form of sexual communication with no serious intent. Typical flirting is usually harmless. However, often flirting is not restricted to such harmless communication and leads to a sexual relationship.

The above contradictory aspects are also characteristic of humor, which is probably the most common variety of playful language activity online.[15] Humor involves honesty, such as when it touches upon the most profound issues in our life; it also involves exaggeration, which may lead to embellishment of the truth and thus to deception. The sensitivity associated with humor indicates that it involves caring for others, but this sensitivity is also associated with not taking others too seriously – sometimes to the extent that other people may be insulted. A sense of humor indicates that we feel good about ourselves, but also that we do not attach too much importance to ourselves. Like flirting, a sense of humor includes a measure of intelligence. The fact that many online affairs are similar to flirting and games, and the fact that humor plays a crucial role in flirting and games, attest to the importance of humor in online affairs.

Flirting is not necessarily a prelude to sexual interaction; it is rather a subtle, sexual communication. Flirting may involve gentle physical contact, but often it does not involve sexual intercourse. Flirting may develop into sexual relationships, but then it stops being flirting in the sense described above. Sometimes sexual talk is considered more sexually offensive than are certain activities involving physical contact, such as kissing and hugging. In flirting, we do not force ourselves on others; it is a kind of enjoyable play having the pleasant atmosphere that is typical of the promise of sexual activity. Flirting also involves the mystery and uncertainty associated with sex. Consider the following description of flirting: "Flirting is more than 'Hi, ya wanna?' It's teasing, playing, innuendos – it's about making someone feel special, it's about being attentive, it's about walking on the edge of danger & getting caught. Flirting is nibbling on the forbidden fruit. It's not blunt straight-to-the point comments. It's playing cat & mouse with each other, and enjoying it."[16] A married woman having an affair with a married man illustrates the move from the playful nature of flirting to the more profound nature of a committed romantic relationship in the following description: "We flirted with and seeked each other constantly, until one day we realized we were not just playing anymore, the flirting had transformed into very deep feelings for both of us. He had reached deep inside my heart and touched where no other man has ever before."[17]

Flirting does not have to be a preparatory activity aimed at an external goal, namely, sexual intercourse. Quite often, flirting is the best available *alternative* – rather than means – to actual sexual intercourse. When people enjoy flirting for its own sake, it may be commendable. Although flirting has its own intrinsic value, it also has certain personal and social benefits (as well as disadvantages). Thus, flirting may help to reduce loneliness and boost one's ego and self-confidence. A recent survey has found that most working-women believe that flirting is good for their health and confidence. Indeed, three out of four of them have flirted with a colleague, while 28 percent have had a sexual relationship with a fellow-worker. Some findings indicate that flirting at the workplace makes people more comfortable around each other.[18]

Although explicit sexual activities and orgasms are secondary in flirting, an orgasm is always possible – sexual arousal is often part and parcel of flirting. A woman having an online affair writes: "In fact, much of the time, actual sexual activity and coming are secondary – the discussion, the being turned on, the mental foreplay is what it's all about. When you meet someone who is like-minded, it's like having your favorite erotic book come alive and become tailored to you personally."[19] Since online sex is essentially a type of conversation, which is also an essential part of flirting, the distinction between online sex and flirting is not clear-cut, and the two activities often overlap.

Cyberspace is associated with flirting not only in the sense that many online affairs are similar to flirting, but also in the sense that the Internet considerably facilitates the process of flirting. Flirting is particularly prevalent in chat rooms as most of them promote flirting and "fooling around."[20]

People are attractive when they are relaxed, feeling good, and enjoying themselves.[21] It may also work the other way around: those who are attractive are more likely to be relaxed, feel good, and enjoy themselves. Since cyberspace offers new dimensions of attractiveness, in addition to that of external appearance, it may break the vicious cycle for those who, because they are considered externally unattractive, are not relaxed and hence are unable to attract people.

When we arrange our everyday life on a continuum, where at one pole we find routine, goal-oriented work, and at the other enjoyable recreation, online affairs are closer to recreation than are offline affairs.

If online-only romantic affairs indeed involve a disinterested love, then we may have found the ideal type of love – a kind of a dream-come-true solution. The situation, however, is more complex in light of the illusory aspects associated with these affairs. When people conduct a love affair in cyberspace, they are aware of its illusory aspect and wish to eliminate that aspect. Accordingly, online romantic affairs often include a wish to ground the illusory fantasy in reality by transforming the online affair into an offline one. This wish indicates the incompleteness of online affairs.

The rules for online dating

> Married, eight children; prefer frequent travel.
>
> Appeared in a résumé for a job application

My characterization of various types of online relationships as intrinsically valuable activities, undertaken for their own sake, is in direct opposition to a prevailing view that online relationships are merely an efficient, transitory, and bothersome means with which to achieve the "real" thing: a face-to-face meeting. This view is clearly expressed in the best-selling book, *The Rules for Online Dating*, by Ellen Fein and Sherrie Schneider.

In 1995 Fein and Schneider published their book, *The Rules: Time Tested Secrets for Capturing the Heart of Mr. Right*, which immediately became a huge commercial success. The basic assumption underlying *The Rules* is that men love a challenge and therefore women need to play hard-to-get. *The Rules* is a set of behaviors for women, which are "guaranteed" to encourage a man, once he has shown initial interest in a woman, to fall in love with her. Some of the basic rules are: Do not talk to a man first; Do not call him; Do not accept a Saturday night date after Wednesday; No more than casual kissing, if even that, on the first date; Do not open up too fast; Do not live with a man unless you're engaged with a wedding date; Do not date a married man.

These rules are clearly contrary to the spontaneous, egalitarian, open, and sincere nature of online romantic relationships. Indeed, in *The Rules II* (1997), Fein and Schneider cannot hide their distaste for online dating. They indicate that these relationships usually do not pan out: "At best women end up with male friends or pen pals, not husbands." In addition, they argue, online dating can be downright dangerous, as the man you correspond with can be "a lunatic, a rapist, a killer, a teenager having fun, or a married man." The great popularity of online romantic relationships succeeded in changing the minds of even these hard-line authors, and in *The Rules for Online Dating* (2002), they admit their mistake: "Only a few years ago . . . we had nothing good to say about online dating . . . But facts speak louder than words . . . We have come to believe online dating is the answer. It is effective, easy, inexpensive, and at your fingertips 24 hours a day."[22]

Fein and Schneider apply their rules to online dating and suggest rules such as: Do not answer men's ads or email them first; You should reveal very little about yourself so that they have to ask you out on a date to find out more; Respond to any emails from potential dates twenty-four hours after you receive them; You should only be available to men on the computer at normal "business" hours; Write light and breezy emails – two or three light sentences and nothing more that shows too much interest and effort; For the first three months, do not initiate emails (after three or four months, you can initiate one quick lighthearted email); Do not open up too fast; Do not let a man log off first; Do not volunteer your phone number first and never call him first; If, by his fourth email, a man has not suggested a face-to-face meeting, do not email him again; After your date zero – the first face-to-face date with an email correspondent – you should date a man for several months before sleeping with him, no matter how you feel or how long you have been reading his emails; Do not break or bend *The Rules* online – even a little bit.

These guidelines clearly indicate that Fein and Schneider still maintain their basic negative attitude toward online relationships; now they only approve of online communication as an efficient, transitory, and unenjoyable method of achieving the goal – to set up Saturday night face-to-face dates. They want online communication to be brief and efficient – just the bare minimum to achieve that date. Hence, the woman's emails should not be "seductive and flirty, but factual." An online relationship is "nothing" until you meet a man – "it's the dates that really count." Fein and Schneider consider as time wasters men who treat their online conversations as an end in themselves, not as a means to an end (dates). Accordingly, they discourage online relationships and recommend that women should "disappear" between their brief and purposeful messages. They also recommend that women refrain from talking about anything that is too personal. This embargo on profound, personal communication will end once the goal – a face-to-face date or, even better, a marriage – is achieved: "When you are married, you can talk to him every day."[23]

We have seen that online relationships typically involve features such as great self-disclosure, sincerity, profound intimacy, and continuous and intense emotional involvement. Fein and Schneider specifically warn their readers against including such features in their online communication, as they are contrary to their strategy of "playing hard-to-get" and of remaining as mysterious as possible. If men, who are by nature pursuers who love a chase, do not consider their female correspondents as challenges that are worth investing a lot of effort in, nothing good – such as the Saturday night date – will come from the relationship. Accordingly, a man should have to invest effort in order to elicit important information from you: "He should at least take you out on a date."[24] In some circumstances, being mysterious may increase excitement, but it also prevents forming a profound personal relationship based upon significant familiarity.

A major disadvantage of "playing hard-to-get" is that it discourages sincerity and spontaneity. The woman refrains from revealing her sincere attitude and emotions; rather she leads the man to believe something else about her. Thus, Fein and Schneider suggest that women should never take part in online dating on weekends; they should pretend that they are fully booked at that time. They specifically warn against responding to email messages on Sundays before 5 p.m. – "men should think you are having brunch or are at a concert or something else equally exciting on Sunday during the day." Almost all the rules intend to mislead the man concerning the woman's real attitude: the man should not "know exactly what you are doing and what you are thinking or feeling about him."[25]

Inhibiting sincerity has other costs, in particular the loss of spontaneity. One of the principal rules is to wait twenty-four hours before responding to a man's message – otherwise, men may get the impression that you are not busy. Fein and Schneider may be aware that such a rule is likely to kill spontaneity and so they "limit" the validity of this rule "only" to the first few months of courtship – after this, an hour or two is reasonable, although waiting till the end of the day is even better. In any case, "anything is better than e-mailing a man a minute later."[26] Interestingly, in a site that offers men tips on corresponding with women in chat rooms, one tip entitled "Let them wait" states that "When talking to a girl online, don't respond quickly at first. Make them think you are so busy talking to many different people. Give a 20 second waiting period between each answer. After a while, make it look like they won your affection and then type quicker."[27] If each person made the other wait, the efficiency of this technique would be reduced and its insincerity would become clear.

The Rules attempt to exclude the expression of any emotional reactions – these are considered harmful to the well-calculated goal of securing a face-to-face meeting. Accordingly, Fein and Schneider urge women to count to twenty before responding to a message and to refrain from expressing intense emotions since these "scare men away." They argue that women should not put their heart and soul into online dating; women should recognize that "Mr. E-mail Man doesn't exist until you see the whites of his eyes."[28]

I will not argue that these suggested rules never work or that they are inappropriate in all circumstances – mystery, challenge, and effort are indeed important characteristics in heightening emotions. Play is part of flirting, and playing hard-to-get may be part of such a play. I also agree that online dating can be an extremely useful tool for finding a suitable mate for an offline relationship and marriage.

I believe, however, that online relationships have their own intrinsic value and are fundamentally different from relationships based upon the tactic of playing hard-to-get. Since online relationships are constituted by conversations, they cannot afford to hide essential information about the agent's attitudes and feelings. They should be, as many of them actually are, open and sincere. For some people it may be the most valuable and meaningful activity they have ever experienced; as one woman writes: "I don't even think I knew what true love was all about until I went on the computer."[29] For others this may be considered a waste of time. The real issue may be that of the correct proportion. I believe that privacy is valuable as well, and therefore personal openness may also have its own limitations. Nevertheless, it appears that online relationships enable a greater degree of openness and sincerity concerning some fundamental aspects of romantic relationships.

The formation of online affairs

> You know what, there is a place you can touch a woman that will drive her crazy . . . her heart.
>
> Melanie Griffith

A typical development of cyberlove is as follows: public discourse, private emails or private chatting, sending pictures, telephoning, and arranging face-to-face meetings. These stages can take a while – sometimes over a year, but typically a few months. This gives the partners an opportunity to get to know each other.

Although not everyone sends a picture to their online partner, many do. One major reason for exchanging pictures is to avoid unrealistic expectations that may cause unpleasant surprises. Indeed, in a survey of people who met on the Internet and then met in real life, several people said that their partner looked just the way they imagined him or her to be, or that they were even better-looking than their self-descriptions or pictures.[30] One characteristic that was slightly different in face-to-face meetings was shyness: in offline relationships, people were more reserved than in online relationships. Generally speaking, however, the preceding online communication had been honest and thus created no significant surprises or deviations from the written presentations of appearance and personality. Accordingly, people had the impression that they had known each other quite well and for a long time.

I have suggested that there is a tendency for online romantic relationships to become more profound. How does this influence the pace of the development of the relationship? In offline relationships, a deep relationship is associated with a slower pace – it takes more time to get to know each other deeply. However, despite often being deeper, online romantic affairs develop at a faster pace than offline affairs. The greater pace is due to online circumstances that enable participants to touch upon the most profound matters of romantic relationships in a more direct and open manner. People are less shy of asking personal, embarrassing questions; they get to the point much faster. Moreover, when meeting people online, you usually meet people with similar needs. Having casual sex is also faster on the Net, as it is easier to find willing partners and it is safer.[31]

One obvious possible result of a face-to-face meeting of online mates is that the imagined physical attractiveness of the partners may be found to be illusory, thereby leading to the termination of the relationship. In this sense, date zero is indeed starting from scratch all over again. However, this new beginning takes place in a most positive atmosphere. In a study of online relationships, many respondents who met their partners in person say that when they got to know one another's inner characteristics first, external physical characteristics did not matter as much. Indeed, most people involved in cyberlove do actually meet each other and many of them state that the meeting went well.[32]

The different ways in which offline and online relationships develop may influence their survival prospects. Thus, it seems that romantic relationships that emerge after getting to know each other are more likely to endure than those that begin as a result of mutual physical attraction.

This is so since the characteristics revealed during the process of getting to know each other – for example, kindness, sensitivity, sense of humor, and wisdom – are more important for enduring love than those revealed by vision, such as a baby face, a good figure, or beautiful hair. It seems that whereas the characteristics revealed by sight are more important for a short-term affair – where sexual desire is more dominant – the characteristics revealed through nonvisual communication are more significant for enduring relationships.

Are the prospects of longevity higher for online affairs than for offline affairs? Let me first discuss those aspects of online relationships that decrease these prospects.[33]

Lower commitment. Commitment is a good predictor of relationship duration – often more so than satisfaction.[34] The lower commitment of online relationships is mainly due to the lack of *shared history* and the *lower cost* of ending them. Shared history is a major factor in building solid and enduring relationships. Friendships emerge between those who share a history. In online relationships, shared experiences are more limited and hence they have less weight when deciding whether to terminate such an affair. The cost of ending an online relationship is lower than that of ending an offline relationship. Since online relationships are characterized by low investment of physical resources, there is less risk of losing significant investment when ending them. Hence, an offline relationship is usually considered as primary and an online one as secondary. Accordingly, the prospects of online affairs are heavily dependent upon the fate of the primary relationship. Thus, when the cyberaffair encounters difficulties, people go back to their primary relationship instead of trying to work out these difficulties.

There is less outside pressure not to end an online relationship. Since no one other than the online partner risks being hurt when an online affair is terminated, there is no one to oppose this termination. There are no children or other family members who will be hurt, and there is no financial cost in compensating those who suffer from such a step.

Cyberspace involves greater availability of desired alternatives. In online relationships, it is easier to find plenty of available alternatives – obtaining them has more to do with creative imagination than with investing actual resources. When a person in a romantic relationship has many desired alternatives, the likelihood of the current relationship enduring is reduced. And vice versa: situations where no attractive alternatives are available cause us to appreciate our current situation more. The many attractive online alternatives available in cyberspace make an existing online relationship less valued.

Online romantic relationships have a *self-destructive nature*. The wish to deepen the online romantic relationship by turning it into an offline relationship expresses the incomplete nature of this relationship and is likely to lead to its termination.

The above considerations indicate that online affairs are likely to be briefer than offline affairs. Let me now examine some aspects of online relationships that may increase their prospects of enduring.

The *cost of maintaining* the relationship is low. Since maintaining an online relationship does not require the investment of many resources, there is little pressure to terminate it, even in cases of temporary disagreement or discomfort.

An online relationship is typically discontinuous, and hence when the relationship encounters difficulties, one can *escape the problem* by freezing the relationship. In this sense, online relationships can escape crises that threaten their existence.

Online relationships are based on *personal characteristics that are deeper* – the partners' compatibility in terms of these characteristics is significant for maintaining relationships. In long-term romantic love, familiarity is more important; accordingly, marital happiness is positively associated with the length of the courtship period. The extended online conversations prior to the face-to-face meeting fulfill such a function and increase familiarity and intimacy. Thus, one study found that people who had discussed a target article online, and then met face-to-face, rated the subsequent face-to-face discussion as more enjoyable than those who met only face-to-face. Indeed, people who communicated for long periods of time before meeting offline are more likely to stay together.[35]

External attractiveness, which is more significant in face-to-face relationships, is less important for long-term relationships – it may even be an obstacle for such relationships, as the availability of tempting alternatives is greater. Indeed, attractive people are less likely to maintain their current marriage.[36]

Taking into consideration the various aspects that influence the prospects of maintaining cyberlove, we may conclude that the probability of online affairs enduring in a continuous and intense manner is not high. Indeed, as indicated, the typical length of such an affair is a few months. After this period, the affair may be terminated or it may be transformed into an offline affair. However, the survival prospects of those affairs that begin online and are then transformed into an offline affair are quite good. In one study, 71 percent of the romantic relationships that had begun on the Internet were still intact two years later – with the majority being reported as closer and stronger.[37] It should be noted that we are speaking here about online relationships and not merely about meeting someone online and immediately setting up a face-to-face meeting. In the latter case, the probability of success is very low, as there are no elements that increase this probability beyond pure luck.

Summary

> I generally avoid temptation unless I can't resist it.
>
> Mae West

Online affairs consist of conversations having elements that are common both to superfluous types of conversations, such as gossip, and to more profound conversations, such as intellectual discussions. Online conversations are similar to gossip in that they are an enjoyable and relaxing dialogue in which interesting intimate information may be shared. In our current offline circumstances, we scarcely have the time for conversations with those dear to us; in online relationships, conversations are once again at the center of human interaction.

Online romantic affairs are similar to flirting. Like flirting, online affairs do not involve interactive physical sex; this is a more subtle activity. Both flirting and online affairs are colored by sexual nuances, and hence both involve sexual enjoyment, but they avoid many of the risks associated with actual sexual activity. Both are often relaxing, enjoyable, and idle romantic activities. They spice up our lives and encourage positive attitudes toward others.

Contrary to my characterization of various types of online affairs as intrinsically valuable activities, some people view online relationships as merely an efficient, transitory means to achieve an offline meeting. Among those who hold this view, the tactic of playing hard-to-get is fairly common. Although online relationships may be beneficial in opening the way to another, less virtual relationship, they also have their own intrinsic value. When they are regarded in this way, they offer the participants an enjoyable, open, and sincere interaction.

The likelihood of an online affair enduring in a continuous and intense manner is low since, if it is successful, the participants often want to transform it into an offline affair, and if it is not successful, there are no compelling reasons to continue the relationship. However, the likelihood of success for affairs that begin in cyberspace and continue in offline circumstances is higher, since when the participants enter the face-to-face relationships, they already have substantial positive knowledge about each other.

8 *Cyberlove*

I know they say love is blind, but does it also have to be deaf, dumb, and stupid?

Unknown

In this chapter I describe the nature of cyberlove in comparison to offline love. The following major issues are discussed: the relative weight of external appearance and personal characteristics in the two types of love; the way we come to know and love our partner; factors that augment online attraction; the possibility of "love at first chat"; the abundance of available partners online and the impact of that on the exclusivity of cyberlove; the role of intimacy, emotional intensity, and commitment in online relationships; the nature of online rejection; and some instances of gender differences. All these issues demonstrate that cyberlove is indeed a great challenge to ordinary love.

Attractiveness and praiseworthiness

I want a man who's kind and understanding. Is that too much to ask of a millionaire?

Zsa Zsa Gabor

The complex experience of romantic love involves two basic evaluative patterns referring to (a) attractiveness (or appealingness) – that is, an attraction to external appearance, and (b) praiseworthiness – that is, positively appraising personal characteristics.[1] Romantic love requires the presence of both patterns. An attractive woman may want to be loved not merely for her beauty but also for her actions and personal traits. An unattractive woman may wish the contrary: that her beloved would value her external appearance as much as he did her kindness or wisdom. People realize that genuine romantic love requires the presence of both evaluative patterns and they want to satisfy both, even if they are at an apparent disadvantage insofar as one pattern is concerned. One would be offended if one's partner said: "You are rather ugly and I am not sexually attracted to you, but your brilliant brain compensates for everything." One would also be offended if one's partner declared: "You are rather stupid, but your attractive body compensates for everything."

Some people would like to change the relative weight of one of these patterns – not regarding the beloved's attitude toward them, but regarding their own attitude. Thus, some people wish that they could attach less weight to attraction, which may carry less value in the long run. Others may wish the opposite: that their love were more spontaneous and less calculated; they wish they could attach more weight to attraction. The familiar unsuccessful experience of trying to love the "right" person indicates the importance of attraction in love. The familiar experience of being attracted to a handsome person, up until the moment he opens his mouth, indicates the importance of praiseworthiness in love.

The relative weight of the two evaluative patterns depends, to a certain extent, on personal and social factors. For example, with age, people typically accord less weight to the issue of attraction. We can also expect to find that a given society influences the determination of the relative weight of the patterns. Factors related to the relationship itself are also important in this regard. Thus, the impact of physical attraction decreases as people move toward a long-term relationship; it is particularly high at the beginning of the relationship.[2]

The two kinds of evaluative patterns involved in romantic love are not independent: a positive appraisal of your partner's characteristics is greatly influenced by his or her attractiveness. There is much evidence suggesting that attractiveness significantly influences ratings of intelligence, sociality, and morality. A common phenomenon in offline relationships is the "attractiveness halo," in which a person who is perceived as beautiful is assumed to have other good characteristics as well.[3] In online relationships, this is replaced by the "personality halo," in which a person who is perceived as having a specific, positive personality trait is assumed to have other good characteristics – sometimes even those connected to external appearance.

In contrast to romantic love, where both evaluative patterns are essential, in sexual desire attraction is far more dominant. Sexual desire is a simpler attitude based largely on spontaneous and non-deliberative evaluations, whereas romantic love often requires both voluntary and deliberative evaluations. Sexual desire is largely based upon perception (and imagination), whereas love also encompasses capacities – such as thinking and memory – that are important for appraising personal characteristics. Sexual desire is typically focused on limited aspects of external appearance; romantic love is more comprehensive.

No precise borderline between romantic love and sexual desire exists. The latter is usually an essential component of the former. Hence, elements that are typical of the one are often found in the other. The close relation between romantic love and sexual desire indicates that we cannot be as unromantic about sex as we are about eating, but it does not deny cases in which sexual desire has nothing to do with romantic love. Many people think that love and sex can be separated, but would prefer to have them combined. Moreover, most people consider sexual involvement between their partner and a rival as a threat to their romantic relationship.

Online romantic relationships differ from offline relationships in that they attach less weight to external appearance, which is revealed by vision, and more weight to a positive appraisal of the other's characteristics, which are revealed by verbal communication. As one woman wrote to her online lover: "I have come to think of you as my lover, without any idea of what you look like."[4]

The emphasis upon personal characteristics rather than external appearance is evident in online communication. Thus, one woman explains that one reason why she fell in love with her online lover is that:

> I really liked the fact that he asked me the type of questions that someone asks when they truly want to get to know. Not the normal "What do you look like/stats" that most guys ask first. I remember one of the sweetest things he said to me was that I didn't even need to send my picture, because he loved me no matter what.[5]

In a similar vein, a married woman, having an online affair with a married man, writes: "I realize that we live in a society that relies on looks more than thoughts and feelings, while here on the Net the true person comes out. I love him for who he is not what he looks like."[6]

Online relationships prevent people from relying on good looks when evaluating other people, and hence they avoid the unjustified advantages that are usually granted to attractive people; these relationships enable people to get to know each other without having to cope with the heavy burden of the attractiveness stereotype.[7] Consider the following email message from a woman to her online lover:

> What I like about meeting someone on the Net is that you don't know what he looks like, and he doesn't know what you look like. The relationship is all about what is happening inside the soul and

> the mind, and the body doesn't get in the way. I believe that people can fall in love through email because they meet their souls first. If you think that what people look like is the most important consideration, you are missing out on the most important things in any relationship.[8]

Since, in offline affairs, men accord significant weight to the woman's external appearance, many women have become obsessed with their appearance, which may impede their optimal functioning – including their sexual enjoyment. External appearance is of less concern in online relationships. Thus, Cabe writes about his online girlfriend: **"She is not even my type when it comes to physical attraction but she is now the most beautiful girl I have ever and will ever meet."** The reduced concern about external appearance enables women in particular to enjoy sex more and to be much freer in this respect. As one woman said: **"It was great not having to worry about being fat and unattractive."**[9]

Some people may be offended by a request to send their photo at the very early stages of an online relationship – such a request implies that the other person is more interested in their looks than in their mind.[10] Thus, Tina, a 24-year-old restaurant hostess, wrote that she had cybersex with someone a few weeks after meeting online, but then the whole relationship ended and they stopped corresponding. Then she got heavily involved with another man online, but this time **"I decided that I would not show this new guy my picture. I really wanted our minds to connect."**[11] Another man told me that although he has a picture of his online friend with whom he frequently corresponds, he hardly looks at it – she has features that are more essential that constantly occupy his mind.

Cyberlove should not, however, be characterized as ignoring physical attractiveness, but merely as giving less weight to this aspect. Thus, in one study of the users of an online matchmaker, women who rated their own appearance as average were less likely to be contacted by men than those who rated their appearance as above average. Among women who rated their appearance as above average or very good, 57 percent received messages from more than 50 men; among women who rated their appearance as average, only 11 percent received messages from more than 50 men. There was no similar relationship concerning the appearance of the men; those who reported average appearance received as many messages as those who reported above-average appearance. (Interestingly, no one, either male or female, described himself or herself as below average.) However, there was no significant difference between appearance and the number of romantic partners they found online: 43 percent of those who rated themselves better-looking started romantic relationships online, and 41 percent of those who reported average appearance did the same.[12] Although an attractive appearance may be a romantic advantage in cyberspace too, cyberspace also provides good prospects for initiating a romantic relationship for those who have an average appearance. In this sense, online matchmaking differs significantly from matches made through video dating systems, where external appearance is the primary criterion in deciding whether to contact another person.[13]

It is difficult to conduct a profound romantic relationship without imagining some aspects of the external appearance of the partner. The concern regarding external appearance is nicely illustrated in the following message sent by John, a married man, to his online girlfriend, Starchild, with whom he had an affair for a while: "I have been wanting to ask you this for a while now – would you mind telling me what you look like? It is hard to just write to a faceless someone, and I have to say I have made up a picture in my mind of what you look like."[14]

Information about external appearance is given in the personal ads or profile of many people, and often pictures are also included. The concern about attractiveness does not disappear in cyberspace; it just has less impact. Accordingly, people who post pictures of themselves online get more dates. The pictures do not reduce the importance of online conversations, but they indicate that in this matter also – a matter that has some importance for future offline relationships – the other person has positive attributes.

Those engaging in online relationships typically wish to actualize the relationships. Since external appearance is the major stumbling block for such a successful actualization, people in online relationships sometimes become – paradoxically – even more worried about their own appearance. Indeed, a site devoted to catching online cheaters claims that one warning sign that someone is engaging in online infidelity is when that person starts exercising and becoming more concerned about his or her appearance. Similarly, a woman who had an online affair with a man she never saw reports that during their affair he had an accident that caused him physical injury; immediately after the accident, he became somewhat distant from her, although his injury did not change her attitude toward him.[15]

In online affairs, people usually do not have a precise and detailed picture of the other's attractiveness, and wishful thinking fills the gap in the data. These expectations create a picture of the online partner that is likely to be more attractive than in reality. Even if the two partners have met previously, during their online correspondence they tend to imagine each other as more attractive than they are. The higher degree of attractiveness may also be related to the aforementioned "personality halo": the perception of one positive personal characteristic is taken to indicate the presence of many other positive characteristics, including attractiveness. Thus, a man involved in an online romantic relationship with a woman whom he had never seen wrote to her saying that she "couldn't be that homely, and that someone with such a heart can only be attractive."[16] As a result of an intimate online relationship, people may also change their standard of attractiveness and find themselves attracted to people to whom they were previously not attracted. In any case, since online correspondence provides scant information about attractiveness, people are not primarily distinguished in light of this feature, and the degree of attractiveness has less weight in choosing a partner.

The reduced importance of attractiveness in online relationships and the increased importance of other personal characteristics is a positive feature in long-term considerations, as the latter are more important for lasting relationships. Getting to know each other's qualities is important in building a strong relationship. An interesting study concerning this issue indicates that when individuals interacted in a darkened room, where they could not see one another, they not only engaged in greater self-disclosure but also left the encounter liking one another more than did those who interacted in a room that was brightly lit. Interacting on the Internet is similar in some respects to interacting in a darkened room, in that one cannot see one's partner, nor can one be seen. In both cases, first impressions are based upon considerable mutual self-disclosure.[17]

While in offline romantic circumstances you get to know someone from the outside in, in online circumstances the direction is from the inside out. As one man describes his online affairs: "It is my favorite way to get to know a person from the inside out."[18] Accordingly, quite a few people, who are considered attractive in offline circumstances, are using the Internet to meet romantic partners because they want to be appreciated for characteristics other than their appearance.[19] Similarly, a colleague of mine told me that a short while after he had divorced his wife she won 14 million dollars in the lottery. She then used the Internet in order to find a new boyfriend – she wanted this person to love her not because of her money but because of her characteristics. (My colleague vehemently denied that he regrets the divorce, explaining that it was a reasonable and sound decision. Whether or not the decision was "reasonable and sound" at the time, it still appears most unfortunate, time-wise.)

Seeing with your heart

> It is only with the heart that one can see rightly. What is essential is invisible to the eye.
>
> Antoine de Saint-Exupéry

In cyberlove, where verbal skills are more important than physical attractiveness, romantic stereotypes concerning these skills are more dominant. One person notes that if someone makes a spelling mistake, it is acceptable since we all make mistakes, "but I can't tell you how much it irritates me when people don't know the difference between their, there, and they're and you're and your. GOD that annoys me and I would never cyber with someone who can't get those straight." In online relationships, "being able to type fast and write well is equivalent to having great legs or a tight butt in the real world."[20]

Which types of stereotypes – the ones stemming from vision or those stemming from verbal communication – have a more profound impact on romantic relationships? It is interesting to note that the root of the word "respect" means "to look at." Respecting a person implies seeing her as she is, being aware of her unique personality.[21] It is not clear, however, whether by just looking at a person we can really perceive her as she is. We should remember that Cupid, the Roman god of erotic love, was blind. People who have successful romantic affairs online declare that it is possible to find true love on the Net and that the surest way to do so is "to listen to your heart," and "to experience rather than to see." In a way, an online romance is like a never-ending blind date.

Visual capacities seem to be more essential for falling in love, since vision provides more information than any other sense. On the other hand, verbal capacities seem closer than visual capacities to properties essential for enduring romantic relationships. Following our visual evaluations may be advantageous in cases of infatuation, but may result in distorted evaluations in the long run; following our evaluation of the characteristics revealed by verbal capacities may be beneficial in the long run, but may be less useful for generating infatuation. The prevailing prejudice, which is typical of face-to-face relationships, that those who are nicer on the outside are also nicer on the inside, has a particularly distorting impact upon long-term relationships in which the "inside" is more significant.

Vision is more closely related to physical attractiveness, while hearing or reading may be related to deeper aspects that refer more to intellectual capacities. If interactive video and voice become more accessible and are more widely used in online relationships, the advantage of being able to ignore external appearance may be lost. Nevertheless, even in this case, spatial distance and the ability to conceal various aspects of our identity may still enable us to focus on those aspects we want to share with other people. It should be noted that, in offline relationships too, people try to present their positive aspects. However, in such relationships, there are more sources of information to verify the validity of the presentation; in online relationships such additional sources of information hardly exist.

In face-to-face relationships, most people fall in love in response to what they see, and then that love is strengthened or weakened as further information is revealed. In online relationships, where self-disclosure is greater and hence intimacy is significant and occurs early in the relationship, most people first get to know each other and only then fall in love.[22] As Somerset Maugham cynically noted: "Love is what happens to men and women who don't know each other." In the prevailing modern ideal of romantic love, love starts with its most intense form: passionate love. Such love is seen as something we do not learn about or prepare for; rather, it consists of a certain magic that happens to come our way. In this view, we stumble clumsily into passionate love and hope the magic will enable us to overcome any hurdle. Accordingly, we date people who are not available or not suitable, being hopeful that nothing will stop that magical love from occurring.[23]

The above view has two basic assumptions: (a) passionate love is our truest guide, and (b) attraction is the hallmark of love – once it is present, praiseworthiness is supposed to emerge naturally. Both assumptions are wrong – or at least too simplistic. Passionate love is a kind of spontaneous evaluation that is based upon a partial perspective and limited information. Like other types of hunches, it may sometimes work out, but in many cases it does not. When a broader perspective based upon extended information supplements the spontaneous evaluation, we are more likely to make better choices.[24] Love cannot be reduced to physical attractiveness. Love is a comprehensive attitude, which must also take into account the evaluation of the other person's personal characteristics. The high rate of divorce these days is one indication of the inadequacy of the two above assumptions – that passionate love is our truest guide and attraction is the hallmark of love. The fact that sometimes the intensity of our love increases as we come to know the other person better indicates that love consists of more than just physical attraction.

Two traditional practices challenge the supposition that physical attraction is more important for generating love than praiseworthy personal characteristics: (a) arranged marriages, and (b) postponing sex until love emerges. In both cases, love emerges, if at all, only after the couple has come to know and to appreciate each other. In arranged marriages, passionate love is not the starting point of the romantic process, but, if the relationship is successful, it will be its result. People learn about each other before their love develops – and in many cases of arranged marriages, love does indeed develop. This is not surprising, since love is based upon knowing each other's characteristics. Similarly, underlying the practice of postponing sex until love has been generated is the assumption that profound love emerges only after we nurture and develop it. In such cases, love develops without any early physical contact – it is too pure to become involved in such carnal matters. Sexual activities follow naturally only later.

In a sense, online romantic relationships mark a return to this traditional order of falling in love. As in arranged marriages, cyberlove is the product of a process in which two people come to know each other. As in the conservative order of love and sex, sexual engagement is the fruit of intense love. In online romantic relationships, people first talk without actually seeing or touching each other, and only then do they move on to sexual activities. This manner of falling in love in cyberspace may greatly enhance the quality of the bond between the two partners. As one woman who married her online lover says: "I am so glad I knew him before I actually got to meet him face to face. Our love is stronger now than ever."[25]

In cases of a one-night cyberstand, the order of love and sex is similar to that typically prevailing in offline circumstances. Thus, Belle, a married woman for twelve years, notes: "It started one morning with me popping in with something like 'anyone for a quickie?' The response was more than I bargained for, the quickie turned into a 3 or 4 hour long, hot and steamy sex conversation. The man I met online has been, and still remains, an inspiration in my life." Marie, who testifies that she is in a very liberal and loving marriage in which she and her husband engage in cybersex (but not together) and enjoy it greatly, writes: "With my first cyberlover, the sexual connection was so immediate and overwhelming that he felt compelled to write me an email saying 'You know we should talk next time. Get to know each other. That might be nice.' Eventually, he became a friend and cyberlover, and the deep affection I will always feel for him is very 'real.'"[26]

In cyberspace the beloved is described by reference to personality traits; accordingly, the beloved is often characterized as the smartest, funniest, sweetest, kindest, most wonderful, sincere, honest, truthful, loving, and caring person; someone who is "a little too perfect." In cyberspace it is easier to possess virtuous traits, as it is just a matter of perfecting your writing skills. In order to explain the popularity of virtuous traits in the

Net, however, we must look for something deeper. The lack of external attraction, such as beauty, forces correspondents to make the effort to be evaluated positively in other realms.

The development of an online relationship is similar to the development of a non-erotic friendship, where we first get to know the other person and only then become friends. It seems that online communication is often more conducive for developing a real friendship, as the communication can touch upon profound and intimate issues that are essential for friendship. As in friendship, in online relationships people spend a lot of time just talking and sharing. Indeed, many individuals report that their online romance was more meaningful because of this friendship. People often describe their online relationship as the most open, rewarding, and exciting friendship they have ever had.[27] Some online sexual affairs later become friendships. Thus, a 51-year-old man, who is in a committed relationship, remarks:

> I find little joy in any kind of 'slam, bang, thank you' experience in the flesh or on line. What has also happened with me is that several of the women I have had cyber sex with have also become wonderful online friends. In fact in several cases though we no longer have cyber sex we continue to chat and share our lives.[28]

Online relationships, which are based on conversations, demand more intense time together – that is, time together without watching television or reading a newspaper. Conversations have a slower pace – they require more time. Online conversations force you to interact with your partner in at least some nonsexual aspects. These aspects, as well as the ongoing nature of conversations, encourage the pleasant atmosphere to spill over to the morning after. Most of the time, the impression of what took place the night before is that of a pleasant conversation, like that typical of flirting.

Online attraction

> You know, I'm not just an interesting person; I have a body, too.
>
> Bumper sticker

According to a prevailing view of attraction, personal relationships begin with attraction.[29] This view seems appropriate for most cases of offline romantic relationships; it is, of course, particularly true concerning love at first sight. Other cases of romantic relationships may develop without initial attraction. You may form a personal relationship with someone whom you do not find attractive, because talking to her (as to any other person) helps you with your problem. You may begin to find her attractive only after you have been together for a while. In this case, the personal relationship does not begin with attraction, but the romantic aspect of the relationship begins to develop only after some type of positive attitude has been triggered.

Such cases are much more common in online affairs. These affairs typically begin by focusing on the value of the conversation itself without finding the other person particularly attractive. Indeed, chat rooms that are designed for singles to meet potential partners may not be the best places to find someone to whom you might be attracted; a better place may be a community that revolves around a subject in which you are interested.[30] Many people who have online affairs began the relationship without the intention of making it a romantic one – they just wanted to talk to someone. The quality of the conversation then created the attraction – which in some cases was unexpected – toward the other person. Online romantic attraction is often a byproduct of an enjoyable, friendly conversation; this is in accordance with characterizing online relationships as intrinsically valuable activities. Indeed, one study of people who used an online matchmaker found that about two-thirds of women users indicated they were mainly interested in starting friendships online; and more than 80 percent of them were successful in doing so. In addition, over half of the women had started romantic or sexual relationships, even though only a third indicated that this had been their main goal.[31] Their success in forming a friendship facilitated the formation of a romantic relationship even though this was not their initial purpose.

One significant sign for the transition from friendship to love is a sense of instability. The correspondence is no longer conducted in the usual manner. Now, the partners send not merely one letter per day, which is written at a specific time; they exchange frequent outbursts of messages of different lengths and natures and at different times. This expresses the fact that each person constantly occupies the mind of the other person.

The development of a friendship into a romantic affair is less common in offline circumstances where external appearance has a greater role, as it does not take time or friendship to reveal such appearance. However, since offline friendship can increase the positive evaluation of personal characteristics, this may overcome a previous average evaluation of external appearance and induce the two friends to become lovers.

The fact that the typical online relationship begins as a profound friendship bodes well for the continuation and intensity of the subsequent romantic relationship. Relationships where the lover remains the best friend have the greatest prospects. People who have had online affairs that survived the actualization into offline relationships and endured a while after it often testify that their online lover remains their best friend in offline circumstances.

Research has found that intimates who initially idealized one another and their relationships also reported a relatively greater increase in satisfaction and decrease in conflicts and doubts later on. In subsequent interactions, people selectively focus upon information that may confirm their original judgments. Hence, love is more likely to be prescient than blind.[32] Idealization of the other is easier in cyberspace where actual constraints do not limit our imagination, and where interactions focus on positive self-presentation. Thus, a 34-year-old woman says about her online lover: "I not only found the man I want to spend the rest of my life with, I have found my best friend, my soulmate and my angel sent down from the heaven."[33] The general atmosphere in online meetings is accordingly calmer and more positive. People feel better about themselves and about their partner. This kind of positive atmosphere may provide a better opportunity for knowing each other and letting the relationship develop in a more intimate and calm manner.

The positive self-presentation that is possible online is in a sense a self-fulfilling prophecy: people put forward an image that they will attempt to live up to – at least in cyberspace.[34] Hence, their self-image is enhanced and they consider themselves to be better. Since people can do what they wish to do in cyberspace, they feel that they can be truer to themselves. A young woman who enjoys cybersex writes: "Cybersex is a release. One finds oneself smiling, breathing quicker, interacting, thinking, feeling, and simply involved. It boils down to being about you."[35]

The positive atmosphere in online relationships is often reflected in the agent's offline circumstances as well. An ethnographic study in Trinidad indicated that it was rare for people to talk about their email messages without a smile.[36] If people are able to continue their positive processes of interaction when their online romantic relationship is transformed into an offline relationship, their new relationship has higher prospects of surviving, as positive processes are at least as important for relationship satisfaction as the processes dealing with negative conflicts.[37]

Another factor increasing the idealization of the online relationship is the comparison with an offline intimate relationship. Since online idealization is easier, the offline relationship is bound to be perceived in negative terms. As one woman whose husband has many online affairs notes about his lovers: "The women are never tired or unhappy, and he can screen out the ones with wrinkles. What chance do real live women have to compete with a world of ever ready women on constant tap?"[38] The decreased idealization of the offline relationship is also due to the fact that this relationship is often the topic of the online conversations (the opposite is rare, as the online relationship is typically concealed from the offline mate). Such conversations force the participants to perceive their offline relationship from a more accurate perspective and hence to abandon their positive biases concerning this relationship. (In the same vein, it has been claimed that counselors who place excessive emphasis on the accurate depiction of their clients' relationship may cause unintended negative consequences for these couples.)[39]

An important phenomenon for a successful romantic relationship is its perceived superiority, that is, the inclination to regard one's own relationship as better than other people's.[40] Perceived superiority is easier to achieve in online relationships – this is particularly true concerning the comparison with one's offline relationship. Indeed, many people claim that their love is far more intense online than with their offline partner. A woman named Rosie notes:

> I am a married woman of 19 years with 2 kids. I have been with my online lover for almost a year and I have such deep feelings for him, it's unreal. Yes I do think I'm cheating in some ways and I do feel bad at times, but I love this man online so much I don't allow myself to think about it too often.

Likewise, Tina writes about her online lover: "I love him sooo much, more than the love I felt being with my ex for 6 years. He has made me a better person. I love him like I have never loved before."[41] As we have already seen, the everyday difficulties of offline relationships are absent from online relationships, which seem to enjoy, on the other hand, most of the benefits of a close romantic relationship.

Online romantic communication may involve some negative information about the participants, but because a general positive attitude pertains, any negative traits are more tolerantly received. The positive perception of the other's personal traits may also affect the perception of the other's external appearance. As one woman testifies, in online relationships, "You focus on the inside. Then if his outside is a little heavier or a little shorter than you expected, it doesn't matter because you already love his soul." The reduced amount of negative information enables people to pay closer attention to many personal traits that may be of great significance in developing a profound relationship.

Online self-presentation is positive not merely because it is largely up to the agent to choose the presented aspects, but also because people have more time to articulate their messages. One may claim that this also makes the responses less spontaneous and more manipulative. Such a risk does indeed exist, but in prolonged relationships, where each partner invests a lot of time and effort to maintain the affair, the incentive to deceive the other is low. The possibility of delayed response enables the participants to make the most of their positive aspects.

One disadvantage of the positive presentation of online relationships is that they can lose touch with reality. As no one is perfect, an overly positive self-presentation makes a person seem less real. Moreover, since we cannot always turn frogs into princes or princesses, cognitive and emotional dissonances are likely to emerge. As the relationship develops further, more negative aspects about the person will be revealed, thus making this person more real. Such negative aspects are revealed, however, when the general attitude is already positive, and hence people are more tolerant toward such aspects. Accordingly, negative aspects that may have prevented the initiation of the relationship in actual circumstances may not ruin an ongoing loving relationship, since they will be perceived as less significant. We may kiss a frog even if there is no promise of a Prince Charming popping out of it – we may just get to know frogs and love them the way they are.

This positive self-presentation online, as well as the positive feedback the agent receives from other people, is likely to increase the problematic nature of self-identity in cyberspace. It may not be clear whether the real self is the one communicating in cyberspace or the one involved in actual activities. The positive character a person displays in online communication may be different from the one revealed in the more tense situation of offline circumstances. Moreover, in cyberspace we have the illusion of overcoming personal limitations.

It should be obvious by now that online attraction exists and that it shares many aspects of actual offline attraction. Deb Levine analyzes five major aspects of offline attraction – proximity, self-presentation, similarity, reciprocity, and expectations – and claims that they are present in online relationships as well.[42]

Proximity is considered to be fundamental to the development of offline interpersonal attraction. In online relationships, proximity is not defined by physical location, but by mental attachment. Indeed, many online partners who are miles away from each other declare themselves to be inseparable. Thus, a married woman describes her online married lover: "He knows my deepest secrets and I know his. We are closer with each other than with our spouses. It's very hard for me to describe the feelings we have for each other."[43] Mental proximity can be measured by the frequency, length, and depth of the partners' conversations. As in offline circumstances, where increased exposure strengthens attraction, repeated online contact with someone increases positive responses to that person.

Self-presentation in offline relationships is expressed first of all in external appearance; indeed, initial attraction in such relationships is based on physical attractiveness. As indicated above, in online relationships, where external appearance is less significant, self-presentation must be based on features such as how you express and describe yourself; here, self-presentation is more under your control. The lack of physical attributes does not necessarily diminish the attraction. Indeed, in a study of human attraction, six out of ten characteristics considered by both women and men to be most effective in attracting opposite-sex partners had nothing to do with physical attributes and could easily be conveyed in an online communication. These include a sense of humor, being sympathetic toward other people's troubles, good manners, being prepared to put effort into spending time together, and willingness to help.[44]

Similarity has an important role in offline attraction; people are attracted to those who are similar to them in certain significant aspects, such as age, family background, religion, education, and political and social attitudes. As suggested, it is easier to detect similarity in online relationships since there are more options and people indicate significant features important for judgments of similarity. Indeed, online partners often testify their great similarity. Thus, one woman writes: "We had so much in common it was unbelievable." Since online relationships are based on conversations, the similarity usually refers to nonphysical characteristics. Thus, a 30-year-old woman describes her online relationship: "It was the most spiritual experience of my life to be with him! I have found a mirror to my soul with him!"[45]

Reciprocity is another feature crucial for offline attraction: we tend to be attracted to people who are attracted to us. The lover wants to be loved – to be kissed as well as to kiss. The lover is ready to be committed, but expects to find similar commitment in the beloved's attitude. The lack of reciprocity, namely, the knowledge that you are not loved by your beloved, usually leads to a decrease in the intensity of love, and, ultimately, to humiliation.

Reciprocity is most evident in cyberlove, which consists of very long conversations – these can sometimes last as much as six hours every day of the week. Conversation is essentially reciprocal activity, and long conversations can take place only when genuine reciprocity prevails. The reciprocal nature of cyberlove is also expressed in the significant mutual self-disclosure and supportive attitudes typical of these relationships.

Expectations and idealizations that act as self-fulfilling prophecies are typical of offline romantic relationships. Positive biases, which are typical of our self-assessment, are also directed at those close to us. Idealizing our partner is beneficial as it makes our partner more attractive to us. High expectations of the relationship are also helpful for promoting the positive prospects of our intimate relationship with that person. (Such expectations are also dangerous as they may lead to severe disappointments.)

Expectations and idealizations are even more significant in online relationships where information about the partner is more limited and there are fewer circumstances that can contradict the positive information presented by the online friend. It is much easier to interpret positively the ambiguous or the unknown than the unambiguous or the apparent.[46] As indicated, idealization is indeed common in cyberspace. Statements like the following are frequent in descriptions of online affairs: "I met the man I thought didn't exist. Sweet, honest, romantic, funny. Everything I ever looked for"; and "I can honestly say he is perfect."[47]

Love at first chat

Smart, sexy, sweet, and relatively sane.
The headline of an online personal ad

Love at first sight is not easy to explain. If romantic love consists of evaluating the other person as attractive and as having positive characteristics, then how can we possibly make an evaluation of their characteristics at first sight? Some of these characteristics, such as kindness and honesty, cannot be revealed in one glance. Knowledge of these characteristics requires familiarity and shared history, which are clearly absent at first sight. It is easier to speak about sexual desire at first sight, since such a desire is based upon the attractiveness of the other person, something that can be perceived at first sight. Although people often confuse love at first sight with sexual desire at first sight, there are nevertheless genuine cases of love at first sight, as many people report.

The fundamental mistake in denying the existence of love at first sight is the assumption that we cannot attribute to a person characteristics that are not present at first sight. Such attribution is done spontaneously by using certain stereotypical evaluations. To activate a schema of an ideal person, not all aspects constituting the ideal have to be present. Sometimes items of seemingly no significance, such as a business suit, a doctor's uniform, a certain smile, or a particular voice, may activate one's schema of an ideal person. These considerations are consistent with the "attractiveness halo," in which a person who is perceived as beautiful is assumed to have other positive characteristics as well. Accordingly, attractive people, who are evaluated mainly on the basis of their appearance, are more likely to be the object of love at first sight. In light of its stereotypical nature, love at first sight can often mislead the participants as it is based more on imagination than on sight.

Love at first sight is similar to other cases in which people fall in love with strangers, about whom they know practically nothing. The little they do know about these strangers does not have to be derived from visual information, as is the case in love at first sight, but may be derived from other kinds of partial information, such as class, race, odor, accent, or resemblance to past lovers. In all these cases, we have scant information about the person – much too little to form a comprehensive, positive evaluation – and we fill the gap by attributing to the person additional positive characteristics.

Falling in love in cyberspace is similar to these cases: we do not have all the required information, but we fill the gap in an idealized manner. In light of this similarity, can we speak about love at first byte?

In online relationships, the weight of the other person's attraction is considerably smaller; getting to know each other is more crucial. As the information in the first message is quite limited, cases of love at first byte are more rare. More common cases are those of "love at first online chat," as such a chat provides more information. For example, one may detect in the first chat a sense of humor and wittiness and instantly fall in love with the sender. The following characteristics, which Sandra described in her online mate (who has now become her husband), can be detected at first chat: "He was romantic, brilliant, poetic, witty, funny . . . everything I'd dreamed about in a man."[48]

Love at first chat is linked with the "personality halo," in which a person who is perceived as having a certain positive personality trait is assumed to have other positive characteristics. People often say that, although they met online, "they hit it off right away." As one man writes: "She was funny and sexy and cute, and I was immediately attracted to her personality." Indeed, it is not unusual for people to declare that they fell in love after their first online conversation. Thus, Lady M. indicates: "We both know that we will be inseparable from the first time we meet (in the chat room)." Similarly, Sara writes: "Phillip caught my heart in an instant." Another woman testifies: "I instantly felt a connection to him for some unknown reason."[49] We may speak here about "Net chemistry." A divorced woman, who spends many hours online every day, told that one day she began chatting with a man (younger than she is) and immediately was greatly attracted to him. After two hours of chatting he asked her: "What are you doing this evening?" "Waiting for you," was her reply. Shortly thereafter, he came to her house and one of her greatest romances began. It was a very intense romance, although brief. She now chats with many men every day, but she has never fallen in love in that way again – although she is still hoping to.

It should be noted that although beauty has a powerful impact at first sight, the weight of this impact decreases as time goes by and once we know other characteristics of the person. Likewise, wittiness has a powerful impact at first chat, but its impact may be reduced once we know other characteristics of the person. When wittiness is perceived to be superficial and more profound characteristics, such as kindness and wisdom, are found to be wanting, the weight of the positive initial impact of wittiness may vanish.

In love at first sight, the high value accorded to the other's external appearance is projected onto her characteristics. In love at first chat, the high value accorded to the other's writing abilities is projected onto other characteristics, including external appearance. Both are instances of real love that is based on scant information and on imagination that fills the missing gaps.

Love at first sight can be the basis for profound, long-term love, provided that characteristics typically revealed in verbal communication later enhance – or, at least, do not oppose – the characteristics revealed at first sight. Similarly, love at first chat can be the basis for profound, long-term love provided that characteristics typically revealed to sight later enhance – or, at least, do not oppose – the characteristics revealed at first chat. The fact that such types of love may perish does not mean that they were not instances of true love. Time is not an exclusive measure for true love.

Availability and effort

> Save a boyfriend for a rainy day. And another, in case it doesn't rain.
>
> Mae West

The availability of an alternative is central for generating emotions. The more available the alternative is – that is, the closer the imagined alternative is to reality – the more intense the emotion. An illustration of the impact of the availability factor comes from research on singles bars: as closing time approached, men and women viewed the opposite sex as increasingly attractive. The looming alternative of going home alone increased the value of those still available.[50] Similarly, a person's greater sexual availability often increases others' sexual desire toward that person. Consider, for instance, the following, very seductive personal profile that a woman from Mansfield, Ohio, posted on an online matchmaking site:

> I am married but we have an open marriage. I love sex, a lot. I need it every day . . . twice on Sundays. Everybody always tells me that I am the best they have ever had in bed. I love to do wild and crazy things when it comes to my sex life. I love to sit in a porn theatre and mess with a guy till he can't take it any more and we have to leave. Intelligence and personality are more important for me than looks.[51]

There are many signals that women and men use to convey their sexual availability. Feminine tactics include darting glances, head tossing, lip-licking, hair-flicking, as well as coy smiles, and dancing alone. Masculine tactics include displaying good manners, offering help, and exhibiting sympathetic and caring behavior. Perceived opportunity is also a significant factor in extramarital sexual affairs. This is in accordance with our general tendency to be drawn to those who show signs of friendliness and cooperation.[52]

Online romantic seduction is just a click away, making seduction far more available than it is offline. This is mainly due to the following factors: (a) it is easier to meet new people in cyberspace; (b) you can choose to communicate with people who are willing to establish the type of emotional relationship you want; (c) self-disclosure is greater in cyberspace and hence it is easier to identify available and willing people.

We have a tendency to initiate relationships with those we interact with most frequently: our neighbors, workmates, fellow students, and the like.[53] Cyberspace has no such spatial limitation; it enables us to increase significantly the number and types of people with whom we interact. Millions of people are willing to meet you in cyberspace. Introducing yourself and asking to initiate a personal relationship is a matter of pressing a button and carries no risk of being considered as sexual harassment or of causing you humiliation.

On the Internet, it is easier than elsewhere to find people with attributes you like. The computer's ability to sort people in light of given characteristics is much greater than the process in offline circumstances, where accidents of proximity are crucial in this matter. For example, an obese woman, who feels insecure approaching new people in face-to-face interactions because of her weight, may interact with people who share her interests and who do not mind her obesity. When she reveals that she is overweight, some people may not want to continue the correspondence, but others may find her physical size irrelevant, or her other characteristics very attractive.[54] For such people, who have to break a lot of eggs to make an omelet, cyberspace provides many such eggs.

As suggested above, online relationships are egalitarian in the sense that external appearance as well as other characteristics, such as socioeconomic status, race, and religion, can be disregarded; the relation is with the people themselves and not with their appearance or background. Cyberspace provides us with the opportunity to interact with the type of people we find interesting. The choice of a partner for an online romantic relationship is typically a "positive" choice in the sense that it is made on the basis of characteristics we appraise as positive and consider as important for such a relationship. Those who do not have these characteristics are simply not candidates for an online relationship with us. This manner of choosing an online partner has the advantage of increasing the likelihood of the relationship's success and decreasing the prospects of painful rejection.

Invested effort refers to the extent of our involvement in the generation of emotions; like availability, invested effort also increases emotional intensity. Generally, the more effort we invest in something, the more emotionally significant it becomes. The opposite is also true: we invest more effort in emotionally significant events. In one sense, however, effort appears to run counter to availability: a highly available alternative is that in which we do not need to invest much effort. This contradiction can be explained by referring to the temporal dimension of the two factors: whereas effort refers to past circumstances, availability refers to present circumstances. An emotional object – say, a lover – in whose obtention we invest a lot of effort has greater emotional significance for us; however, if attractive available alternatives to that object then appear, its emotional significance decreases and the significance of the alternatives increases. Whereas effort increases the emotional significance of the offline partner, the great availability of online partners decreases the emotional significance of their offline counterpart.

The issue of invested effort plays a lesser role in online affairs. Having a monitor-to-monitor relationship needs fewer resources than those required for a face-to-face relationship. This applies both in choosing the partner and in maintaining the relationship. In light of such a lesser role, personal involvement – and, in particular, the commitment and seriousness of online partners – is lower than in offline relationships.[55]

The lesser effort required by an online affair can be viewed not as one of its advantages, but rather as a flaw, since something that is easily available may not be greatly valued. As popular wisdom puts it: "Easy come, easy go," and "The more you pay, the more it is worth." Freud objected to masturbation because he was concerned that it allows the person to achieve satisfaction while avoiding hardship.[56] When no effort or hardship is involved, there is the risk that the relationship will be less valued. It seems that, before enjoying your handsome prince, you have to kiss a lot of frogs. The issue here is not merely that, in order to be happy, you need to know what sadness is. Rather, it is that the construction of a healthy relationship also involves an engagement with its painful aspects.

Whereas conducting an online affair requires the investment of minimal effort, transforming this affair into an offline relationship requires a great deal more effort and other types of resources. It is easy to write to a cybermate about taking her on a romantic trip to Paris; organizing such a trip requires more resources and effort. The actualization of online relationships often involves many hurdles that must be overcome – for instance, leaving families and jobs, burning bridges that support your current relationships, and traveling long distances to unfamiliar environments. A woman who married her online friend notes: "The important thing we have going for us is our firm commitment to make this marriage work, and there is no doubt in my mind it will. Believe it or not, there have been hurdles to overcome already, and we have accomplished them one at a time."[57] Overcoming such hurdles may be an additional reason why people who met each other initially in cyberspace tend to maintain their liking for each other over time – more so than if they had initially met in person.[58]

The factors of availability and effort are evident in the romantic realm. In light of the *availability effect*, greater romantic availability generates more intense emotions. In light of the *effort effect* (which can also be termed the "Romeo and Juliet effect"), when people are unattainable, their emotional significance increases. Given these effects, we can discern two major tactics in attracting a partner: "playing easy-to-get," which is in accordance with the availability effect, and "playing hard-to-get," which relates to the effort effect. Both tactics are effective in different circumstances. The tactic of "playing hard-to-get" is most effective when used in the context of long-term love in which a person wishes to be sure of his partner's commitment. Long-term romantic love has great emotional significance and hence we are ready to invest much effort in attaining it. Playing hard-to-get forces the other person to make significant investments and ensures that this person is indeed ready to make a commitment to an enduring relationship. The tactic of "playing easy-to-get" is most effective when used by someone in the context of casual sex, where availability is the most important commodity. In this context, people are not ready to make significant investments since the benefits are smaller and more temporary; hence, playing hard-to-get here will not be effective at all.[59]

The availability and effort effects are evident in online relationships. The availability effect is a major reason for the seductive nature of online affairs. The effort effect is a major reason for the emotional significance that people attach to their enduring online relationships, particularly when these are transformed into a committed offline relationship.

As indicated above, the tactic of "playing hard-to-get" is in contradiction to a central feature of online relationships – that is, their great degree of sincerity. Sincerity means hiding nothing (or almost nothing) and revealing one's real desires. The value of "playing hard-to-get," however, lies precisely in not revealing one's real desires. Although cyberspace imposes different rules on the game of love, people's emotional structure remains the same; consequently, this tactic is still effective and can be useful in online affairs as well. However, in light of the greater availability of online partners, this tactic may be less useful in cyberspace.

The abundance of available partners online, which seems to be merely a quantitative factor, has a profound qualitative impact upon romantic relationships and in particular upon the issue of romantic exclusivity.

The exclusivity of cyberlove

> For Sale: A complete set of Encyclopedia Britannica.
> 45 volumes. Excellent condition. $1000 or best offer. Do not need it anymore. Got married last week. Wife knows everything.
>
> An ad in *The New York Times*

Can the beloved be replaced? Can we love more than one person at the same time? It is easier to defend the claim that love is replaceable than that love is nonexclusive. "Replaceable" is used in a diachronic sense – that is, replacing the object after a certain period of time; "nonexclusive" is used in a synchronic sense – that is, having different objects at the same time.

While it is certain that we would not describe every love affair as genuine romantic love, there is no reason to suppose that one can only experience a single instance of genuine love in a lifetime; one may find a new and more compatible partner. After all, Adam and Eve are the only couple who were truly made for each other. The fact that the beloved is replaceable does not deny the existence of cases in which people have only one genuine love throughout their lives.

The claim that romantic love is not exclusive – that is, that one can love several objects at the same time – is less self-evident than the claim that love is replaceable. Exclusivity plays an important role in love – for example, it ensures mutual commitment, the investment of sufficient resources, and confidence in paternity. In comparison to other emotions, romantic love requires more resources, such as time and attention, and hence its objects need to be more limited. One does not have enough free time and attention, not to mention sexual energy, to love many people simultaneously. Commitment to more than one person reduces available resources. Moreover, nonexclusive love may generate jealousy and the (justified) fear of losing one's partner to someone else.

A major factor opposing the exclusivity of romantic love is that of change. I have suggested that change is the major cause of emotions. Whereas exclusivity increases stability, nonexclusivity increases change; however, both factors increase emotional intensity. The demand for romantic exclusivity is understandable in light of the partial nature of emotions and in particular the need to focus resources in order to sustain the great intensity required by the relationship. However, emotional partiality does not necessarily limit the emotional object to merely one object. From a conceptual point of view, there is no contradiction in loving more than one person at the same time. Indeed, the temptation to deviate from romantic exclusivity is common. External considerations referring to practical limitations and prevailing moral norms are a major obstacle to such nonexclusive love.

The possibility of loving several people at the same time is evident in another type of love, that is, parental love. It should be noted, however, that even in parental love there is a limit to the number of intimate relations one can maintain at a given time without reducing the quality of each relationship.

Multi-loving may express a revolt against human limitations; it involves the belief that we can have it all. This belief is not realistic and is bound to generate difficulties. Limitations are part and parcel of the human condition, as human beings have limited resources and multiple goals. Indeed, a successful romantic relationship requires a degree of sacrifice that is not easy to make. Multi-loving seems to ignore this requirement.

In cyberspace, where human limitations are considerably reduced, the belief that we can have it all is somewhat more realistic, and multi-loving is easier. The non-physical nature of online relationships provides a different type of relationship that may be focused upon different aspects in one's life. Nevertheless, the multi-lover does not live entirely in cyberspace – hence, it is highly probable that her actual everyday relationships will be harmed as a result of her multi-loving.

The loss experienced when a partner engages in a romantic affair is often described as a loss of resources, such as love, time, attention, sexual energy, and financial resources. The unfaithful person is described as transferring such resources from the spouse to the lover. In accordance with this description, it has been claimed that infidelity consists of taking sexual energy of any sort – thoughts, feelings, and behaviors – outside of a committed sexual relationship in such a way that it damages the relationship.[60]

There are here two empirical assumptions: (a) we have a given amount of sexual energy, and (b) having an affair decreases the sexual energy directed toward the spouse. These assumptions should be empirically examined, and it is not evident that they are always correct.

There is no doubt that in many circumstances, such loss of resources occurs. However, it is not clear whether the loss of resources, rather than the loss of exclusivity, is the focus of concern here. There are situations in which the mate, for reasons of guilt, personal considerations, or a better emotional state in general, lavishes extra attention on a spouse while developing an outside attachment. In these cases, too, the spouse may develop negative emotional attitudes such as jealousy and hostility. This suggests that the value of certain activities is enhanced if people engage in them only with each other, despite the fact that they may reap some benefit in violating such exclusivity. Certain rewards may lose much of their value if they are not exclusive. This is true even when the violation of exclusivity is only imaginary. Jealousy exists also when the spouse is merely sexually interested in someone else, even when this interest is restricted to the level of fantasy.[61]

Another considerable obstacle to multi-loving is the attitude of the partner, who may be jealous because someone else shares the love of his or her beloved. A woman named Joyce notes: "My husband has a friend online. They talk every day. They both have videocams and can see each other quite clearly. Of course I get jealous. I've asked him to stop talking to her but he says he enjoys it. I just can't help myself for being jealous. I just wish he would concentrate more on our relationship."[62] Jealousy is concerned not merely with the quantity of things that one expects to receive, but also with their quality – and in particular the attitudes and intentions of the giver. In this sense, an emotional affair can be as painful as, and sometimes even more painful than, a sexual affair that has no emotional implications.

There are types of exclusivity other than those that forbid all social relationships or those that forbid merely sexual ones. These types may refer not merely to sexual relationships, but also to going to a movie, having a meal together, working together, or spending a lot of time together. The personal and cultural differences associated with jealousy are expressed in the type of exclusivity that underlies jealousy.

In cyberspace, major obstacles to the nonexclusive nature of romantic love – that is, practical limitations, the partner's attitude, and moral norms – are of lesser weight. Accordingly, jealousy may be less intense in the case of online relationships. Another reason for this is that the cost of ending an online relationship is smaller and hence the pain of that event is less intense as well. Moreover, the great availability of online alternatives makes it easier and more common to have several online relationships with various people at the same time.

These considerations do not eliminate the presence of jealousy online. The profound degree of intimacy developed in online affairs may generate intense jealousy. Consider the following description by a woman having an online relationship that later developed into a successful marriage:

> My feelings for him began to grow stronger and I could tell he felt the same about me. I began to get jealous if he talked to others in the chat room and he was doing the same with me. He finally told me he didn't want me to talk to any other men because they did not know me as he did. He didn't want his lady to be talked down to. I respected his wish and refrained from talking to other men.[63]

It seems that, because the lines are not clearly defined in cyberspace, and the desired alternative is readily available, it is important for people to draw their own lines. Thus, many people make a choice to be a cybercouple and may even announce this to their online friends.

Romantic exclusivity may refer to various aspects: attention (for example, thinking and fantasizing about another person or looking at pornographic pictures), verbal activity (such as offline and online flirting or cybersex), nonsexual physical activity (like going to a movie or to a restaurant), and sexual physical activity. Although attention seems to constitute the least serious violation of romantic exclusivity and sexual physical activity the gravest one, various societies may have different criteria for such violations. From a psychological point of view, the gravest violation is that involving the greatest emotional involvement of the betraying partner. Since sexual physical activity often entails the greatest involvement, it is generally considered to be the greatest violation of romantic exclusivity. However, this does not have to be the case – sex with a sex worker may generate less emotional involvement than an enduring romance with no physical sexual activity.

It seems that cyberlove has dramatically increased the level of emotional involvement in chaste relationships. This makes current concerns about romantic exclusivity highly relevant. Consider the following statement:

> In some ways, I'd have an easier time understanding why he would want to have an affair in real life. At least there I could say to myself, "Well, it's for somebody with a better body, or just for the novelty." But he's saying that he wants that feeling of intimacy with someone else – the "just talk" part of an encounter with a woman – and to me that comes close to what is most important about sex.[64]

Barking dogs may not bite, but online talks are often highly emotional and sexual. Emotional involvement may be much more intense in online love than in the primary offline love.

Another relevant issue in this regard is the degree of loyalty associated with each type of relationship. In offline relationships, loyalty is a central characteristic of friendship. Friendship is based on shared history and implies various commitments concerning the present and the future. Since the role of shared history in online relationships is marginal, loyalty is typically insignificant. It is true, however, that when an online relationship is developed over an extended period of time and involves meaningful communication, loyalty and certain obligations are expected.

It is obvious that romantic exclusivity is harder to maintain in cyberspace, as opportunities are highly available and tempting. When people are looking for a romantic association on the Net, they often establish contacts with many people at the same time. Personal ads posted in cyberspace can be seen by many people, and so one can expect to receive dozens of responses from people who may suit one's romantic needs. One woman reports that she had over 900 replies to ads she had placed on the Net and, at first, she corresponded with 10 of the respondents. Another woman, who describes her love for her online friend as "the most beautiful, precious love there is," nevertheless admits that "There have been other men in my life during the course of all of this online relationship, and yet, my heart belongs to only this man."[65] It is not unusual for a person to have more than a dozen initial romantic explorations ongoing at the same time.

Even a somewhat conservative writer on online affairs, who suggests focusing on writing high-quality messages rather than on a large quantity, testifies that she personally can handle no more than half a dozen men at the same time.[66] Initiating offline romantic affairs with half a dozen men at the same time is practically impossible, not to mention morally unacceptable in current society. In cyberspace, it is much easier and more acceptable. Another woman suggests: "Send out many emails. It is like a fishing expedition. You don't really know what is out there until you bait your hook."[67]

In order to increase the chances of having many responses, some people post several personal ads describing themselves from somewhat different perspectives. Since it is likely that many of these initial communications will not materialize into satisfactory romantic relationships, making so many contacts at the same time is a useful and accepted strategy. The tendency to conduct several romantic affairs at the same time is an instance of how online communication combines features of both interpersonal and mass communication.

The above tendency is not limited to dating. There is no clear-cut boundary between exploratory communication intended to find out whether the person is suitable for an online romantic relationship and the communication that actually constitutes such a relationship. People are not certain whether they are in the preliminary stages of courtship or whether they are already engaged in an intimate relationship. Moreover, it may happen that only one person feels a great degree of intimacy; in this case, the other person may feel entitled to pursue several romantic communications at the same time. These clear-cut boundaries are also absent in offline relationships, but since those relationships require many resources, it is physically more difficult – although not completely impossible – to conduct many romantic relationships at the same time. There is also a practical problem of confusing the several lovers. Based on her personal experience, an author of a survival guide to online dating recommends avoiding double-dipping – at least when it concerns face-to-face meetings resulting from online dating: "I recommend spreading your dates apart at least by a day or two."[68]

Even when both people feel that they have already established a significant, intimate, and committed romantic relationship, they may not be able to end their other romantic relationships. A married woman having an online affair notes: "I could not divorce my husband because he does love me so much and I love him too. It would kill him if I did. He is a good father to my son." Another woman, while having an intense romantic affair, tells her lover that she is married and is happy with her husband, but nevertheless claims that "if I ever lost him [her online lover, Jim] my heart would never be the same. I LOVE YOU JIM. SO VERY MUCH. ALL MY DEEPEST LOVE, YOUR PRINCESS." The following account describes a similar case:

> I am a married man who has fallen hard for a woman who lives 3,000 miles away. She says she loves me and I know I love her. Tonight, my new love confronted me with the fact that she caught me in a place online that I shouldn't have been. She's ready to stop talking to me altogether. What should I do?[69]

It seems that cheating on his online mistress worries this man no less than cheating on his wife. This indicates the great emotional significance he attaches to the online relationship.

It should be remembered that many online relationships begin while at least one of the partners is having an ongoing offline relationship with another person. Sometimes the online affair is justified as the best available means for avoiding an offline affair. Take, for instance, the following statement:

> Chat gives me the opportunity to be sexual with people I could never be sexual with in real life. I'm married and monogamous, so I cannot and will not have sex with others physically; however, online I can have sex without guilt or pretense. My spouse is aware and approves and does the same himself. We consider it a healthy pressure valve for monogamy and we are brutally honest with our online partners about our unavailability in real life.[70]

Netizens are more accepting of non-monogamous sexual relationships, but only some of them may be able to love two people at the same time.

José Ortega y Gasset argues that, whereas sexual desire involves superficial knowledge and the evaluation of many objects, love involves a more profound knowledge and the evaluation of very few objects.[71] We have seen that online love is similar to offline love in being profound and in involving very few objects (although the former involves more objects). A more fundamental difference may exist between offline sex and cybersex. Contrary to offline sex, which may involve superficial knowledge of the object, cybersex typically involves detailed knowledge of the beloved's body. The detailed knowledge of one's online partner includes not merely the partner's psychological attitudes and fantasies, but also their physical features. Thus, a woman who was having an online sexual affair argued that her online lover "who has never seen or touched me, knows my body and its responses better than either of my two former husbands."[72]

Online intimacy and commitment

Happiness is having a large, loving, caring, close-knit family in another city.

George Burns

Robert Sternberg has suggested that romantic relationships characteristically have three major components: intimacy, passion, and commitment. Intimacy expresses closeness, bonding, and connection. Passion is largely the expression of desires and needs and is expressed in physical and mental arousal. Commitment is the extent to which a person is likely to stick with someone and see her or him through to the end.[73] In this section, I examine whether these components are present in online love as well.

In online relationships, intimacy is high – probably higher than in offline relationships. Intimacy has to do with self-disclosure, and this is significantly present in online relationships. Sternberg notes that self-disclosure is often easier in same-sex friendships than in loving relationships, and between strangers than between spouses – probably because the costs of self-disclosure can be high. It appears that self-disclosure is as profound, and possibly even more so, in online romantic affairs as in online same-sex friendships. This is because in both cases, there are no costs involved in such disclosures, and closeness is often greater in the former.

In discussing offline relationships, Sternberg indicates that there is a curvilinear relationship between reciprocity and self-disclosure. The rewards of reciprocity in self-disclosure increase up to a certain point. When a couple becomes very intimate, though, the costs of self-disclosure become so great that it often decreases. Accordingly, intimacy develops slowly and is difficult to achieve. The result is a balancing act between intimacy and autonomy.[74]

This problem does not exist in online relationships, where the relationship between reciprocity and self-disclosure can be more or less linear. Intimacy can increase despite the greater self-disclosure since there is no significant price to pay and no autonomy that is threatened. The linear correlation becomes curvilinear only when the two lovers have face-to-face meetings and begin to plan their common future. At that point, their romantic relationship begins to acquire characteristics typical of face-to-face relationships.

The second component in love is termed by Sternberg "passion." Sternberg sometimes refers to this component as psychophysiological arousal. The term "passion" is ambiguous, and I suggest replacing it with "emotional intensity." Sternberg claims that, in some romantic relationships, the passion component develops almost immediately, and intimacy, only after a while. In some other close relationships, passion develops only after intimacy. Sometimes, intimacy and passion work against each other. This is so, for instance, in a relationship with a sex worker or when strangers are more sexually exciting than our familiar partner is.[75]

In cyberlove, emotional intensity usually increases as intimacy increases. Since the partner is to a large extent unknown, increased familiarity and intimacy is correlated with increased emotional intensity. Generally, emotional intensity of online affairs is as high as in offline affairs and often even higher – major reasons for this are the high degrees of self-disclosure and familiarity, the incomplete nature of online relationships, and the great role that the imagination plays in them. In cyberspace, people may not give their physical body to their lovers, but they certainly give their heart. Indeed, the term "my soul-mate" is frequent in descriptions of online mates. This type of emotional involvement more than compensates for the lack of physical contact.

People often testify to the great intensity of their online affairs – many of them indicating that they had never felt this way before. The following are a few examples of such testimonies. One woman stated: "I feel a love for this man more powerful than I have ever loved anyone and we've never met. It's like being a teenager all over again." Another woman writes: "I really started feeling strongly towards him, the emotions were overwhelming, I didn't know I could EVER feel about anyone the way I felt about him." A married woman having an online affair writes: "I have never felt this way for anyone, including my husband and my first lover over 10 years ago." The same claim is repeated by many netizens; thus, another person declares: "I have never loved a man as I do this one. I feel more for him than I ever have for my husband." Another person writes: "Our mutual love for each other is so immeasurable that it seems as though no other person on this planet has or ever will feel the way that we do." A woman having an affair with a man ten years younger than her, testifies: "All my life I was convinced that real true love was the stuff of silly romance novels and country western songs. (I had been married for almost 13 years and *knew* there was no such thing as 'fireworks.') Now suddenly I found myself thinking of this man constantly. I loved him so much, it was almost painful." She adds that they finally met face-to-face and about a year later got married; they have recently celebrated their second anniversary, and "our love has grown to unbelievable proportions."[76]

The great intensity of cyberlove and the fact that there are many millions of people populating cyberspace lead those who fall in love on the

Net to feel as if their meeting was a miracle: a precious gift that God sent or evidence that they were destined to be together. Accordingly, people often believe that such an affair is something they cannot resist; some kind of internal or external genuine voice forces them to pursue the affair.

In Sternberg's view, the third component of love is a commitment to maintain that love. Generally, commitment is lower in online relationships than in offline circumstances. In online affairs, people are much freer than in offline affairs and this freedom implies less commitment. Indeed, in one survey many cyberspace respondents said that their online romantic relationships were fun, stimulating, and gratifying in their own right; nevertheless, they claimed a lesser sense of seriousness or long-term commitment.[77] This does not mean that online affairs are never taken seriously with long-term commitments in mind. However, in these cases, people usually consider the affair as a means for achieving a fulfilling offline relationship.

Esther Gwinnell speaks about three major levels of commitment in romantic relationships: (a) commitment to continue and develop the relationship, (b) commitment to exclusivity, sacrifice, and long-term planning, and (c) commitment to marry and live together. She argues that only the first level is clearly evident in online relationships.[78]

The initial stages of online relationships involve the first level of commitment, that is, to continue the communication in a prompt and caring manner. In this sense they are similar to offline relationships. The deepest level of commitment – that is, to marry and live together – may be the result of online relationships, but the actualization of this commitment means the termination of the online relationship: it means transforming the online relationship into an offline one. Whereas the first level of commitment is obviously present in online relationships, and the third level is typically absent, the second level may be present, but to a lesser degree than in offline relationships.

The second level of commitment, which involves exclusivity and long-term planning, is problematic for online relationships. Cyberspace provides an alternative world to the actual one. People do not live exclusively in one world; rather, they move from one world to the other. This lack of exclusivity is also evident in the romantic realm. Cyberspace enables participants to explore exciting alternatives without necessarily violating significant personal commitments. Indeed, many online affairs are conducted while at least one of the participants is having an offline relationship with another person. Married people comprise a surprisingly high percentage of visitors to the most popular dating websites. This is also compatible with findings suggesting that more people living with a sexual partner masturbate than people living alone.[79] Cyberspace provides an outlet for developing alternative emotional ties, without completely ruining the primary offline relationship. When people confuse cyberspace with the actual world, the issue of commitment becomes problematic, and emotional and moral difficulties emerge.

Sternberg indicates the presence of three major possible conflicts concerning romantic relationships: (a) real versus ideal, (b) self-perceived versus other-perceived, and (c) feelings versus actions.[80] Let us see how these conflicts are expressed in cyberspace.

The first conflict in romantic relationships concerns the discrepancy between what the lover expects the beloved to be (the ideal beloved) and what the beloved actually is (the real beloved). As long as the online affair is limited to cyberspace, this discrepancy is not significant, as the online lover is depicted and imagined to be close to the ideal type. Only when the affair is transformed into a face-to-face relationship can this discrepancy become evident.

The second conflict is expressed in the discrepancy between the way you perceive yourself and the relationship and the way the beloved perceives you and it. This discrepancy is less frequent when the online affair is limited to cyberspace, because, in this case, the other perceives you as almost identical to the way you describe yourself. There may, however, be discrepancies concerning the attitude of each partner toward the development of the relationship. This conflict may arise when one participant hopes that the online affair will become an offline relationship or that a "solely sexual" relationship, or a solely platonic friendship, is "going somewhere" – that is, that it is going to develop into a committed romantic relationship.

The third conflict refers to the discrepancy between the way the beloved feels toward you and the way he translates his emotions into actions. This conflict is also less evident in online relationships, as the available activities are limited. However, this conflict may become crucial when plans are made to transform the relationship into actuality.

Thus, we see that the three major conflicts associated with offline romantic relationships are less prominent in cyberspace, mainly because imagination plays a more crucial role in online affairs.

To sum up: in comparison to offline relationships, online relationships usually involve greater intimacy and emotional intensity, but less commitment. Since intimacy and emotional intensity were found to be the best predictors of satisfaction, it is likely that romantic relationships in cyberspace provide greater satisfaction. This perspective, together with the perspective concerning the lack of major conflicts, may further explain the lure of cyberspace. However, this advantage may prove illusory once the online relationship is transformed into an offline relationship.

Online rejection

> The best way to remember your wife's birthday is to forget it once.
>
> E. Joseph Cossman

The ease of online communication makes it an important tool not only for maintaining romantic relationships, but also for ending them. Indeed, terminating relationships through email is becoming quite popular. Such a non-personal manner of ending the relationship may be easier for the sender, but may be stressful for the receiver. One such example is the case of British solicitor Richard Holt, who committed suicide after receiving an email from his mistress terminating their relationship. However, in most cases, online rejection is less painful than offline rejection. Major reasons for this are: (a) the rejectee's anonymity, (b) the ability to explain the rejection by referring to external circumstances, (c) the greater prospects of obliterating the pain by finding a new partner, and (d) rejection is very common.

Rejection is painful not merely because of the event itself, but also because of the damage it inflicts upon our self-esteem, which is determined to some extent by the way people evaluate us. Public knowledge of our failures typically hurts our self-esteem. The anonymity of cyberspace often eliminates this type of psychological harm.

I have indicated that when our responsibility for a certain event is reduced, emotional intensity decreases as well. Accordingly, people are less distressed by rejection when it is due to external circumstances. Such circumstances reduce the relevancy of the event to the rejectee's self-esteem and hence reduce the event's strength.[81] Online rejection can easily be attributed to external circumstances. Thus, the rejectee can believe that the rejection is based upon circumstances such as children, work, or a change in the partner's environment, which are beyond the control of the beloved. The rejectee can also believe that the rejection is based upon the leaner channel of communication, which fails to reveal valuable information about the rejectee and therefore does not actually reflect the rejectee's real worth.

The pain of online rejection is also reduced by the greater prospects of finding a new online partner. In this sense, the rejection can be perceived as having a less damaging impact upon the rejectee's romantic life.

In cyberspace, rejection is a common experience as each person posts many requests to date many people. The greater prevalence of romantic rejection makes it a normal and routine event that everyone experiences many times and which they can therefore adjust to; accordingly, it is a less emotional occurrence and causes less pain. Similarly, cyber-etiquette is such that most people are not offended by a lack of response to an initial email asking for a cyberdate.[82]

The above reasons mitigating the pain of online rejection also mitigate the guilt over rejecting others. In this sense, online relationships are more romantically oriented. Considerations external to the mere romantic wish to be together – such as practical considerations, guilt feelings over hurting other people, or worrying about their well-being – are of lesser weight in such relationships.

There are, of course, many circumstances in which online rejection is very painful. We must remember that online relationships involve real love; the termination of such love may be painful, especially when intense, profound love is involved (which is often the case in online relationships). One woman, who testifies that "I have never given anyone my heart until I met him," says after her online friend broke off the relationship: "Boy that killed me. I didn't know what to do. For a few days I was unable to eat or sleep. I cried for 2 days straight. I can never love anyone else, because I gave this man my heart, and he crushed it. I have no heart to give to another human being." When the rejection occurs after a few face-to-face meetings, the pain is even greater. One woman, who experienced this situation, writes: "My heart broke into a million pieces afterwards. It still hurts today. I'm severely depressed and can't understand how he could just 'let' go so easily?" A married woman describes her situation after her online lover got married: "For me it's like it's the end of the world; every day I cried & cried & cried just to think of him, because I lost him."[83] Although online rejection is typically less painful, virtual love can easily break real hearts.

Another issue is that of ending an offline relationship by sending an email or even an SMS message. Here the pain of rejection may be augumented by the feeling of humiliation stemming from the lack of the decency to discuss the matter in a more serious manner.

Gender differences

Things you'll never hear a man say:

1. Here honey, you use the remote.
2. You know, I'd like to see her again, but her breasts are just too big.

3. While I'm up, can I get you a beer?
4. Sex isn't that important; sometimes, I just like to be held.
5. We never talk anymore.

<u>Things you'll never hear a woman say:</u>

1. Ohh, this diamond is way too big!
2. And for our honeymoon we're going fishing in Alaska!
3. Can our relationship get a little more physical? I'm tired of being "just friends."
4. Aww, don't stop for directions, I'm sure you'll be able to figure out how to get there.
5. I don't care if it is on sale, 300 dollars is too much for a designer dress.

Jane Oneill

Do online relationships have an impact on the gender differences that are typical of offline relationships? There is no simple answer to this question. Some of the basic gender differences seem to be preserved in this new type of relationship, but some changes may be detected as well.

Concerning the relative weight of the two basic evaluative patterns, that is, attraction and praiseworthiness, the typical feminine attitude toward romantic relationships is closer to the attitude prevailing in online relationships than is the typical masculine attitude. The fact that women generally give less weight to the external appearance of their partner accords with the fact that external appearance is of less concern in online personal relationships. It has been argued that men love the women to whom they are attracted, whereas women are attracted to the men they love. Oscar Wilde, for example, claimed that women fall in love with their ears and men with their eyes. Personal ads placed by women who are seeking to attract men are most likely to advertise their beauty; a man seeking to attract a woman is more likely to mention his sincerity, friendship, and financial security. One study found that, although both men and women preferred good-looking partners, women considered other qualities, such as status and money, as compensating for looks. This was not true when men evaluated women: unattractive women were not preferred, no matter what their status.[84]

Cyberspace may change the traditional weight given to attractiveness and praiseworthiness. Thus, a study on online personal ads has found that men respond more to an ad describing the woman as "financially successful and ambitious" than as either "very attractive" or "passionate and sensitive." This is different to the response generated by newspaper personal ads. One explanation for this difference may be that Net users are more educated and affluent, and are simply looking for someone of a similar background.[85] Another reason may be that physical attraction is less important in cyberspace.

Although the issue of attractiveness is less significant in cyberspace, there are nevertheless some gender differences in this regard. On the Net, women often receive messages from men asking for their physical description. Some men are especially visually reliant and ask for intimate descriptions, such as "What is your bra size?" Women, conversely, pay more attention to the content of their chats and show less interest in knowing about an individual's external appearance.[86]

In other ways, too, online relationships are more similar to the type of relationship generally preferred by women: women tend to self-disclose to others more than men do, and they place greater emphasis on talking and sharing emotional attitudes. Women tend to engage in intimate conversation with their good friends, whereas men tend to spend time in common activities with theirs.[87] As one woman said, "My husband has Playboy and other things he can use. But the words do it for me. It is seduction at its best." Another woman, who had a long (over six years) online affair with a man she never saw or spoke to, writes: "At one time I even thought he was a woman. He just seemed too emotional to be a man, I don't know why."[88] Because women have a greater tendency to discuss their emotions, they often become responsible for maintaining relationships among family and friends. Online communication is particularly useful for this purpose. Indeed, women use email more than men in communicating with family and friends; accordingly, the use of email has increased women's social contacts (including an increase in phone calls and personal contacts).[89]

The distinction between expressiveness and instrumentality, which denotes two styles of relating to others, is relevant in this regard. Expressiveness is associated with emotional intimacy and sharing in personal relationships, whereas instrumentality indicates a more agentic style of relationship oriented around common activities. Women have been found to be more expressive and men more instrumental in their relationships. It has been found that women talked more frequently than men about sexual matters including sexual behavior, sexual feelings, dating, and romantic relationships.[90] Accordingly, women use the Internet more for interpersonal communication than do men and they derive more psychological gratification from this activity than men do. Men use the Internet primarily for purposes related to entertainment and leisure. It seems that males and females use the Internet equally often, but differently.[91]

The novel nature of online communication may change some stereotypical gender behavior. Thus, while women are not as sexually expressive as men in online relationships, they nevertheless express greater sexual freedom than they do offline. Indeed, the crudeness and brashness of women in cyberspace often surprises men who encounter them there. Moreover, the phenomenon of women making the first move is more common and acceptable in cyberspace. Men, on the other hand, when making connections with women on the Net, should learn to do so through verbal and emotional routes and not through impressing them with their status and wealth. Hence, they may become more sensitive to intimate, emotional issues.[92]

I have indicated one type of gender difference concerning the connection between sex and love: it seems that men tend more to separate sex and love whereas women tend to believe that love and sex go together. Thus, it has been suggested that X-rated pictures generate more arousal in men than in women, whereas pictures of romantic couples generate more arousal in women than in men. Similarly, women's extramarital sexual involvements are more likely to be love-oriented and those of men to be pleasure-oriented. Accordingly, men are more likely to engage in extramarital sex with little or no emotional involvement, whereas women are more likely to engage in extramarital emotional affairs without sexual intercourse. It has been argued that a wife usually commits adultery when her feelings are deeply involved or likely to become so.[93]

The above gender differences are also expressed in cyberspace: men were more likely to prefer visual erotica (50% men to 23% women) while women preferred chat rooms (49% women to 23% men) where they can "get to know" men.[94] More often, it is the woman who will try to transform the online sexual relationship to an offline relationship.[95] These findings are compatible with the fact that the sexual fantasies of women tend to be more verbal and interactive, while those of men are more visual.[96]

Some gender differences are less pronounced in cyberspace. Thus, in light of the imaginary nature and the prevalence of cybersex, women may feel that there are fewer moral obstacles to sex online than offline and may be more comfortable with separating such sex from true romantic love. Nevertheless, when they are dissatisfied with a relationship, women are more likely to feel shame about their online sexual affairs.

Online relationships include not only casual sexual affairs, but also extramarital emotional affairs. Cybersex is in many respects imaginary, but it often entails profound emotional involvement. This may be of more concern to women for whom emotional involvement has greater weight. Consider the following complaint of a 39-year-old woman, whose husband of 14 years had online affairs:

> He did have affairs, although not physically. He had affairs of the mind, and that to me is as much a violation as if he actually had a physical affair with someone. Moreover, in one sense I feel that having an affair of the mind is worse than having an actual partner. My husband can, at any time, have an "affair" without leaving the house or seeing another human being.[97]

The ease and legitimacy of engaging in pleasure-oriented sexual activities online may encourage a larger percentage of women to participate in cybersex. Because cybersex is imaginary, more people engage in sexual activity for pure pleasure online than would participate in such activities offline. In this sense, the gender difference concerning the connection between sex and love is becoming narrower in online relationships.

Another gender difference in this regard concerns the use of sexual imagination: men fantasize about sex roughly twice as frequently as women do and they are more likely to fantasize about strangers as well.[98] The imaginary nature of cyberspace offers a more convenient outlet for sexual fantasies, and indeed men visit sexual sites more frequently.

Summary

> Birds do it, bees do it, and now people with computers do it.
> Gloria G. Brame

Romantic love consists of two basic evaluative patterns: attraction and praiseworthiness. In cyberspace, where conversation is more important than vision, attraction has significantly less weight than in actual-space: the positive appraisal of characteristics other than external appearance is more important. In cyberspace, you first get to know the other person and only then are attracted to her; in actual-space, the order is reversed. In online affairs, familiarity with the more profound aspects of one's personality is greater, as self-disclosure is greater. While in offline romantic circumstances you get to know someone from the outside in, in online circumstances the direction is from the inside out.

Attraction in online relationships is significant and it shares many aspects of offline attraction. The major aspects common to both are proximity, self-presentation, similarity, reciprocity, and expectations.

Love at first sight is more common than love at first chat, as the characteristics revealed by first sight can easily generate great attraction. Nevertheless, it is possible for some messages to generate love at first chat.

The availability of an alternative is central for generating emotions. In cyberspace, this is greater due to a few major factors: (a) it is easier to meet new people in cyberspace; (b) you can choose to communicate with people who are willing to establish the types of emotional relationship you want; (c) self-disclosure is greater in cyberspace and hence it is easier to identify available and willing people. The issue of invested effort, which is also important for emotional intensity, plays a lesser role in online affairs.

The abundance of romantic availability makes romantic exclusivity difficult to maintain in online romantic relationships. Indeed, many such relationships are conducted simultaneously with other offline or online romantic relationships. This may contribute to the more transitory nature of online affairs and the less painful nature of online rejection.

In comparison to offline relationships, online relationships usually involve greater intimacy and emotional intensity, but less commitment. This may lead to greater emotional satisfaction.

Some of the basic gender differences seem to be preserved in this new type of relationship, but some changes may be detected as well. The typical feminine attitude toward romantic relationships is closer to the attitude prevailing in online relationships than is the typical masculine attitude. There are, however, indications that some gender gaps may be decreasing in cyberspace.

9 *Chatting is sometimes cheating*

> A man can have two, maybe three love affairs while he's married. After that it's cheating.
>
> Yves Montand

The moral aspects of online relationships are raising greater interest as such relationships become more and more popular and their moral implications ever more evident. Thus, more and more people are seeking divorce on grounds of virtual infidelity: their spouses are having online affairs. The fact that their spouses never met their lovers does not seem to eradicate the emotional and moral harm.

This chapter begins to examine the morality of online relationships by discussing the morality of imagination: is our imagination subject to the same moral criticism as that directed at our actual behavior? I demonstrate that the so-called "virtual relationships" are real in important aspects. Accordingly, there are considerable risks in becoming involved in such relationships. Nevertheless, their popularity, as well as their positive aspects, indicate that we cannot altogether avoid them. We must learn how to cope with them while reducing as much as possible their moral and emotional harm.

The morality of imagination

> I remember the first time I had sex. It was very frightening. I was all alone.
>
> Rodney Dangerfield

Imagination has an important role in our life. It is impossible to conceive of human beings without imagination. Imagination fulfills cognitive and affective functions crucial for human existence. Evading imagination would be harmful for human existence and in any case is impossible to achieve.

The extensive use of imagination raises interesting moral questions concerning the assumed reality of the imaginative environment and its implication for our actual environment. If the imaginative environment were in no sense real to us, it would be of less relevance to moral discussions. Imagination, however, has a powerful impact precisely because it is considered to be in some sense real, and hence may have a harmful impact upon our actions.

What is the moral status of imagination? Can we criticize imagination in the way we criticize actions? Most people would agree that, concerning issues of morality, actions speak louder than imagination (or thought). Accordingly, the central moral question is not "What ought I to imagine?" but "What ought I to do?" Most people would acknowledge that imagination has some relevance for morality, but there are no moral ground rules to regulate sexual fantasies. As one man writes: "If cybersex is cheating, then so is any imaginary stimulation; the only difference is that there is someone actively involved in your imagination. If someone thinks this is cheating, then they shouldn't even be reading sexually stimulating material."[1]

As indicated, imagination may be broadly characterized as a capacity enabling us to refer to what is not actually present to the senses or to nonexistent events. There is nothing inherently wrong in referring to events that are not present to the senses or that do not exist. On the contrary, one cannot imagine human beings without imagination – complex imagination is one of the central characteristics distinguishing human beings from animals. However, since imagination has a crucial impact upon actual behavior, it is not morally irrelevant.

Many philosophers have emphasized the importance for morality of a person's attitudes and states, such as beliefs, desires, intentions, emotions, thought, and imagination. It seems that their principal significance, however, is related to their tremendous impact upon actions. A change in the agent's attitudes or states may make the agent a bad person who is more likely to behave immorally.

Imagination is not typically subject to moral criticism and guilt feelings because it is often not translated into actual behavior. However, imagination is not completely immune to moral criticism, since some practical implications are evident as well.

Lust, which is a kind of imagination, may be defined as "the desire for sexual activity for its own sake."[2] Lust is condemned in cases where sex is perceived as something that should always be a goal-oriented activity. Accordingly, in certain religious societies, the only legitimate type of sex is that intended for procreation. In such a view, any type of lust is condemned. Indeed, some religious people even believe that a man who lusts after his wife commits adultery with her in his heart.

A more common predicament concerns the impact of sexual fantasies upon actual behavior. Consider the case of a married man who indulges in sexual fantasies about a woman other than his wife, but does not act upon them. Can we say that such fantasies do not influence his actual behavior? Although the man may not have a physical affair with the woman, these fantasies influence his behavior and emotional attitudes toward his wife. The more he thinks about the married woman, the stronger is the influence. Accordingly, we are more critical of someone who indulges in sexual fantasies all day long than we are of someone who fantasizes more rarely. If, however, we assume that the fantasies in no way influence his behavior, there are fewer reasons – if any – to criticize morally the occasional appearances of such fantasies. If the man's fantasies are directed at a fictional character, our moral criticism would be less severe than if they were directed at his neighbor. The reason is again related to the fact that, in the latter case, it is more likely that these fantasies will influence actual behavior.

Another interesting case in this regard is that in which one of the partners fantasizes about someone else while engaged in lovemaking. An obvious problem caused by such a fantasy is that the focus of attention of the fantasizing lover is not on her or his partner at what is expected to be the most intimate moment between them. Accordingly, if during lovemaking someone else's name slips out, the partner may be deeply hurt – and rightly so, we may say. Some people may even consider such fantasies as a moral defect and even as betrayal – it may not be actual betrayal, but it can be considered as imaginary betrayal.[3] The issue, however, is more complex. Quite often, such fantasies are the only means for some people of getting excited about their own partners. Therefore, in order to excite the partner during lovemaking, a person may describe to his (or her) partner how the partner is making love to another person. For similar reasons, many couples watch X-rated movies before making love. In these situations, fantasies are not entirely selfish and inconsiderate, as they include the wish to satisfy the partner.

Extreme religious and conservative societies prohibit the use of lustful emotional imagination since they assume that such imagination has great probability of leading to immoral behavior. Avoiding lustful fantasies is realistically impossible. Even Jimmy Carter admitted that, although he was very religious, he had lusted after a woman in his heart. Sometimes, trying to repress a certain image – for example, imagining that a pink elephant is standing in the corner – simply makes that image even more irrepressible. It is also doubtful whether prohibiting lustful imagination is morally just. The above extreme approach assumes the validity of the slippery slope argument: once you take the first step on a slippery slope you are bound to fall all the way down the hill. Thus, a woman wrote in a discussion group: "Once you agree to spend the rest of your life with a person you should not have friends of the opposite sex or be flirting."[4]

The slippery slope argument is flawed since our lives are full of slopes and hills and avoiding all of them is tantamount to ceasing to live. We must make compromises without conceding the extreme pole. We can make a few steps on the slope without necessarily falling all the way down. Living involves taking risks, but these can be calculated risks with certain safety valves. Drawing lines is an inevitable everyday activity, which should take into account the given context. Indeed, the more prevailing moral approaches draw flexible lines concerning the use of imagination. These approaches do not prohibit – at least not completely – lustful fantasizing; it is the enactment of such fantasies that may be morally wrong.

The active role of the participant in an online relationship raises the issue of whether electronic correspondence has already left the imaginary realm; if so, online fantasizing could be considered to constitute immoral behavior. Taking a stand on this issue depends upon the degree of reality we ascribe to such relationships. Although online affairs are similar in some aspects to lustful fantasies, people treat such affairs as being real, and, in this sense, their moral status becomes problematic.

Chatting about sex

> Dear Abby,
> I suspected that my husband had been fooling around, and when I confronted him with the evidence he denied everything and said it would never happen again.
>
> Appeared in a newspaper

In a stimulating paper entitled "Chatting is not cheating," John Portmann defends online lust and characterizes cybersex as talk about sex; he maintains that such talking is more similar to flirting than to having sex. "Talking dirty," whether on the Internet or on the phone, does not amount, he believes, to having sex. Portmann does not deny that words can seduce others and that dirty talk can fall within the realm of sexual harassment, but nevertheless he holds that talking is not equivalent to sex itself. In his view, such talking is merely flirting since it lacks the essential element of sex: physical penetration.[5]

There are two issues here: (a) whether chatting about sex should be considered as sex, and (b) whether chatting is cheating.

Not all chatting about sex is equivalent to sex. You can talk about philosophical or psychological aspects of sex – as this book does – without considering it as having sex. Having sex cannot remain abstract: it must be more personal and specific. Some such personal and specific chatting may be considered as flirting, but not as having sex. Flirting is not an explicit sexual activity, but rather an enjoyable, subtle prelude to – or substitute for – it.

Although the chatting typical of flirting should not be regarded as having sex, some other types of chatting may be regarded as such. Flirting is full of sexual connotations, but these are subtly hinted at. Cybersex and phone sex usually include detailed descriptions of hard-core sex. Describing in an explicit manner to your phone or online partner what you are doing to her body is not subtle flirting; rather, it is imaginative sex that has features similar to actual sexual interaction.

Unlike masturbation, cybersex and phone sex are conducted with a real person, and this real interaction is what makes these contacts sexually real and morally problematic. A married woman, who enjoys open relationships, remarks:

> How would you feel if you walked into your living room and found your partner with someone and they were both masturbating? If they were not touching one another but were merely watching and mutually enjoying the act and the fantasy – the fantasy more than likely being that they were engaged in ACTUAL sexual intercourse. How would that make you feel? This would, after all, be a form of sexual interaction. Wouldn't you feel betrayed?[6]

While penetration of a male's penis into a female's vagina is considered the typical sexual act, there are other activities that are as sexual, if less typical. Many people, especially women, consider looking at porn to be an act of infidelity, and even adulterous. Some would argue that masturbation is a sexual act, while others – like Bill Clinton – deny that oral sex is a sexual act. Similarly, a group of Taiwanese judges and lawyers have argued that oral sex is not intercourse and so is not adultery. They support the view that intercourse means genital-to-genital contact; the opposing camp believes that sexual intercourse refers to any form of genital contact.[7]

One may delineate a continuum from activities that are obviously not sexual, such as a professional discussion, to those that are evidently sexual, such as physical penetration. Since the differences along the continuum are ones of degree, drawing a precise borderline between sexual acts and non-sexual acts is impossible and of little value. Moreover, such a borderline may depend upon personal and circumstantial factors. This line may be necessary for implementing certain practical decisions, for example legal proceedings; in that case, a somewhat arbitrary line may have to be drawn.

Cybersex has the basic characteristics of actual sex – except for the physical contact. Thus, it has the excitement, anticipation, satisfaction, and orgasm associated with typical sexual activities. Cybersex does not merely involve typing – it is a whole emotional experience similar to that we enjoy while having physical sexual contact. Physical penetration is no doubt important for sex, but other characteristics are significant as well. Accordingly, we may say that cybersex is a sexual activity – albeit not the typical one.

An activity should be regarded as sexual not according to the mere presence of physical contact, but according to other aspects as well: for example, its emotional nature (that is, the presence of intimacy), or its results (if orgasm is achieved). There are cases of physical penetration that do not involve intimacy or do not lead to orgasm; on the other hand, there are cases of cybersex that involve intimacy and result in orgasm. Indeed, the prospects of achieving real intimacy and orgasm during cybersex are no less, and often even higher, than in physical sex. There is no doubt that if an activity involves physical penetration, intimacy, and orgasm, it is a more typical sexual activity than an activity that lacks one of these elements. However, it is arguable which of the elements is more significant. All these elements are significant for sexual activities, but none is sufficient to constitute the prototypical sexual activity.

The discussion so far has indicated that, although "dirty talk" is not equivalent to sex itself, when such talk is part of an intimate process, cybersex may be regarded as a kind of sexual activity – although not the typical one. It still remains to be seen whether such chatting is cheating.

If indeed physical contact is not the sole essential factor in sex, then nor can physical contact be the sole factor in determining whether cybersex involves cheating. Other criteria should be taken into account. When extramarital affairs are conducted with the knowledge and acceptance of the other partner, no cheating is involved, even if physical penetration occurs. A necessary – although probably not a sufficient – condition for identifying certain chatting with cheating is the presence of deception. If no such deception exists, chatting about sex cannot be regarded as cheating. There is nothing intrinsic to chatting that makes it cheating, but the same holds for sex. Before examining this issue further, I will first discuss activities such as casual sex, adultery, and infidelity.

Casual sex, adultery, and infidelity

> With me, nothing goes right. My psychiatrist said my wife and I should have sex every night. Now, we'll never see each other!
>
> Rodney Dangerfield

Casual sex can be characterized as "sex between partners who have no deep or substantial relationships of which sex is a component . . . If sex becomes an essential part of their relationship, then they are no longer just friends (but lovers) and their sex is no longer casual sex."[8] The most extreme example of casual sex is that between complete strangers. Although this is common in specific offline circumstances – such as among particular sections of gay culture, or among heterosexuals who visit sex workers – people typically have some acquaintance with those they sleep with.

In casual sex, sex is typically not a goal-oriented activity, but an intrinsically valuable activity having no significant practical goals. One may say that the goal of casual sex is to reach an orgasm, but it is likely that the goal of casual sex is the enjoyable sexual activity itself; in this sense, it is an intrinsically valuable activity. Although casual sex is often condemned, it seems that there is more to criticize when sex is a goal-oriented activity. When sex is used merely for attaining goals such as money, improving social status, or having children, it may become a mechanical activity lacking intimate connection. Hence, people try to complete this necessary evil as soon as possible. In such circumstances, the other person is often perceived as a means for achieving this goal, and real intimacy is often absent.

In purely casual sex, the attitude of the other person is often significant; the other person is frequently not treated as a means, but as a partner in an enjoyable experience. Listening to the other person and being sensitive to her needs are more typical of reciprocal intrinsically valuable sex than of goal-oriented sex. In the latter case, only the goal, but not the other person, is significant. A mere desire for the woman's (or man's) body and not for her as a whole person is more typical of goal-oriented sex than of intrinsically valuable sex, as expressed in pure casual sex.[9] The invalidity of criticizing casual sex on the basis of its alleged focus upon the person's body is even more evident in the case of cybersex, where no body is actually present or is at risk of being harmed. The connection is purely mental, having no physical contact. A pure form of casual sex is less frequent in offline circumstances which are loaded with practical implications, such as risking diseases, pregnancy, the need to change one's ordinary schedule, financial considerations, and so forth.

One criticism voiced against casual sex is that its interest is focused on a partial aspect of a person and not on his or her whole personality. This criticism may be descriptively correct, but is nevertheless invalid. Most emotional attitudes are partial – their intensity is achieved by focusing on a very narrow target. Not all our relationships should be comprehensive – the value of a relationship is not necessarily measured by its extent. Hate is comprehensive, but typically morally wrong. I can have a stimulating intellectual relationship with someone, which is not extended to the sexual realm. We do not need to do everything with everyone; in fact, it would be harmful to do so. The desire to form various types of relationships with different people is a healthy instinct.

Online sexual relationships are even more partial than offline relationships, as many aspects of one's partner are not known. Again, the limited extent of a sexual affair is not necessarily a flaw. Online romantic relationships are more comprehensive than are online sexual affairs, but are still partial as they do not involve all aspects of face-to-face relationships. Nevertheless, online relationships may be profound.

Adultery has an objective definition that is independent of the participants' attitude. Adultery involves extramarital sex; it is a voluntary sexual relationship with someone other than the person's spouse. Infidelity is related to the participants' attitudes and to their explicit or implicit agreements; it involves unfaithfulness, which violates the spouse's trust. There are cases of consensual adultery, such as in open marriages, where adultery is not regarded as infidelity. There are also cases in which an activity may be considered to involve infidelity although it is not adulterous – for instance, some people may consider a man attending a movie with a woman without the knowledge of his wife as a type of infidelity.

Infidelity (and often adultery) typically involves betrayal, which has always been considered among the worst offenses people can commit against their kin. Betrayal is painful not merely because it disrupts an ongoing, meaningful relationship, but more importantly because it indicates that our partner prioritizes his or her interests over ours. Indeed, a large percentage of divorces involve sexual infidelity. Betrayal strikes a devastating blow to our self-image as it shows how little our partner cares for us; it also shows our partner's willingness to deceive us.[10]

Cyberadultery involves having an extramarital sexual liaison via the Internet; cyberinfidelity entails unfaithfulness that violates the spouse's trust by using the Internet. Major reasons for the popularity of cyberadultery and cyberinfidelity concern their greater accessibility, lesser vulnerability, and apparent lesser moral severity, compared with their offline counterparts. Cyberadultery and cyberinfidelity are easier to perform and put the agent in a less vulnerable position, as the chances of getting caught or being hurt in other ways are considerably reduced. They are also perceived to involve a lesser degree of betrayal as they involve more imaginary elements; the degree of neglecting the partner's interests may also be lesser. Cyberadultery and cyberinfidelity enable you to nibble on forbidden fruit, served with anonymity in the comfort of your home, while paying a smaller moral and emotional price.[11]

The private nature of online affairs may make them less painful for the betrayed partner as well. Since online betrayal is not public, certain repercussions that accompany adultery and that often cause considerable shame and distress – such as the phenomenon of the betrayed partner being "the last to know" about a partner's infidelity – are less likely to occur in cyberspace. It may take some time for people to discover their partner's online affair, but when they do they are often the first to know. However small, this is at least some consolation.

As in offline relationships, in cyberspace, adultery can also occur without infidelity. Some online affairs are similar to an open marriage in that they do not involve deception, but are merely extramarital affairs – that is, cybersex takes place with the full knowledge of the actual partner and sometimes with the participation of this partner. A married man writes:

> We are a married couple, I am 52 she is 51, married 29 years, who have just found the joys of cybersex. We have signed on individually, and as a couple, and have had a ball! It took some convincing to get my wife to do this, but now we have found out that SHE is the one in demand! We both have had several "great" sessions, individually, and as 3somes, with another female! Cheating? Definitely NOT! This is the greatest thing since sliced bread! The sex we have AFTER cybering is fantastic![12]

We can also speak about cyberadultery or cyberinfidelity not concerning an offline relationship, but concerning another online affair. The moral condemnation here will be less severe, as cyberspace has less strict normative limitations concerning the types and numbers of romantic affairs.

Cheating involves infidelity, that is, violating the partner's trust; adultery is often associated with cheating. In the next section, I discuss whether cybersex is a form of cheating.

The morality of online affairs

We ought never to do wrong when people are looking.
Mark Twain

In discussing the morality of online affairs, two central aspects are most relevant: (a) whether such affairs involve cheating, and (b) whether they are harmful. The two issues are independent. An online affair may not involve cheating if the offline partner knows about it, but it may still be harmful to that partner. And cheating does not necessarily have harmful consequences.

Online sexual activity involves various types of activities, such as viewing explicitly sexual materials, participating in an exchange of ideas about sex, exchanging sexual messages, and online social interactions with at least one other person with the intention of becoming sexually aroused. The issue of cheating is most relevant to those types of sexual activities involving social interaction with other individuals. Some people take a more extreme stand and view any sexual stimulation online of their partner that precludes them as a breach of trust.[13]

I have suggested that moral norms are less rigid in cyberspace; this is due to the fact that the damage done in cyberspace is typically less severe and that certain types of deception are more likely to occur. This does not mean that there are no moral norms in cyberspace. The power of such norms is often connected to the degree of reality ascribed to events in cyberspace.

People consider their online romantic and sexual relationships as real, as they experience psychological states similar to those typically elicited by face-to-face relationships. Accordingly, cybersex is not merely a conversation about sex, but is a form of sexual encounter itself; it involves experiences typical of sexual encounters, such as masturbation, sexual arousal, satisfaction, and orgasm.[14] Indeed, people consider cybersex to have a high degree of reality. Thus, one woman describes her first experience with cybersex in the following way: "I shouldn't have had cybersex on the first date. Big sin. I should have waited. It would have meant more to me if I'd waited."[15]

The psychological reality of online affairs does not necessarily lead their participants to think of them as cheating. On the contrary, such affairs may be considered as a sincere and profound expression of the participant's true self, which is remarkably different from cheating. It would appear that for many, preventing your heart from speaking honestly is no less of a sin than preventing your (offline) partner from knowing about all your actions. A woman who had an online affair notes: "I fell in love with this man on IRC [Internet Relay Chat]. I felt like I was cheating on my fiancé, but I thought that my IRC-lover actually loved me more than the man I had in my arms."[16] When it comes to more than just getting to know each other and corresponding, the moral situation becomes even more complex. In such cases, the online affairs cannot be considered as "harmless little online flings."

Despite the great *psychological* reality felt by participants in cybersex, most of them do not consider it to be *morally* real – at least not as real as offline affairs. One survey found that over 60 percent of netizens do not consider cybersex to be infidelity.[17] Many of these people believe cybersex to be similar to pornography; it is an extension of fantasy, keeping them from physically being with other people. Consider the following statement from a 41-year-old married man from Oklahoma City: "My wife doesn't care if I have relationships (even sexual) on the Internet. It's like it's not real. I can get away with it. But I'm sure she'd get upset if we were to meet for a drink or something."[18] Here a cyberaffair is considered to have less moral reality than does an offline, nonsexual clandestine meeting with a member of the opposite sex.

Many people even consider cybersex as a means not to cheat. It is something that may add spice to their offline relationship. They believe that if they do not know the real name of their cybermate and never actually see them, their affair cannot be regarded as real from a moral point of view; it should be considered as not any different from reading a novel or other kind of mere entertainment – a way to play out fantasies in a safe environment. People may say to themselves: "Hey, what's the big deal – I look at porn, masturbate, who's getting harmed? No one." Others may explain that it is only a machine they are talking to. Consider the following typical statement by a man, who is married (to Jody) and is having an online affair: "I'm not actually cheating. I'm not having real sex with anyone else, and I'm not at risk for catching a sexually transmitted disease or exposing Jody to one. I'm just having some fun, and no one is being hurt."[19]

Other people may admit that cybersex done without the knowledge of the other partner is cheating as it involves deception; nevertheless this is a type of positive cheating: "having cybersex with someone other than one's spouse IS cheating, but it's OKAY cheating." In some circumstances cybersex may help a person through rough periods in an offline, loving relationship. In such circumstances, cybersex may be recommendable, but can still be regarded as cheating. There are indeed circumstances in which cheating can be regarded as morally defendable. As a 29-year-old married woman, who often engages in cybersex, says: "People need to ultimately and

consistently remind themselves that 99% of fantasy is WAY better than the actual reality."[20] When people feel trapped by their current circumstances, but they still do not want to ruin everything around them, cyberspace may offer a parallel world in which things are better. Being in that parallel world can help them preserve the actual one, while not giving up exciting emotional experiences. Living within the two worlds is not easy and may become risky when we do not realize the limitations of each world.

In discussing the moral nature of cyberspace, people seem to separate psychological reality from moral reality. Psychological reality refers to the person's own mental experiences, such as emotions, feelings, desires, and beliefs. These experiences are no doubt intense and real – sometimes even more intense than in actual circumstances. Moral reality refers to the other's – that is, their primary partner's – situation, which is the main concern of morality. People who are having online affairs believe these affairs are psychologically real but morally unreal. They believe that although these affairs provide them with real psychological satisfaction, their offline partners should not be hurt since from a moral point of view such affairs are merely imaginary. Similarly, mere fantasies may excite us, but they have no moral bearing upon our actual environment.

Whereas people having online affairs tend to reduce their problematic nature, their offline partners often do not see any difference between online and offline affairs: the lack of physical contact and face-to-face meetings does not diminish the sense of violation of their vow of exclusivity.

At the heart of moral harm is the harm we impose upon other people. Just as casual sex is not inherently harmful, neither are online affairs. They may be so, when participants are also involved in another primary offline relationship. In this regard, the following aspects are particularly significant: (a) the resources invested in such affairs, (b) the wish to actualize them, and (c) their degree of intimacy.

A major moral objection to online extramarital affairs is that such affairs ruin the established relationship by diverting *resources* from the primary offline relationship to the online affair so that it becomes increasingly difficult to sustain the offline relationship, as someone else is competing for the time and attention of the partner. The more intense the online relationship is, the more resources are diverted to it. Thus, too much cybersex may make offline sexual activity a rarity: the person having the online affair may be less enthusiastic, less energetic, and less responsive to lovemaking with the offline partner, as it is difficult to compete with the novelty and excitement of a new, fantasy partner. In a survey of cybersex addicts, in only 30 percent of the offline relationships involving such an addict were the two partners still interested in offline sex with each other.[21]

The major resources invested in an online affair are not physical but mental. Online lovers are constantly thinking about their online beloved and paying less attention to their offline mate. After a stimulating online exchange, they may become happy; after an online tiff, they may become angry with their offline intimates. If, for some reason, their online beloved does not respond for a few days, the lover may become depressed, and nothing in her offline environment may interest her. Consider the following complaints of a woman whose husband is having an online sexual affair:

> My husband is using sexual energy that should be used with me. The person on the other end of that computer is live and is participating in a sexual activity with him. It is one thing to masturbate to a two-dimensional screen image. But to engage in an interactive sexual encounter means that you are being sexual with another person, and this is cheating.[22]

The more varied and interactive the communication is, the more it is perceived to be real and to require further resources. Sometimes even the participating person admits the transfer of sexual resources from the partner to the Net. A 45-year-old man, who spent much time masturbating to online nude pictures, wrote: "My sexual energy was 'saved' for the Internet. I lost interest in sex with my wife because I knew there were an unlimited number of photos on the Net that could 'get me off' any time I preferred."[23]

There are, however, cases in which getting involved in cybersex may improve people's comfort with their own sexuality and their offline sexual relationships. This is especially true for people, who are often less comfortable with sexual issues. One woman notes: "I've been happily married for four years, but recently I found an old boyfriend on the Internet. Sometimes we have cybersex and I think it has made my sex life with my husband better. Even though we will never meet in person, doing this makes me feel like I'm cheating."[24]

Online relationships are also a potential rehearsal tool, in the sense that they enable us to practice various romantic activities – and in particular, sexual activities – in order to improve our behavior in actual circumstances. In the words of a married woman in an open relationship: "Cybersex helps you flex your erotic muscles and that just makes sex better."[25] Consider the following advice of Deb Levine: "No matter what you think, the key is to use cybersex as a tool – take your reawakened desire off the computer and into your real life." Levine notes that cyberaffairs provide certain specific benefits such as the opportunity for sexual experimentation and exploration. The anonymity of cyberspace offers people the chance to experiment and explore and then to apply what they discover to their offline relationships. She describes the discoveries we make in cybersex as similar to the type of self-discovery we enjoy while reading a new book of culinary secrets.[26] Indeed, many people consider their online affairs as a romantic and sexual learning experience.

A related issue is that raised by cases in which partners have different sex drives. In Japan, Kim Myung Jun has addressed this problem by establishing sex volunteer corps whose members give their time and money to pursue relationships with women in sexless marriages so they can repair their damaged self-esteem.[27] Although Kim's noble activities may be praised, more efficient and less morally problematic results can be achieved via the Internet. Indeed, as Armand, a 58-year-old dentist, confesses: **"Frankly, I'm relieved that my wife gets satisfied online. I don't have a sex drive anymore, and she does. I'd rather she gets it at home than if she were to go outside our relationship in our small town."**[28] Consider also the following predicament of a male seminary student who wants to be a minister:

> I am 38 and have been married since age 18, for almost 20 years now. My wife is the only sexual partner I have ever had . . . physically. Due to incest on both sides, our drives differ greatly. She would be very happy with sex twice a month when she really physically desires it. I would be perfectly happy with 2–3 times a day! Cyber sex, with a small group of women who are in the opposite situation with their spouse's sex drives, keeps our marriage working. I see it as an extension of fantasy, keeping me from physically being with other women. Sex is a gift from God, and if you are using it as a means of enhancing your relationship with God and your spouse, then it is not cheating. I am a better husband and father, lover and believer because of my on-line loves. I no longer hassle my wife for sex and cause problems in our relationship for it, and I am better able to truly appreciate our lovemaking when it happens on her schedule. Meanwhile, I am blessed with helping and being helped.

In some cases then, cyberadultery is the best way to prevent actual adultery.

Sometimes sexual interest online may indeed increase sexual interest in the offline spouse.[29] Thus, a 42-year-old woman, who loves to cyber, notes: **"The sexual appetites of some men are not being fulfilled by the wife and rather than resort to REAL physical cheating they come online and explore things in the fantasy realm. Some wives of my 'cyberlovers' even say it actually enhances their performance, therefore they love it when I cyber their husbands just before sex."**[30] Once cybersex becomes more dominant, though, the interest in the offline spouse is typically reduced if it does not completely cease. Thus, one man said that, after buying a computer, his 28-year-old wife would stay up late, and "at 1am or so she would crawl into bed and I would be awakened with 'lets have sex.' I enjoyed that." Later on, she "asked for something in bed that shocked me; excited yet, but very unlike her. I enjoyed the sex." However, after a few months "she has no interest in sex with me any longer. She is flooded with it all night long; I'm the only rest from it she gets."[31] Only if a measure of moderation is applied to the use of cybersex can the resources devoted to the offline spouse be maintained. The problem is that, as with taking drugs, such moderation is very hard to sustain.

An even more crucial factor in this regard is the loss of emotional exclusivity, which is most hurtful. Online affairs seem in many cases to damage the emotional attitudes toward the offline spouse. In light of the exclusive nature of emotions, romantic intimacy with someone is likely to impair such intimacy with another person. From a moral viewpoint, it matters less that you do not actually touch your online partner; what matters is that, as a result of the online affair, you do not touch your offline partner in the same manner as before.[32]

Intense online involvement increases the risk of becoming addicted to cyberspace, making coping with everyday reality harder. Like other types of addiction, the addiction to cybersex involves an element of self-destruction. Thus, one woman reported that she spent sixteen hours a day visiting sex sites on the Internet, which resulted in her marriage breaking down. Therapists testify to the growing number of marital problems caused by online activities, and various support groups, such as one called "CyberWidows," have been formed for dealing with this problem. There is, indeed, a significant increase in the number of people who cite their spouse's online sexual and romantic activities as grounds for divorce.

Another major moral difficulty in having online affairs is the wish to actualize them. As indicated, this wish is dominant in such affairs – especially in the more successful ones. This wish, which may prevent us from truly enjoying the online affair, can also ruin our offline relationships. In old-time fantasies about a mythological character, a fictional persona, or a famous movie star, the realization of such fantasies was not a significant issue within the fantasy, as such realization was either conceptually impossible or highly improbable. In this sense, these fantasies did not inflict much harm on offline relationships, since they were never perceived as a real alternative to them. The situation is different in online romantic affairs. The degree of reality of these relationships is high, as they are conducted with real people, who, like us, want to actualize these relationships. People may consider the implications for the established offline relationship as the basic issue underlying any moral evaluation of cyberlove.

One way of facing this difficulty is to distance the online affair from offline reality, by refraining from exchanging personal, actual details or by having other types of limitation upon the online affair. These types of limitations are hard to obey. Consider, for example, the limitation upon the duration of an online sexual affair – such an agreed limitation also prevails in open marriages. Thus, one couple has agreed that both partners can have an online sexual affair but must limit such an affair to merely one encounter. As one woman in a committed relationship remarks about her online sexual affairs:

> I've had this discussion with my boyfriend and we both agree that as long as it's not with the same person more than twice, it is really masturbation. It's like reading an erotic story and masturbating to it. I think, however, if you do it with the same person more than once there is a risk of getting attached to them.[33]

This woman wants the online affair to be just pure sex; however, such an affair lacks one of the greatest advantages of online relationships: intimacy. Indeed, many other women want to know their online partner before having cybersex with them.

Another aspect expressing the moral difficulty of online affairs is the *degree of intimacy* achieved in them in comparison with the degree prevailing in face-to-face relationships. If, in the course of an online affair, two people reveal to each other sexual fantasies or secrets that they do not reveal to their offline partners, it is not clear in which relationship there is greater psychological intimacy, and this may threaten the prospects of the face-to-face relationship.

The above considerations indicate the reality of online affairs and hence the actual harm done to the primary, offline romantic relationships. Indeed, people are likely to be just as disturbed about their partner's online sexual affairs as they would be if they discovered that their spouse was exchanging steamy love letters with someone else. Such an online affair is painful for two major reasons: (a) it indicates that something is unsatisfactory in the offline relationship, and (b) if it develops further, it may injure or end the offline relationship.

There is no doubt that online affairs may be hurtful and harmful for the non-participating spouse. Many such spouses describe the outcome of such affairs for them as some combination of devastation, humiliation, isolation, rejection, hurt, betrayal, loss of self-esteem, abandonment, mistrust, suspicion, fear, and lack of intimacy.[34] The fact that most of these affairs are concealed from the offline spouse is indicative of such possible harm. Consider the following reaction of Melissa: "I glanced at the screen and was shocked to find John talking to some woman about how he'd like to throw her on the bed and make wild, passionate love to her. I was furious and hurt. We had quite a blow up about it."[35] A similar attitude is expressed in the following message: "I recently found a love letter my husband sent to a woman via email. I know there has been no physical contact because she lives across the country, but I still feel betrayed, humiliated, and hurt."[36] Another person, Susan, voices a more liberal, and less common, attitude: "I don't really care if Alex is playing around online. We are both secure in our relationship and I see it as a harmless outlet as long as it stays on the computer. We have an agreement on that point. No exchange of identifying information and no phone calls."[37] Susan and her husband can live with the husband's affair because they draw some lines and the affair is not going beyond those lines. They draw a line between what they consider reality and fantasy and do not cross it. They feel that their behavior is moral because they keep what they determine to be their moral standards. The issue is whether Susan can keep her liberal attitude for an extended period of time, and whether her husband will stay within the lines in the future. As one woman notes: "I cannot for the life of me understand how someone can share sexually explicit fantasies with someone who they know is real, and remain detached from that."[38]

Another suggested boundary is that of honesty. The man writing the following message requires his wife to be completely honest concerning her online affairs:

> I allow my wife to have cybersex as long as she is honest with me about it and tells me when she does. It has really improved our sex life a lot. I put an activity monitor on our pc to watch what was going on and she was always honest with me and told me daily what went on. The activity logs backed that up 100%. I trust her online and look foward to the days when I get home from work and she is standing in the hallway naked.[39]

It is ironic to note that, although honesty and openness is what enables the wife to have cybersex, her husband does not trust her and is monitoring her. It seems that the husband assumes – and rightly so – that in these circumstances it is difficult to comply with artificial constraints, for example to avoid the wish to actualize the affair. This is indeed one of the major moral problems of online affairs.

In light of such difficulties, there are some situations where both online partners agree to keep their online affair within certain boundaries, and if it goes further to break it off. They agree not to develop a profound relationship, permitting themselves only a virtual one-night stand, or an uncommitted affair. However, keeping within such boundaries is not easy.

On the whole, when the online affair is revealed to the significant other, it cannot be considered as cheating. However, since people do not consider online affairs as mere fantasy or as mere interactions with an anonymous series of computer links, such affairs are highly emotional and can be harmful.

Cybersex with software

Good sex is like good Bridge. If you don't have a good partner, you'd better have a good hand.

Mae West

One moral complication concerning cybersex relates to attempts to develop automated software programs and new "body suits." Software companies have begun developing interactive dialogue, voice-responsive commands, and virtual reality programs to augment communication with a virtual lover. Such programs will become so sophisticated that those engaged will usually not be able to tell whether they are flirting with a real person or just software. The new body suits, which are at their initial stages of development, will be able to stimulate many different erogenous zones simultaneously, thereby simulating physical sexual experiences. We can expect further developments that will increasingly make the virtual more realistic.[40]

From a psychological point of view, this raises the issue of whether people will continue to experience intense emotional satisfaction while knowing that they are having an affair with software. Most people will not experience the same satisfaction, as they will realize that their interaction is a mere sophisticated fantasy. The attitude of the partner is an important factor in generating sexual desire; knowing that "the partner" is no more than software may prevent one from attributing an appropriate attitude to the machine. It may be possible to hide successfully the mechanical nature of the software in cybersex, but it is hard to imagine conducting, over an extended period of time, an online romantic relationship with software; such relationships may go beyond online communication, and hence far beyond the boundaries of computer software. In short, software may be useful for providing immediate sexual satisfaction, but not for providing the deeper sense of satisfaction associated with romantic relationships.

Is having cybersex with such software less immoral than having cybersex with a real person? Many people will answer in the affirmative, as the former is more like buying a sexual device, like a vibrator, than like having actual sex. In this sense, it is more similar to masturbation and fantasies than to actual adultery; hence, it cannot be described as cheating. Indeed, the popular and liberal media sex counselor, Ruth Westheimer, has declared extramarital sex as taboo while approving practices such as threesomes, orgies, and sex with inflatable dolls. The absence of a special personal relationship is crucial for the above approval of these practices while rejecting extramarital relationships. Such absence is also significant in judging the morality of cybersex. Thus, Lisa notes: "Cybersex is NOT cheating; it is the alternative to cheating. I personally think cybersex is just another form of masturbation (as long as you keep it at home and never, ever have contact or give personal information to your online friend)."[41]

Judging the morality of sexual activities only by their relative position in the continuum between actual adultery and masturbation is problematic, as moral judgments are complex and depend on other factors, such as future consequences for the relationship, treatment of other people, and indications of a corrupting character. Thus, many people consider having sex with animals as more immoral than adultery, as it inflicts more pain upon another creature than does adultery. Similarly, raping one's wife is very far from adultery, but many people consider it more immoral. The use of force on an unwilling party for the purpose of sexual satisfaction is indeed a criminal offense, whereas adultery is in many circumstances not such a crime. It is also debatable whether an orgy is morally superior over adultery. In an orgy, the tender and exclusive emotional concern for the mate is absent, and the negative consequences may be as bad as those of adultery.

Without going into such subtleties, it can be asserted that cybersex with software is less dangerous to the primary relationship than cybersex with a real person. Hence, it may be a more acceptable option for those involved in a primary offline relationship. However, once the real nature of the software is revealed, it is likely that sexual satisfaction will be much harder to achieve. The novelty of the software does not eliminate all the risks and the moral problems associated with sexual activity without one's partner.

The risks and prospects of online affairs

> Don't have sex, man. It leads to kissing and pretty soon you have to start talking to them.
>
> Steve Martin

Online relationships are regarded as something exciting that provides an enjoyable alternative to the more dull aspects of our everyday life.

These relationships are particularly valuable in cases where no offline relationship is available. It has been found that the physical effects of sex produce health benefits that can dramatically reduce mortality.[42] The ability of many people, who cannot have offline sex, to have cybersex may be beneficial from this perspective as well.

Together with the beneficial aspects of online relationships, there are also risks that we should be aware of if we want cyberspace to become a prosperous human environment.

Despite its youth, the psychological flaws of cyberspace are already evident; most of them have to do with the negative impact on the participants' actual environment. Cyberlove can lead to marital discord and divorce. In this regard, a married person who has had many cyberaffairs notes: **"Cybersex with shared knowledge and acceptance is not cheating, but is asking for trouble. The problem is that any kink in one's real relationship may result in a deepening in the relationship with one's cybersex partner(s)."**[43] Some participants in online relationships gradually spend less and less time with real people and neglect their everyday responsibilities. Studies indicate that about 10 percent of people engaging in online relationships manifest signs of sexual compulsivity, and about a third acknowledged that their online sexual pursuits had interfered with at least one important dimension of their actual lives.[44]

Online relationships seem to be the most serious challenge that long-term romantic relationships have ever been faced with. This is due to the private, easily accessible, and inexpensive nature of cyberaffairs.

A major danger inherent in using the Internet is that of becoming addicted to it. This is particularly true concerning those engaged in online affairs. Some people, who are careful to avoid actual extramarital affairs, are more easily drawn into online extramarital affairs. One reason for this is that the latter are considered to be less real than the former. When something is considered to be less real, its risks are considered to be less significant.

Another reason for the compulsive nature of online affairs is the lack of an established and familiar mechanism to warn us against being involved in affairs we do not want to pursue. The permissive nature of cyberspace gives rise to fast online sexual affairs without leaving much time for the participants to hesitate about their willingness to be involved in such relationships. Online romantic affairs take much longer to develop, but the gradual development of intimate connections does not indicate to their participants that they are falling in love with each other. The trouble with online affairs is that by the time you realize you have gone too far, you are too involved to retreat. In offline circumstances, we know that we are being drawn into a romantic or sexual affair and we may choose to avoid it in its initial stages of development. Thus, if we do not want to have an extramarital affair, we may avoid spending a lot of time with an attractive person.

Despite the compulsive nature of cyberspace, the major problem is not concerned with cyberspace itself, but with the way we use it. Likewise, the problem of excessive eating is not with food, but with our eating habits. In both cases, moderation rather than avoidance is the optimal solution. We should not avoid the Internet, but we should learn how to use it to our benefit while reducing its risks.

It should be remembered that the Internet is still a novel tool for personal relationships. The excitement and immature use of this tool are associated with the risks of its use. Maturation of the participants, changes in the way they use the Internet, and changes in the Internet environment may somewhat reduce these risks. On the other hand, there may be some harmful consequences in the long run, which are still not evident.[45]

The Internet has become a prime vehicle for social interaction, and, alongside the risks associated with it, there are many social advantages. These advantages are not limited merely to those who have successful offline relationships – in the spirit of the rich getting richer. The Internet is also advantageous for those who have difficulties with face-to-face encounters; here, the socially poor are getting socially richer.[46]

One can use online romantic relationships in three major ways: (a) as a means of escaping from forming offline relationships, (b) as a means of forming and enhancing meaningful offline romantic relationships, and (c) as an intrinsically valuable activity having no other end beside maintaining these relationships.

The first usage is helpful in cases of actual crises. However, its cure is often temporary and it has little therapeutic value. Escaping into an imaginative environment is of little value in coping with everyday problems. Such an escape can be a useful initial step at the very beginning of the crisis, but, after this, more profound steps are required.

The second way of using online affairs, that is, as a means for arriving at a subsequent offline relationship, has various objectives, such as: (1) locating the suitable partner, (2) enhancing the online romantic connection, and (3) enhancing the current offline primary relationship. As indicated, all these objectives have their own advantages and shortcomings.

The third way of using online romantic relationships treats the relationship as an intrinsically valuable activity. We engage in this activity because we enjoy it and are immensely gratified by it, and not because we would like to achieve a certain external goal. Using online relationships in this way is, on the one hand, easy: we just have to continue doing what we enjoy doing. On the other hand, it is extremely difficult to continue using the Internet this way for any length of time because we have a tendency not to be satisfied with our own lot. We want to be happier than we are now and to move the enjoyable relationship into new dimensions. In the case of online romantic relationships this means turning them into offline relationships. The value of cyberspace is in providing a partial alternative, of being the next best thing to actually being there. When we are so close to Paradise, though, we always want to enter it; when this attempt is unsuccessful, our affinity to Paradise may be ruined as well.

Another moral issue regarding online relationships concerns the anonymity associated with them. It may be argued that although anonymity can assure privacy, it typically encourages immoral conduct.[47] Hence, the anonymity in online relationships may lead to such conduct. This may be true when people use the online connection as a means for achieving certain goals – especially actual goals, for example cheating, raping, and even murdering the online partner. In such cases, there is no moral fault in the online relationship itself; however, the anonymity associated with this relationship facilitates the execution of the crimes. If people do not use online relationships for achieving external goals, the moral harm associated with their anonymity is less significant.

This is not to say we should not under any circumstances attempt to transform online romantic relationships into offline relationships; we may do so when we feel profound trust and love toward our online mate. However, people should not treat every online affair as a prelude to an offline relationship. People may enjoy the intrinsic value of the affair, and the decision to develop it further into an offline relationship should be postponed until the time is ripe for such a decision.

It is up to people engaged in such relationships to draw the appropriate lines and make the necessary compromises so that online communications can be integrated with actual encounters. Consider the following complaint of a husband whose wife is having an online affair: "My wife cybers all the time on America On Line. She has even called one guy on the phone! She lies about her age and only uses her real first name. She says there's nothing wrong with it, but it definitely makes me jealous." In her response, the sex-educator Deb Levine indicates a few possible compromises to his wife's cybersex forays:

- Once a week, sign on as a couple and play sexually online together.
- Send erotic e-mail to each other to put a little mystery and anticipation back into your marriage.

- She closes her America On Line account and opens a new one, with new screen names.
- She can have cybersex online with men, but not phone sex.
- She can meet men online, but not tell them any defining facts about herself.
- Each time she goes to turn on her computer, she has to kiss and cuddle with you first.[48]

There are, of course, many other types of compromise; no single one will be suitable for everyone in all circumstances. Coping with a new type of personal relationship is not an easy task, however, nor are there any readymade solutions. It is something that must develop over the years and it depends on the individual nature of the people involved.

In order to avoid some of the harmful consequences of cyberspace, it is useful and morally commendable to moderate the visit to such a space and in particular to the sexual sites on the Net. Turning off the computer for extended periods of time is a good way of acquiring the appropriate perspective about our offline and online relationships.

Summary

> How much sin can I get away with and still go to heaven?
>
> Unknown

Online relationships constitute a serious challenge to offline romantic relationships. This is due to the private, easily accessible, and inexpensive nature of cyberaffairs. These relationships are regarded as exciting novelties, which provide a pleasant alternative to the more humdrum round of daily life. They are especially important in cases where no offline relationship exists. In addition to the considerable advantages of online relationships, there are also hazards that we should be wary of if we want cyberspace to become a beneficial human environment.

Imagination lets us wander through the jungle of our wishes and desires. This in itself is not morally bad and may even have certain advantages, such as letting you overcome some of your personal inhibitions. In the imaginary jungle, many of our actual moral prohibitions are absent, and hence violating them in online affairs is not perceived as so immoral.

Developing emotional ties with other people is not in itself a sin; some ties, however, are improper as they may be harmful. Romantic ties between an adult and a small child may be harmful even if no sexual activity is involved. Moreover, since emotional ties consume considerable mental (and often physical) resources, developing new ties may harm existing ones, which typically have moral priority over the new ties. Thus, our moral commitment toward our offline partner is typically greater than toward our online partner.

Distinguishing between a harmless relationship online and an affair involving infidelity is somewhat similar to distinguishing between them in offline circumstances. Is physical sex the defining factor? When does flirting cross the line and become romance? What constitutes emotional investment in a relationship? Does spending time together – offline or online – constitute infidelity? Although the lines are not always clear, in many circumstances cybersex clearly does cross some lines and may be regarded as infidelity – especially when it is done with the same person again and again, thereby developing enduring emotional bonds that pose a real threat to the primary offline relationship.

When analyzing the harmful consequences of an online affair, we should remember that in many cases such an affair typically does not appear out of the blue, but, rather, it expresses an underlying problem in the primary offline relationship. Of more interest, however, are cases – about half of reported users – in which couples report having no significant marital problems prior to getting involved in a cyberaffair; they began the affair mainly for recreational purposes. However, the more they were exposed to online sexual materials, the more they began to compare the attractive online lover, who seemed to fulfill every emotional need, with the current partner, who seemed dull and boring in comparison. In many cases, the online partner turned out to be an unrealistic and self-created persona.[49]

The morality of online affairs is mainly determined by whether they involve cheating and harmful consequences. Chatting is not cheating when the significant other knows about it; but cheating does not cover all the possible harmful consequences. Honesty can be harmful as well. However, there are many circumstances in which online affairs do less harm than offline affairs and hence may be preferable. There are, no doubt, many risks in online affairs, but it is not obvious that the risks are greater and more severe than those associated with offline affairs.

Only a better understanding of cyberspace and the limitations of human nature may enable us to cope with the brave new world we are facing. So far, human history has been characterized by our ability to learn how to cope with painful and usually harmful circumstances; it is now time to learn how to cope with the enjoyable and often beneficial environment provided by cyberspace.

10 *The future of romantic relationships*

Give me chastity and continence – but not yet.

Augustine's plea to God

It is hard to predict the future – for one thing, the future (as Paul Valéry said) is not what it used to be. Indeed, many past predictions now provide us with amusing reading. Thus, an 1868 survey of traffic in Victorian London seriously estimated that vehicular traffic would squelch to a nasty halt by 1925 because the roads, by then, would be covered in horse manure to a depth of 12.652 feet.[1] In 1977, Ken Olsen, President of Digital, made a similarly mistaken prediction when he famously remarked: "There is no reason for any individual to have a computer in his home." Accordingly, I do not intend to present a detailed forecast of romantic relationships. However, when examining past and present circumstances – and in particular some of the new processes elicited by cyberlove – it is possible to anticipate a few of the tendencies that are likely to emerge in the future.

Stability and change in romantic relationships

Some people ask the secret of our long marriage. We take time to go to a restaurant two times a week. A little candlelight, dinner, soft music and dancing. She goes Tuesdays, I go Fridays.

Henry Youngman

Emotional meaning is generated by the interplay between stability and change. Emotions typically arise when we perceive significant changes in our personal circumstances. However, an event can be perceived as a significant change only when compared with a stable background framework. Together with change, stability – and in particular familiarity, which expresses some stability – also increases emotional intensity: the familiar person is emotionally closer than the stranger. The unique combination of change, which is related to excitement and risk, and stability, which is related to commitment and security, is crucial for emotional excitement. Thus, romantic relationships consist of both change, which increases excitement, and familiarity, which enhances commitment and liking. The integration of change and stability is reflected in the notion of spiraling change, which combines both a directional change (movement from somewhere to a different situation) and a cyclical change (patterned repetition).[2] In both types, the meaning of the change is related to a stable framework.

The role of familiarity in emotional experiences should not be underestimated. Familiarity is positively related to liking, at least to some extent. It has been shown, for example, that children's liking for new food increases with the number of times they are served this food, regardless of whether they actually eat any of it.[3] The correlation between liking and familiarity need not be linear – that is, a given increase in familiarity does not necessarily result in a similar increase in liking. Moreover, from a certain point onwards, there is an inverse correlation between familiarity and liking. Up to a point, "the more the merrier" remains true, after which "one can have too much of a good thing."

A study concerning familiarity in music indicates that the frequency of listening to a certain kind of music may increase the preference for this kind. However, too much familiarity produces boredom. In order to explain the different effects of familiarity, the factor of complexity should be taken into account: simple music is liked less with increased exposure, while a complex piece is liked more. The interaction of familiarity and complexity causes listeners to dislike the incomprehensible, enjoy the newly understood, and be bored by music that is too well known.[4]

Romantic love may be explained along similar lines. Familiarity often correlates directly with romantic love. Mere exposure, in the absence of anything else, makes people more favorably inclined to each other.[5] However, mere exposure only sets the scene for falling in love. People become lovers not just because they happen to see each other every day. Rather, frequent meetings enable them to deepen further their concern for and attachment to each other. As in the case of music, the complexity of the object is an important factor in determining whether love will be more or less intense as a result of greater familiarity: a simple psychological object is liked less with exposure, while a complex object is liked more. Romantic relationships that are more profound are then more likely to endure. Online relationships that involve profound communication have in this regard an edge over offline relationships; this also explains how online lovers can exchange frequent and lengthy messages without becoming bored.

Profound love is a complex psychological state, with numerous aspects, whereas sexual desire is a more superficial state, with fewer relevant aspects. Accordingly, replacing the object often increases sexual desire, but not profound love. For love, replacing the object is often a temporary and elusive remedy. An indication of this is that very few people who leave their marriage for a lover eventually remain with that lover. Enhancing novelty and excitement in romantic love does not necessarily mean replacing the object; indeed, knowing the object better can make for heightened novelty and excitement.[6]

The integration of change and familiarity is also present in sex. As suggested, there is a considerable amount of evidence indicating that sexual response to a familiar partner is less intense than to a new partner. Consequently, the frequency of sexual activity with one's partner declines steadily as the relationship lengthens, reaching roughly half the frequency after one year of marriage compared to the first month of marriage, and declining more gradually thereafter. The fact that this phenomenon can also be found in cohabitation, homosexual relationships, and online relationships indicates the universality of this phenomenon.[7]

Stability and familiarity, however, are also important in sex as is evident from the fact that monogamous married couples report greater emotional satisfaction from their sexual lives than do single people or married people having affairs on the side. Ironically, married people having affairs often report better sex in their primary relationship than in their secondary relationship.[8] Moreover, extramarital sex can increase the risk of having a heart attack – about 75 percent of cases of sudden death during sexual activity involved people who were engaged in extramarital sexual intercourse. For these people, the emotional excitement of change – of being with an unfamiliar partner in an unfamiliar setting – was too much.[9]

We may distinguish in this regard between sexual desire (or drive) and sexual satisfaction. Sexual desire is a relatively simple desire, and as such can be generated by many objects, whereas sexual satisfaction is a complex emotional experience in which familiarity plays a more significant role. Familiarity is important for sexual satisfaction, as it makes the relationship less stressful and more comfortable, enabling a more intimate acquaintance with the partner's needs and desires. Accordingly, in marriage there is a decrease in sexual desire, but not in sexual satisfaction. Indeed, research has found that married men who spend time with their wives and children have less testosterone – the hormone that stimulates the sex desire – than bachelors do.[10]

The increase in life expectancy implies that in the future there will be an even greater need for both stability and change in romantic relationships. Elderly people benefit from living together in a committed framework, where helping each other is central; for this, a stable relationship is necessary. However, the need for change also becomes more pronounced when the marriage endures much longer.

The dynamic nature of cyberspace upsets the delicate balance between change and stability in our life, particularly in the romantic domain, as it significantly increases the role of change. Offline boundaries that delineate, for instance, place, time, social and moral behavior, are not applied online and more people feel that everyone is free to do whatever they please. Consider, for instance, the following confession:

> I am 57 and, as happens with most 57-year-old ladies, I need something to keep me sexually "peak." My husband is 48 and VERY sexually active. I am bi-sexual, and only became so 2 years ago. My husband does not know about my lover, who is my best friend. I use Cybersex to keep me in peak condition so that I can satisfy both my husband and lover. I am very lucky as I can orgasm on words alone and nearly always do when I am Cybering with either men or women. Neither of my partners knows what I do but then again, neither of them is disappointed when I have finished living out what I fantasize in the net. It is nothing for me to multi-orgasm and, when I have the real thing, I am thinking of my (online) experiences.[11]

The many available romantic bonds considerably reduce the meaning of each bond, since meaning is related to some stable background. The frequent changes associated with cyberspace are becoming a permanent feature of our life. This feature is likely to have a greater impact in the future because, in addition to the increasing number of people who are connected to cyberspace, the mobile phone further increases the number of people who are almost always online.

Cyberspace lacks a closed and unitary structure. Being in cyberspace involves a perpetual state of searching, an endless chase that will rarely settle into a stable form of life. Online events often lack a stable narrative, with an expected beginning and end. Such never-ending events, which are analogous to unfinished business, increase uncertainty and hence emotional intensity.[12] Similarly, immoral deeds often share certain characteristics of unfinished business; accordingly, the Bible warns: "There is no rest for the wicked." In cyberspace, it would seem that there is no rest for anyone. The dynamic environment makes everyone restless.

The restless nature of modern romantic life is further exacerbated by the widespread participation of young people in cyberaffairs and cybersex.

Such greater sexual flexibility will further augment the flexible nature of their future romantic bonds. As a young woman remarks about cybersex: **"My generation was the first to have computers in school. I do not have such moral dilemmas about online communication, nor do I question it. It just is."**[13] Empirical findings suggest that if a person has a previous history of multiple sex partners, the likelihood of him or her having a secondary sex partner during a current relationship greatly increases.[14] It will, therefore, be increasingly difficult to fulfill the romantic ideal of satisfying all one's emotional needs in a single relationship throughout one's lifetime. Couples will have to bring new experiences into their lives, together and apart, and further develop their friendships with others so as to cope better with the stability–change conflict. If marriage is to survive, it cannot be an isolated, static island in our current dynamic environment. Marriage must also become a dynamic form that is able to handle a greater number of meaningful relationships and that is not expected to satisfy all the needs of the participants.[15]

The dynamic character of cyberspace does not mean that it is a place of total chaos. The online experience is neither chaotic, nor homogeneous: online groups and activities possess their own unique characteristics and develop their own sets of distinct rules.[16] The rules may be more flexible than in offline activities, but, nevertheless, they exist – a group or activity with no stable framework is unlikely to be able to sustain meaningful interaction. The brave new world is not without rules, but these are much more unstable and transient.

The dissolution of some borders in cyberspace has created legal, psychological, and social difficulties. Thus, since online activities cut across territorial borders, the feasibility and legitimacy of laws based on geographic boundaries is undermined.[17] Similarly, the dissolution of psychological borders in cyberspace has created mental difficulties. The feasibility and legitimacy of rules based on stable social and psychological boundaries is undermined. Hence, social structures, such as marriage, which are based upon a stable framework, will face further difficulties.

The marriage paradox

> Love is an ideal thing, marriage a real thing; a confusion of the real with the ideal never goes unpunished.
>
> Johann Wolfgang von Goethe

Linda Waite and Maggie Gallagher provide impressive empirical evidence indicating not only that a happy marriage is one of most people's important objectives, but that married people indeed live longer, have better health, earn more money, accumulate more wealth, feel happier, enjoy more satisfying sexual relationships, and have happier and more successful children than those who remain single, cohabit, or get divorced.[18]

To take the example of the sexual domain, it has been argued that married people have both more and better sex than singles do; only cohabitors have more sex than married couples, but they do not necessarily enjoy it as much. Married people are more satisfied with sex than cohabiting or single people are. This is due not merely to convenience, but to commitment. Thus, people who expect their current relationship to last at least several years are more likely than less committed people to find sex extremely satisfying emotionally. Satisfaction with a sexual relationship is increased when the partners do not have sex with others. Accordingly, married people with more traditional views concerning sex out of wedlock are more likely to be sexually satisfied than married people with less traditional views.[19]

The above findings illustrate what we may term "the marriage paradox." Despite the enormous benefits of marriage, about half of all recent marriages now end in divorce and many people choose to be single parents. Although marriage is greatly beneficial, many people cannot or do not want to be married. If sex within marriage is so good, why do so many people seek extramarital sex? Extramarital sex prevails despite the enormous risks it carries for those involved in it, including risks to their health, family, financial resources, and status.

Waite and Gallagher explain the marriage paradox mainly by reference to external factors. They blame various private and public forces who they maintain have been parceling out to the unmarried many of the rights and benefits previously reserved for the married. They further accuse clergy, counselors, psychologists, educators, family scholars, and media figures of claiming that the main issue in deciding whether or not to divorce is whether it would make one happy. In such a view, marriage is demoted from a uniquely honored relation to just another option. Such permissive attitudes toward divorce encourage it and make happy marriages less likely.[20]

The above explanation is problematic. Historical and cultural comparisons reveal substantial changes in love styles and family forms. The problems associated with marriage are evident throughout history.[21] One cannot keep alive a certain social form by artificial means such as exclusive rights and benefits for those adhering to that form. The rejuvenation should come from more profound and natural factors. The marriage paradox is not the result of the attitudes people have toward marriage: after all, most people still believe in the value of marriage as a romantic bond and aspire to achieve happy marriages, and many divorcees remarry.[22]

Analyzing the empirical findings concerning the marriage paradox requires a more subtle approach. Indeed, a recent longitudinal study of the impact of marital transitions on life satisfaction reveals that people who get married and stay married are indeed more satisfied than on average, but they were already so, long before the marriage took place. It seems that, often, happy people are more likely to get and stay married. On average, people get only a very small boost from marriage; most people are no more satisfied after marriage than they were prior to it. (Although it should be noted that the events of widowhood, and perhaps divorce as well, appear to have long-lasting negative effects.)[23] These findings do not mean that, after marriage, all people retain their starting level of satisfaction. Instead, while many people end up happier than they were before marriage, just as many end up less happy than they were, as marriage can be pleasant but also stressful. Various psychological factors are involved in determining such results. These findings suggest that some of the differences concerning happiness in marriage are due to pre-existing differences in satisfaction – these individual differences can easily be overlooked if only average trends are examined. Contextual and individual differences are thus crucial for determining long-term, as well as short-term, life satisfaction.[24]

Several implications can be drawn from the above findings. First, for many people marriage is a suitable social framework for maintaining a high level of happiness; it is a most suitable one for those who are typically happier. Second, marriage is not suitable for many other people – typically, those with lower levels of happiness. Third, the existence of romantic bonds, as well as other life circumstances, can make a difference to our happiness. Although for many people marriage is a beneficial romantic form, for others it is not. Cyberspace may be beneficial for both groups either by enhancing marriage or by promoting alternatives to it.

Historically, the social framework of marriage has been considered beneficial because it offers life satisfaction, sex, children, and financial benefits. Not all these factors have had a similar weight through history. Thus, in some sectors of certain societies, life satisfaction and sex were not significant in marriage. Our current society provides alternative forms of relationships that can offer these benefits, too. Thus, there are plenty of sexual opportunities outside marriage, children do not have to be raised within marriage, and people ensure their financial security without being married.

It seems that the gradual process of dissociating marriage from its significant relative advantages in terms of factors such as sex, children and financial security will continue. Accordingly, I believe that the survival of marriage will depend upon (a) its ability to fulfill its intrinsic emotional function – that is, offering a more satisfactory form of life, and (b) its ability to be at least as beneficial as other alternatives regarding the other factors. I think that marriage can easily be at least as beneficial as other forms of relationship in the matters of raising children and financial security. Society in general and married couples in particular should give more time to a consideration of what greater efforts need to be made to ensure the emotional benefits of life satisfaction and sex within marriage. Here, the stability–change conflict must be dealt with in light of the rapid normative and technological changes in current society. As I indicate in the next sections, an appropriate use of cyberspace could be beneficial in this regard.

Proclaimed monogamy with clandestine adultery

Half the lies they tell about me aren't true.

Yogi Berra

The classic solution to the stability–change conflict in marriage is to support monogamous marriage while from time to time committing clandestine adultery. For many people this solution is beneficial. Thus, in one study of people who were currently engaged in extramarital sex, 56 percent of the men and 34 percent of the women said that their marriages were happy. Despite having an extramarital affair, these people said that they love their partners and enjoy good sex with them.[25] However, the high rate of divorce and extramarital affairs indicates the decreased utility of this centuries-old solution.

This solution is responsible, at least in part, for the popular cultural idea of an opposition between the "dullness of marriage" and the "thrill of romance." The ideal of courtly love advanced by medieval troubadours was essentially adulterous. Almost always, true love could exist only between unmarried people. The classic pair in this literature was an unmarried knight and the wife of a great lord. In his treatise, *On the art of honorable loving*, Andreas de Capellanus records the following verdict from a "court" of noble ladies: "We state and consider as firmly established, that love cannot assert its powers between two married people. For lovers give everything to one another freely, not by reasons of force or necessity. Married people, on the other hand, have to obey each other's wishes out of duty, and can deny nothing of themselves to one another."[26] From a different perspective, Catholics were taught the sinful nature of sex and that the main purpose of marriage was not love but procreation. The separation of marriage and romance is also evident in cases where the custom of marriage is maintained for practical rather than romantic concerns, including instances where people marry for reasons of status or wealth.

One way of combating the stability–change conflict in marriage has been to reject the prevailing assumption that marriage is a potential threat to the "thrill of romance." Thus, in the first half of the twentieth century, advertising and movies advanced a new vision of love as a utopia in which marriage could be exciting and romantic. For example, a 1921 advertisement for soap shows a man and a woman in a close embrace; the caption reads: "You would never guess they are married." The message implies that if you buy the soap, your dull marriage will be revitalized and filled with passionate romance. Another ad from the early twentieth century, in this case for a deodorant, claims: "Love cools when husband or wife grows careless about body odor." The implication is that passion dies in a marriage because of trivial oversights that can easily be rectified by external factors, such as an efficient hygiene product.[27]

Such "heroic" attempts to overcome the opposition between the "dullness of marriage" and the "thrill of romance" have not made much impact upon divorce rates. On the contrary, denying this opposition created expectations that could not be fulfilled and led to increased frustration, which became an additional reason for the increase in divorce rates in the second half of the twentieth century. On the other hand, acceptance of this opposition has legitimized the pattern of proclaimed monogamy with clandestine adultery – after all, some proclaim, it is not natural to live without the thrill of romance. Getting a kick out of exciting extramarital sex often provides the energy required to continue in a dull marriage. This pattern was reasonable as long as adultery was limited and clandestine, when adultery could be regarded as an occasional deviation that does not threaten the foundations of marriage. Whenever the secret deviation becomes a prevailing overt practice, it threatens marriage to the point of becoming the problem rather than the solution.

Cyberspace drastically increases the popularity of adultery, as it provides easy access to sexual encounters that involve reduced cost and risk. People can engage in adultery within the comfort of their own homes or offices. At any moment, any person can be swamped with tempting sexual invitations. Given the prevalence of AIDS, this type of casual sex is even more tempting. Whereas in offline circumstances romantic and sexual stability is the rule and transitory relationships are considered exceptions, in cyberspace transitory relationships are the rule and stable boundaries hardly exist.

Although cybersex may somewhat reduce the problematic nature of extramarital sex, it still touches upon the most sensitive and intimate aspect of the romantic bond: romantic exclusivity. For most people, maintaining this exclusivity is the most profound commitment of the romantic bond. Violation of such exclusivity is most painful emotionally.

The classic solution to the stability–change conflict in marriage – that is, proclaimed monogamy with clandestine adultery – leaves the social form of marriage intact while finding individualistic psychological outlets that reduce the emotional problem of the sameness of marriage. This solution is increasingly becoming unsatisfactory since adultery has become so prevalent – one reason being the popularity of cybersex – that many marriages cannot remain intact. Another solution to this conflict is to alter the social form of marriage itself by introducing fresh and flexible elements into it. Cohabitation is one such solution.

Although my discussion has focused upon heterosexual marriage, many of its various claims are also valid for same-sex committed relationships (or marriage). It is not yet clear whether same-sex committed relationships will provide all the benefits that heterosexual marriage does, but many of them are likely to accrue.[28] This is especially true of the benefits associated with greater commitment.

Cohabitation and online affairs

> I can't mate in captivity.
>
> Gloria Steinem on why she had never married
> (later, she did get married)

Cohabitation – that is, living together in a sexually intimate relationship without being married – is now more popular than ever and its popularity continues to increase. Thus, research estimates that, in the United States, the present pre-marriage cohabitation rate is 50–60%. At the same time, more people are marrying later in life – or not at all – than in the past. In addition, there is an increasing separation between childbearing and marriage.[29]

Cohabitation is attractive since it provides some of the benefits associated with the stability of marriage – such as convenience, increased sexual access, and lower financial costs and risks – while allowing for greater change in the short term. Cohabitation is often perceived to be a kind of inexpensive, but exciting, testing ground for crucial long-term decisions.

A major attraction of cohabitation is that it involves less of a long-term commitment, which in turn allows greater access to emotional changes. For instance, one survey on sexual fidelity found that 4% of married men, compared to 16% of cohabiting men and 37% of single men in ongoing sexual partnerships, said they had been unfaithful over the previous year. Only 1% of married women said they had had an affair in the past year, compared to 8% of cohabiting women and 17% of single women in ongoing sexual relationships. Moreover, cohabitation before marriage is still associated with reduced sexual exclusivity after marriage.[30]

Cohabitation is a flexible form of personal relationship. Indeed, it has been found to be selected by individuals less committed to marriage and more approving of divorce. Similarly, people who reject the constraints and demands of traditional gender roles are more likely to choose cohabitation than marriage. Cohabitors value more independence within a relationship, whereas people who marry value and rely more on interdependence. Sex, which is a crucial element in the quest for short-term change, is more significant in cohabitation. As compared with marriage, cohabitors have more frequent sex, although they are not necessarily more satisfied (this also holds true when the length of the relationships is similar in both cases). Furthermore, while celibacy is extremely rare among the married, it is virtually unheard of among cohabitors.[31]

The greater flexibility of cohabitation, and hence the lower commitment, increases emotional intensity but also uncertainty. The lesser commitment increases people's autonomy and is associated with novel changes, but it also reduces the sense of belonging that is crucial for human personal relationships – hence, the likelihood of maintaining successful stable relationships decreases.[32] The lesser commitment is also expressed in the fact that the probability of divorce among cohabitors who marry is greater than for those who did not cohabit prior to marriage. One possible explanation of such surprising findings is that cohabitors carry to their marriage their lower degree of commitment and their less favorable attitude toward marriage and less negative attitude toward divorce.[33]

It is interesting to compare, in this regard, cohabitation with commuter marriage. The definition of a commuter marriage is one in which employed spouses spend at least three nights per week in separate residences. Commuter marriage, in which people are still married and intend to remain so, is a growing form of distant relationship. Unlike some kinds of cohabitation, commuter marriage does not reject marriage, but merely the prevailing assumption that co-residence is necessary for marital viability. Whereas, in cohabitation, co-residence is perceived as essential to the romantic relationship, in commuter marriage, commitment rather than co-residence is more important. Indeed, the commitment in commuter marriage is high and accordingly the percentage of extramarital affairs is similar to that of standard marriages; the satisfaction from sex is also similar.[34] Online relationships are similar to commuter marriages in assuming that co-residence is not necessary for loving relationships.

It is not surprising that, as well as the current increase in cohabitation, we are witnessing an even greater increase in online relationships. The two types of relationship, which share various attractive features, pose alternatives to marriage in that they offer greater flexibility of traditional moral and social norms – in particular, they are less sexually exclusive. This is compatible with social changes that have reduced the costs of not marrying by greatly increasing tolerance for pursuing all types of sexual activities, including sex outside of marriage.[35]

In marriage, time horizons and commitments are usually considerably greater than in cohabitation and online relationships. Most people – even those who have separated or divorced – believe that marriage should be for life and hence that it involves significant commitment. In both cohabitation and online relationships, the time horizon is typically shorter and commitment is lower as well. Indeed, most cohabitors either break up or marry within two years.[36] Most online affairs either break up or are transformed into offline relationships even within a shorter timeframe.

The lack of significant commitment is one of the biggest attractions of both cohabitation and online relationships. One can get emotional satisfaction without necessarily paying the full price in terms of invested resources and future commitments. The reduced commitment is also one of the significant shortcomings of these relationships, as it is associated with a reduced level of the emotional and economic security that is involved in more committed relationships. Without firm commitment, there is an increased likelihood of difficulties, such as divorce, financial problems, and cheating, occurring. The absence of firm commitment also reduces the likelihood of one partner making sacrifices for the other.

Although cyber-marriage exists, it cannot solve the marriage paradox. Cyber-marriage is the phenomenon in which two people declare their online marriage. This declaration may give their relationship a romantic or sexually exclusive status in cyberspace and so increases the couple's commitment to each other. Since the commitment is limited to cyberspace, however, its impact is similarly restricted, and it is still significantly lower than that of cohabitors.

In cohabitation, there is relaxation of practical obligations in order to leave more room for passionate love. In many cases, the results are not encouraging. In online relationships, practical obligations hardly exist and love is intense; however, such unfettered, isolated love cannot endure for long.

Cyberspace presents a major obstacle to successful offline marriage, as it provides exciting alternatives. I have suggested that the major factors contributing to the great seductiveness of cyberspace are imagination, interactivity, availability, and anonymity. The first two features are expressed in the ability to conduct exciting affairs online, and the second two are to be found in the low cost and the low risk in doing so. In comparison to offline circumstances, finding an exciting romantic partner online is easier and involves lower cost and lower risk. The great availability of people willing to form new romantic relationships endangers marriage since, in marriage, the romantic partner is expected to be permanent. In this sense, the Internet intensifies the modern trend toward greater mobility and, in particular, the opportunity to meet more people as we spend more time outside home, at work or elsewhere. As Katie notes:

> Why bother going out to a place with 200 strangers, gambling on the slim chance of establishing something meaningful with one of them, or the even smaller chance of anything resembling real sex, when you can go to a place with a million or so people, meet someone in less than 30 seconds . . . and have a solid 85% chance of scoring! How's that for odds?[37]

This greater availability of choices further advances another trend that is harmful for marriage: the inability to be satisfied with your romantic lot. People are no longer settling for Mr. or Mrs. O. K.; it's Prince or Princess Charming or nobody.[38] If Prince Charming is just one message away, it is emotionally intolerable to leave him there. As I have indicated, the imagined condition of "it could have been otherwise" intensifies emotional experiences.

Online relationships also threaten marriage because their risk is not easy to detect. Some online relationships are not considered immoral, as they are not romantic or sexual in nature; however, they can easily become so – often without the explicit intention or awareness of the participants.

Cohabitation and online relationships are both about midway between platonic relationships and the strictest social form of romantic relationships, that is, marriage. Participants in both types of relationships can enjoy some of the benefits of marriage, while paying a lower price for them. However, both may lack the more profound benefits of marriage;

accordingly, many people in successful relationships of these types may wish to transform them into marriage. Nevertheless, cohabitation and online relationships may prove an important stepping stone for examining the compatibility of the two partners and hence providing a smoother road to profound committed relationships.

Both cohabitation and online relationships offer some of the emotional benefits of marriage, but, in the long run, people in these relationships may be in a worse emotional situation than if they were married. The short-term benefits may have costly consequences. One such cost is that breaking up with a live-in or an online lover carries many of the same emotional costs as divorce but happens far more frequently.[39]

Cohabitation and online relationships are not likely to replace marriage completely, but they indicate tendencies in coping with the stability–change conflict in marriage in that they facilitate a greater flexibility of the prevailing romantic norms. The classic pattern of proclaimed monogamy with clandestine adultery leaves marriage intact, and provides a secret outlet in which intimate activities take place. The failure of this pattern and the greater accessibility of sexual experiences – particularly on the Net – offer various ways in which marriage itself may become more flexible. In the next section, I discuss a certain type of online sexual arrangement that represents an important stage in the development of such romantic flexibility (or romantic tolerance).

Whetting your appetite outside while eating at home

A man in the house is worth two in the street.

Mae West

The relatively new practice of engaging in cybersex with the awareness and approval of the offline partner facilitates greater romantic flexibility in a marriage. This practice may be described as "Whetting your appetite outside while eating at home." As one married man notes: "It does not really matter where you get your appetite from as long as you eat at home." Indeed, some people testify that their cybersex actually increases sexual activity with their primary partner. The question is whether whetting your appetite outside will not encourage you to leave home. (The man quoted above admits: "My first marriage ended because my wife just had to see what it would be like to sleep with her online lover.") A married woman, who participates in cybersex both with her husband and without him, notes: "If there were more 'safe' sexual outlets that couples could enjoy together, maybe less people would stray into destructive behavior."

I believe that engaging in cybersex with the awareness of the offline partner is a revolutionary step in the search for greater romantic flexibility. It provides circumstances in which the monopoly of marriage (or another type of committed relationship) over sex is broken in a limited manner that can be normatively and emotionally acceptable to both spouses. In these circumstances the violation of sexual exclusivity is not clandestine (as in typical extramarital affairs), but it does not completely deny the privileged sexual status of the significant other (as is often the case in open marriages).

The above practice may be considered as a sexual sharing in which you can have your cake and eat it, too. A key issue for the success of this practice is the assumption that it will not hurt the primary relationship offline. Cyberspace provides some partial measures with which to deal with this difficult issue. The assumption that everyone is satisfied and no harm is done is particularly dominant in cyberspace. The virtual nature of cyberspace indeed reduces risks such as unwanted pregnancy, disease, physical injury, and significant financial expense. Thus, a woman whose husband "allows" her to engage in cybersex writes: "I have been with my husband for almost 18 years. Our sex life is great with the exception of a lack of it during the week because of work exhaustion. This is when I 'play'... and it takes nothing at all away from him."

If indeed the practice of "whetting your appetite outside while eating at home" harms no one, then romantic affairs may not be in conflict with a committed relationship. A woman whose husband had an affair notes:

> When a man has an affair, what is unbearable is the belief that someone else makes him happy and you are no longer the center of his world. But if you can overcome the initial pain and think reasonably, you may be able to see that you can stay within his world even if he loves another woman as well. When a woman marries a painter or a pilot, she does not demand that he give up his love of painting or of flight, since she understands that such love is necessary for the integrity of his happiness. Having another woman is perhaps similar.[40]

It is interesting to note that the opposite attitude exists as well: people who prefer their work to their partners may also provoke some sort of jealousy.

A liberal attitude toward romantic affairs is more rare in offline circumstances where two simultaneous relationships can cause more conflicts. Such conflicts are less evident in cyberlove, as its unique features may provide novel experiences that do not compete with prevailing offline experiences. Thus, the essential role of conversation in cyberlove may touch upon personal aspects not satisfied in offline relationships. One woman writes:

> I have a great husband and I love him dearly. As he does me. I am very sure he has never cheated on me. Well . . . I met someone online. I could talk and connect to him about things my husband will never be interested in, like poetry, karma, life, and death. We feel good together. Yes, by now we have had cybersex.[41]

People testify that online affairs have opened other ways to use their mind and even to make them better people.

The Internet greatly facilitates the option of having a few simultaneous relationships in a convenient, confidential, and relatively safe environment. There are various ways of utilizing this option. Thus, some people may pursue online affairs only at those times when they are temporarily dissatisfied with their offline relationship; others may pursue them when they temporarily want to experience intense sexual excitement. Others may participate in online affairs as a means of learning about and exploring sexual experiences.

Having cybersex with the awareness and knowledge of the offline partner provides a novel type of excitement to marriage. Consider, for instance, the following testimony: **"I personally get turned on by watching my wife having cybersex with another person. Just thinking that there's a guy somewhere feeling himself due to her excites me."** Perhaps because of overfamiliarity, this man has so forgotten his wife's sexual attractiveness that the mere knowledge that another man responds to her is sufficient to excite him. The practice of sexual activity between threesomes offline is different from this cybering since such offline activity involves actual physical sex and is less accessible.

Two major types of issue arise from the practice of an online affair in addition to the primary offline affair: one is moral, the other emotional. From a moral perspective, the issue is whether having an affair that is limited to cyberspace is morally wrong. The emotional issue concerns both the emotional impact of an online affair upon our attitude toward the offline partner and the ability to resist emotional temptations that may lead us to cross the boundaries between our on- and offline worlds. The emotional issue appears more significant than the moral one.

I have discussed the moral issue in the previous chapter, where I suggested that chatting is cheating when it is done without the knowledge of the primary partner. Since morality is mainly concerned with not hurting other people, such a deception may hurt your partner. However, when two people in a committed relationship agree that one or both of them will have cybersex, no harm seems to be done to anyone. As a married man argues:

> I strongly believe that if you're open and honest about what you are doing with your mate there should be no problems. However if you try and hide it, that could lead to some serious problems. As with anything in life, honesty is the best policy! I believe if you're honest and open with it, it could be exciting for both people.

A 43-year-old woman voices a similar attitude:

> If both partners are honest with each other about what they are doing, it could be very exciting to watch one's lover becoming aroused through the words of another person. I enjoy seeing my lover receive pleasure, and I would watch with delight! Then, while he was enjoying his conversation online, I could play with him, and do the actions that the person on the screen was doing to him. I think it would be fascinating!

Honesty, which is a key element here, should also be part of the relationship with the online lover. In this regard, a married person notes: **"I do not think of cybersex as cheating. It's just harmless fantasy, as long as the other person doesn't get the wrong idea. I enjoy it, it adds spice to my significant other at home. To me, cybersex is no different from reading novels."**

Candor is indeed beneficial providing the other partner can live with it; otherwise, such honesty may be harmful. Consider the following testimony of a 45-year-old man: **"I think a cyberaffair is cheating when it is hurtful to the other partner. I am currently in a cyberaffair with a woman who lives very far away, but my wife knows how I feel about her, because I told her, and she was hurt. But I continue to do it."** It is debatable whether honesty is the best policy in these circumstances.

Some people may disagree with the permissive view assuming that online affairs that are accepted by all involved parties are not morally wrong. However, taking into account the prevailing permissive attitudes in current society, this view is likely to be acknowledged, if not always approved of, by many people. The major issue arising from such a view is emotional: can people keep all aspects of their affair within online boundaries? Will such an arrangement not hurt the emotional bonds connecting the couple? These are difficult questions to answer.

The circumstances of cyberspace conveniently separate the online affair from the offline relationship by offering natural and clearly marked boundaries between the two relationships – that is, the boundaries of cyberspace. Cyberspace can also help to delineate clearer boundaries between different types of personal relationships, such as romantic and sexual. A 33-year-old married woman comments:

> I don't think cybersex is cheating if you can keep it on the computer and not let it move into real life. If it's kept strictly on the computer, if there's no physical touching, it's a good way to act out fantasies of being with someone new, being with a stranger, etc. without actually doing it. People just have to be very careful because it can be very tempting to make the online thing a real thing and there are always people throwing the temptation at you.

Despite the presence of clear boundaries, it is extremely difficult to remain within their limits. One woman remarks: **"I found myself truly surprised that mere characters on a keyboard could carry with them such an erotic and emotional charge. But the guy was married and although we did establish ground rules, I ended up 'coloring outside the lines' in a way I never thought I would."** A married woman recalls her unsuccessful attempt to keep cybersex within the online boundaries:

> We had all the proper conversations an average, educated couple would have on the "rules" of cybering. We both enjoyed the stimulation of new encounters and fully understood that it was never to go any further than just fun!!! Unfortunately, reality is a bitter pill to swallow. Now, two years later, with a broken heart, one year separation, countless tears, and the dejection of knowing that even the best intentions do not prevent the biggest mistakes, I cannot help but to come to the hard core conclusion that cybering IS cheating. I don't care what means people use to justify their online activities, people are just that, people!!! and as long as the human factor comes into an activity that falls slightly outside of the "rules," someone is going to get hurt!

As suggested in a previous chapter, being happy is not sufficient if we can conceive of a situation in which we might be happier. The pleasure induced by cybersex is not sufficient if we can envisage a greater pleasure in offline sex or in serious romantic (offline or online) relationships. Hence, it is extremely difficult to keep the following advice from a woman practicing cybersex: **"Type one handed if you like, just don't make it an emotional relationship."**[42] Drifting into serious personal and emotional involvement is natural when participants enjoy their cybersex immensely. In such circumstances, the online affair gets (metaphorically and literally) out of hand. A 39-year-old married woman who initially had cybersex without her husband's knowledge and then, later, while her husband watched her, writes: "My problem is that I also want a bond with my sexual partner, as many women do, and that makes the issue more complicated." Likewise, another married woman who does not hide her cybersex from her husband testifies: "I would rather not have different partners all of the time. Sex of any kind is important to me, but I prefer not to be a 'cyber slut.' I would rather find someone who I can get to know and with whom I can develop a sincere and caring friendship." Many people are carried away and, before they know it, find themselves in an emotional affair. In cyberspace, people are easily carried away and can misunderstand the nature of the environment they are in or underestimate its risks. Like drugs, the Internet affords easy access to pleasure, which in the long run may cause great distress or compulsive behavior.

The practice of "whetting your appetite outside while eating at home" may then not be suitable for all couples in all circumstances. Some may uphold marriage's monopoly on sex from the moment of their vows until death; others may not apply that monopoly to cyberspace. Others may stick to the good old-fashioned practice of proclaimed monogamy and clandestine adultery. Still others may adopt an open relationship in which sexual exclusivity is not demanded.

The failure of open marriage in the sixties is an indication of the difficulties inherent in maintaining multiple relationships. Love is both exclusive and comprehensive – the object of love has a unique status and it also requires full attention. Having multiple lovers may make it impossible to retain this exclusivity, which would lead to a concomitant reduction in the intensity of emotions. The lack of a firm commitment might endanger the comprehensive nature of love and raise questions about whether this is a deep romantic relationship.

Cyberspace offers an environment in which the major traditional concerns about romantic exclusivity are reduced, but do not disappear. Cyberlove does not threaten paternity, does not transmit diseases, and does not divert physical resources from offline relationships. However, mental resources such as time and attention are invested in an online relationship and hence can harm the primary offline relationship.

Cyberadultery occupies a midpoint between adulterous fantasies and actual adulterous affairs. This may encourage people who would never get involved in an actual adulterous affair to participate in an activity that is more than mere fantasy, but less than actual adultery. However, this may also divert those who might become involved in actual adultery from doing so, as they have a more moral and less dangerous alternative. From this perspective, it is not evident that cyberspace will necessarily increase the net weight of "sexual sins" in the world – assuming that online affairs are lesser sins than offline affairs. The validity of this conclusion depends on whether the move from actual adultery to online adultery becomes less common than the move from adulterous fantasies to online affairs. At the point on the morality scale where cyberadultery is located, the slope is very slippery; at this point, people can easily slide downhill, to where actual adultery is located. Indeed, there is some initial evidence indicating that cyberadultery is leading to an increased number of divorces.[43]

In light of the fact that the Internet facilitates greater access to infidelity and adultery at lower costs and lower risk, we should expect further modifications in moral and social norms. Such modifications may legitimize some practices currently considered as improper, and especially those prevailing in cyberspace. Adopting such norms may enable marriage to become at least as sexually satisfying as other forms of relationship.

Greater romantic flexibility

Q: Did you ever stay all night with this man in New York?
A: I refuse to answer that question.
Q: Did you ever stay all night with this man in Chicago?
A: I refuse to answer that question.
Q: Did you ever stay all night with this man in Miami?
A: No.

An actual court transcript

Marriage's monopoly on sex has been violated throughout history by extramarital affairs, but these were typically secret and contrary to prevailing norms. A normative change in this monopoly took place in the mid to late twentieth century and can be seen in the currently widely accepted practice of premarital and nonmarital relationships. The next step in the sexual revolution will perhaps normatively legitimize some violations of the sexual monopoly within marriage itself. The seeds of this step are already evident in open marriages and other forms of alternative relationship. More limited changes are those that overlook what are considered to be minor violations of the monopoly. Thus, couples may not object to extramarital affairs in certain circumstances, such as when one of them is abroad; in this way, no daily deception is practiced and the affair does not interfere with the family routine. Likewise, for some people their spouse's extramarital affair has limited emotional significance as long as they and other people do not know about it. Accordingly, people may prefer not to hear about their partner's affair – as long as they do not know about it, it is not emotionally real for them.

The practice of whetting your appetite outside while eating at home is a significant element in the process of violating marriage's monopoly on sex. As cybersex is seen as a lesser sin – since it can be considered merely a process of talking that involves no actual physical encounter – some offline partners will tolerate or even support it. Letting your partner know about, and even watch, your sexual activity with another person is significant in the sense that the committed couple knowingly accepts that sexual exclusivity is not a one-degree category that should never be violated. Sexual exclusivity is thus seen as a continuum, and, in some circumstances, certain points along that continuum may be violated. Such an attitude may solve the problem of change in the stability–change conflict and the emotional advantages of stability and shared history will become more evident, thereby increasing overall life satisfaction.

Violations of marriage's monopoly on sex are more frequent in cyberspace, which enables participants to conduct several online affairs while still maintaining the primary offline relationship. People may have an online relationship that is different in nature from their offline relationship, and hence the two may not be in conflict – at least not significantly enough to force the termination of one of them. If the offline relationship is more pragmatic, with only a dash of romance, the online affair may be full of romance and with little or no practical implications. One relationship may be merely and entirely sexual, while in the other the sexual aspect may be marginal. Since the two types of relationship fulfill different needs, their coexistence may be beneficial.

In order to reduce the risk of ruining their primary offline relationship, some married people may accept their partner having an online sexual affair, but not an online romantic affair. Others may further limit the sexual affair to a one-night cyberstand. All such limitations are intended to minimize the harm done to the primary relationship. It seems, however, that a more substantial change in our emotional makeup is required for coping with these sexual opportunities while still maintaining some stability in the primary relationship. A woman, married for twenty years and having cybersex with a man who has been married for thirty years, says: "I told myself that cybersex is adultery, sin, etc. and for a while I would feel guilty. But I have never felt guilty enough to stop talking to him. I will never be sorry that I have these feelings for him."[44] Overcoming the discrepancies between moral norms and emotional responses requires a long social and personal process of emotional and moral development.

It should be clear by now that there is no single solution to the stability–change conflict. Certain solutions may be more suitable for some people; different ones will suit others. Some people's marriages may be happy and filled with the thrill of romance so that neither spouse needs outside stimulation; some may employ the classic solution of proclaimed monogamy with clandestine adultery; some may choose the cohabitation route, and still others may choose to remain single. Other people may choose serial monogamous marriage – they may choose to marry, then divorce, then marry and divorce again. These choices can be found in heterosexual, homosexual, and bisexual relationships.

The Internet greatly encourages such enhanced flexibility and in particular the conjunction of a few options at the same time. As one woman says: "I don't cyber with men; I am bi, and I prefer to explore that side of myself via the web. I assumed that this would make my boyfriend more accepting of my cyber hobby." The Internet facilitates all types of sexual and romantic behavior – this is true concerning solitary and communal sex, orgies, bi- and homosexual relationships, and superficial and profound romantic relationships. Thus, one man notes: "My wife and I have been having cybersex for quite a while now and it has really made our sex life better and we are starting to try many new things. We are considering meeting some of our contacts personally as we are both bi-curious."

The Internet presents a serious threat to monogamous relationships in general, and marriage in particular, since it facilitates not merely pleasurable sexual activities but deep romantic relationships as well. A one-night cyberstand is more available and easier to keep secret, and people are not oblivious to this advantage. On the other hand, the conditions for nourishing a deep loving relationship have also been improved. The Internet provides a most enjoyable and efficient means by which various people get to know each other intimately without the distractions of external factors, such as appearance, age, geographical distance, race, nationality, religion, or marital status. This will increase the number of international, intercultural, and interreligious marriages, ultimately modifying global social norms – in the main, making them more flexible.[45]

In the near future, we shall witness a significant increase in the low-cost and low-risk sexual opportunities that are accessible to all types of people. Accordingly, online infidelity and adultery will drastically increase and will often have a negative impact on marital relationships. The quantitative increase in online extramarital affairs may cause a qualitative change in the agreed meaning of "infidelity" and "adultery." The criteria for inclusion within these categories will become more limited.

The Internet is not unique in providing opportunities for meaningful romances and also superficial sexual affairs; its main novelty is that it offers an environment in which – given a wise and moderate use of cyberspace – both types of relationship can coexist. Indeed, initial findings suggest that Internet users who engage in online chats are usually people who are satisfied with their offline social relations and, for them, socializing in online chat rooms does not substitute for offline emotional or social needs; rather, it complements their offline relations.[46]

In addition to acceptable boundaries, the greater romantic flexibility that cyberspace affords needs to be placed within an order of priority. In such an order, online affairs should be granted lower priority than the offline, committed relationship. As one woman says: "I have had many relationships with people online, all types. But I always put the person who is in front of me on a higher priority level. And everyone online should expect to be relegated to second priority."[47]

The question of whether offline romantic relationships will withstand the online revolution is somewhat similar to the question asked in the 1960s: would people still have sexual fantasies after the sexual revolution of that time? It is also similar to the question of whether marriage will survive the high rate of divorce or whether people will retain any privacy after the current information revolution. I believe the answer to all these questions is yes, as they refer to significant aspects of human life: face-to-face, tangible relationships, fantasies, and privacy. Revolutions typically modify, but do not eliminate, the relevant basic human characteristics that generate the demand for these aspects.

There are many ways in which the Internet has extended our options in the way in which we pursue romance. Although cybersex may be compared to phone sex, the Internet gives us an alternative to face-to-face relationships and provides us with opportunities that the telephone cannot. The Internet makes the fulfillment of our desires easier and hence online affairs have become more prevalent. The Internet is likely to increase romantic and sexual activities, as it provides easy, low-cost, and low-risk circumstances for them. We will see an increase in all such cyberactivities: superficial sex, serious romance, and all the different shades of flirtation.

The increase in flirtation will probably be a most significant element of the online romantic revolution, as online affairs are similar to flirting in many respects. Thus, neither involve actual, physical sex, but both are tinged with sexual nuances; both are relaxing and enjoyable romantic activities that encourage positive attitudes toward others. Indeed, surveys indicate that about half of workers flirt online while on the job; many of them are in committed relationships.[48] These numbers are likely to increase. This new kind of flirting is in a sense a revival of the courtly love invented by the troubadours and characterized as a kind of "tender, extramarital flirtation which (ideally) was sexually unconsummated and which, therefore, made the chaste lovers more noble and virtuous."[49]

The Internet encourages other types of changes in romantic relationships. Thus, the prominence of verbal communication in online affairs is likely to increase the value placed on intellectual abilities in romantic interactions. Accordingly, online romances are likely to depend more on the combination of emotions and intelligence, including verbal and intellectual features such as wit, a sense of humor, and good articulation. The value of personal characteristics – as compared to the value of external appearance – will probably increase. The change may have rather less impact once most computers are equipped with a Webcam, but it will be evident even then as long as distant online relationships continue to be based upon written text.

It is highly unlikely that, in the future, either offline or online romantic relationships will cease to play an important role in people's lives. The increased lure of the Net lowers the likelihood that those with access to the Net will restrict themselves solely to offline relationships. Because of the inherently incomplete nature of online relationships, satisfying offline relationships will continue to be considered as much more full and desirable. Learning to integrate cyberspace with actual-space in the romantic domain will be a major task for our society.

Concluding remarks

> There are times not to flirt. When you're sick. When you're with children. When you're on the witness stand.
>
> Joyce Jillson

Cyberspace currently attracts many types of people who, on the whole, have positive emotional experiences while surfing. It is likely that, in the future, a greater variety of people will enjoy such experiences. Today, different types of personalities gain different degrees of satisfaction from visiting cyberspace. If Internet designers were aware of these differences, the emotional satisfaction available on the Internet would increase.[50] The Internet would thus offer more diverse types of positive experiences to more people. However, the greater emotional excitement provided by the Net will also increase negative emotions. Accordingly, the Net will elicit a greater variety of contrasting emotional responses.

Cyberspace has a profound impact upon our emotional experiences. For one thing, it increases intense emotional experiences. So far, we have not observed the generation of new kinds of emotions, but this possibility should not be ruled out. It should be noted that the development of new types of emotions and the increase in the complexity of existing emotions have characterized our evolution from non-human animals to humans; nevertheless, in this evolutionary process none of the animal emotions ever completely disappeared. It is not clear yet whether online relationships will generate such significant changes in our emotional life.

I have discussed several major types of online romantic relationship: (a) online relationships intended to find an offline sexual or romantic partner; (b) enjoyable (though superficial) cyberflirting and cybersex; and (c) serious online romantic relationships. These relationships will become more prevalent in the near future and even more so in the more remote one when most of the population will have begun their online activities in their early youth.

Integrating offline and online relationships in a way that will increase both satisfaction from serious personal relationships and excitement from more transitory relationships is a great challenge for society in general and for specific individuals in particular. Unlike previous periods, when humans adapted to change through evolutionary processes, today these changes occur too rapidly for evolutionary processes to catch up. We cannot wait for millions of years while such processes allow us to adjust to our new environment. A more conscious and deliberate strategy is required.

The Internet has dramatically changed the romantic domain; this process will accelerate in the future. Such changes will inevitably modify present social forms such as marriage and cohabitation, and current romantic practices relating to courtship, casual sex, committed romantic relationships, and romantic exclusivity. We can expect further relaxation of social and moral norms; this process should not be considered a threat, as it is not online changes that endanger romantic relationships, but our inability to adapt.

The relaxation of such norms will be particularly evident in matters pertaining to romantic exclusivity. It will be difficult to avoid the vast amount of available tempting alternatives entirely. The notion of "betrayal" will become less common in connection with romantic affairs. Together with the increase in romantic flexibility, the values placed upon stability and stronger commitment will increase as well. The chaotic and dynamic nature of cyberspace will never replace the more stable nature of actual-space, as we cannot live in complete chaos: like other types of meaning, emotional meaning presupposes some kind of stable background against which meaning is generated. Nevertheless, the romantic realm will become more dynamic and it will be more difficult to achieve the emotional advantages of a stable romantic framework.

The test of the Internet will be whether it can complement ordinary romantic activities, just as the telephone complements ordinary social activities, or whether it will merely replace them with less valuable activities, as the television frequently does. Society faces a great challenge if it is to integrate cyberspace successfully into our romantic relationships. It also faces great danger, for, if we fail to meet that challenge, it will cost us dearly.

Notes

Quotations from people describing their online experiences are taken either from websites or from books about online affairs; they are quoted here as they were originally written, except for minor grammatical and stylistic changes and certain abbreviations.

1 The seductive space

1. On these issues, see also Fink, 1999: 23, 191–194.
2. Wysocki, 1998.
3. Fink, 1999: 192–194; Lombard & Ditton, 1997.
4. Csikszentmihalyi, 1990: 59–62.
5. Cited in Semans & Winks, 1999: 166.
6. Marx, 1869: 15.
7. Cited in Semans & Winks, 1999: 159.
8. www.infidelity-infidelity.com, Stories.
9. The survey was done by Dateable.com in 2000.
10. Cited in Semans & Winks, 1999: 169.
11. Doering, 2000.
12. www.infidelity-infidelity.com, Stories.
13. Hawaii Chat Universe, www.lovelife.com, Cyber Love Stories, "You're the one."
14. Cited in Levine, 1998: 135–136.
15. C. Worthington, "Making love in cyberspace," *Independent on Sunday*, October 6, 1996.
16. *Self-help Magazine*, www.shpm.com/articles/cyber_romance/cbrsxsrv.html.
17. See also Joinson, 2003: 6–19.
18. www.clitical.com/how_to/cybersex.php, Cyber sex.
19. Gwinnell, 1998: ch. 1.
20. Standage, 1998: ch. 8.
21. Maheu & Subotnik, 2001: 60.
22. B. A. T. Brown & Perry, 2000; Gerstel & Gross, 1984: 58; Joinson, 2003: 23, 165; J. W. Moore, 2002: 44–45.
23. DeAngelo, 2002.
24. Whitty & Gavin, 2001: 627.

25. Cited in Maheu & Subotnik, 2001: 59.
26. Cited in Wysocki, 1998.
27. Semans & Winks, 1999: 165.
28. CollegeDates.com, "What?????" December 15, 1999.
29. Joan Elizabeth Lloyd's website, www.joanelloyd.com/fbcheat.htm.
30. Goodson et al., 2000: 253.
31. Kraut et al., 1998; see also Graham, 1999: 33–35.
32. Kraut et al., 1998.
33. N. H. Nie et al., 2002: 231; Robinson et al., 2002.
34. For the negative influences, see, e.g., J. N. Cummings et al., 2002; Kiesler et al., 1984; Kraut et al., 1998; N. H. Nie, 2001; N. H. Nie et al., 2002. The positive influences are found, e.g., in Amichai-Hamburger & Ben-Artzi, 2003; Kraut et al., 2002; LaRose et al., 2001; McKenna et al., 2002; R. H. Shaw & Gant, 2002a; Wellman & Haythornthwaite, 2002. See also Birnie & Horvath, 2002; Joinson, 2003: ch. 2; Whitty & Gavin, 2001.
35. Birnie & Horvath, 2002; Peris et al., 2002.
36. Chen et al., 2002; Copher et al., 2002; Hampton & Wellman, 2002; Katz & Rice, 2002; Quan-Haase et al., 2002; Robinson et al., 2002.
37. Mobile SMS, www.mobilesms.com/main.asp.
38. Eldridge & Grinter, 2001; Schiano et al., 2002.
39. Rheingold, 2002: 195–196.
40. Ibid.: 26.
41. Ibid.: 164–166, 194.
42. Joinson, 2003: 164–165.
43. Katz & Rice, 2002. The idea that cyberspace is egalitarian is disputable; see, e.g., Ebo, 1998; Fink, 1999: 256–261; Semans & Winks, 1999: 174.
44. www.infidelity-infidelity.com, Stories.
45. L. H. Shaw & Gant, 2002b; Weiser, 2000.
46. www.infidelity-infidelity.com, Stories.
47. Lovingyou.com, "An online love."
48. Gloria G. Brame, "How to have cybersex: Boot up and turn on," http://gloriabrame.com/glory/journ7.htm.
49. In an interview in the *Jerusalem Post Magazine*, August 16, 2002; see also Fein & Schneider, 2002.
50. For such implications concerning gender differences, see, e.g., Gergen, 1991: 143; see also Fink, 1999: 168–170.
51. Cooper speaks about the three A's responsible for the lure of the Net: accessibility, affordability, and anonymity (A. Cooper et al., 1999; A. Cooper et al., 2000; see also J. Schneider & Weiss, 2001: 13–16). I have combined accessibility and affordability into the notion of "availability" and added the factors of imagination and interactivity. Barak & Fisher (2002) propose to add to Cooper's list acceptability and aloneness. Young (Young et al., 2000) has proposed that anonymity, convenience, and escape are the major features responsible for cyber sexual addiction.
52. See also Dreyfus, 2001.
53. Cited in Semans & Winks, 1999: 169.
54. Cited in Levine, 1998: 124.
55. Buss, 1994: 44.
56. Robinson et al., 2002.

57. www.infidelity-infidelity.com, Stories.
58. A. Cooper & Sportolari, 1997; Doering, 2000, 2002; Gwinnell, 1998; Levine, 1998.
59. www.infidelity-infidelity.com, Stories.
60. www.infidelity-infidelity.com, Stories.
61. *Self-help Magazine*, www.selfhelpmagazine.com/cgibin/cyber_survey.cgi?congo.
62. Sunstein, 2001.
63. The survey was commissioned by the leading UK children's charity NCH, and the results were announced on April 15, 2002; see www.nchafc.org.uk/news/index1.asp?auto194.
64. Copher et al., 2002.
65. Joan Elizabeth Lloyd's website, www.joanelloyd.com/fbcheat.htm; www.geocities.com/Paris/6278/, "Take it slow."

2 The paradoxical nature of online relationships

1. Cairncross, 1997; Kellerman, 2002.
2. Hawaii Chat Universe, www.lovelife.com, Cyber Love Stories, "Anonymous 2."
3. Csikszentmihalyi, 1990: 53; Maheu & Subotnik, 2001: 10.
4. Joinson, 2003: 168–169; McKenna & Bargh, 2000; McKenna et al., 2001.
5. Cyberlove101.com, "I can't function till I check my email"; Hawaii Chat Universe, www.lovelife.com, Cyber Love Stories, "Distant love"; Gloria G. Brame, "How to have cybersex: Boot up and turn on," http://gloria-brame.com/glory/journ7.htm; Cyber-Relations, www.geocities.com/Paris/6278/, Immigrating. See also Ron Polland, "Internet romance: Mystique or mistake," Mystique 4, www.myloveneeds.com.
6. For review and critique, see Baym, 2002.
7. Tidwell & Walther, 2002.
8. Donn & Sherman, 2002; Lea & Spears, 1995; Savicki & Kelley, 2000; Sherman, 2001; Whitty, 2002; Whitty & Gavin, 2001.
9. This term was coined by Azy Barak (personal communication, March 15, 2003).
10. The above citations are from Hawaii Chat Universe, www.lovelife.com, Cyber Love Stories, "Married but not to each other," "Love online," "Maggie," and "Two married people"; and Lovingyou.com, "My hero."
11. Danet, 2001: 12, 90–94, ch. 2.
12. Joinson, 2003: 187–191; O'Sullivan, 2000.
13. Cited in Miller & Slater, 2000: 68.
14. Joinson, 2001, 2003: 130–133; Parks & Floyd, 1996; Tidwell & Walther, 2002.
15. Ava Cadell, "Is cybersex being unfaithful?" www.gaynetsa.co.za/jan03/is_cybersex_being_unfaithful.htm.
16. Joan Elizabeth Lloyd's website, www.joanelloyd.com/fbcheat.htm.
17. Baxter & Wilmot, 1985; McKenna et al., 2001.
18. Lovingyou.com, "My hero."
19. Dindia, 1998.
20. Ibid., 1998.

21. Gwinnell, 1998: 94.
22. McKenna et al., 2002; Rubin, 1975.
23. Bader, 2002: 265; see also Merkle & Richardson, 2000; Wysocki, 1998.
24. Danet, 2001: 33.
25. McKenna et al., 2002.
26. Hawaii Chat Universe, www.lovelife.com, Cyber Love Stories, "Lady Shelby."
27. "Favorite ways to flirt, date and interact online revealed in Lycos Matchmaker Survey," *Business Wire*, January 28, 2002.
28. Cited in Gwinnell, 1998: 73.
29. Amichai-Hamburger, 2002.
30. Baker, 2002; Byrne, 1997.
31. Cited in Mary E. Behr, "High-tech sex," *PC Magazine*, September 4, 2001.
32. Barry Fox, "I know what you're feeling," *New Scientist*, June 29, 2002.
33. Suler, "The online disinhibition effect," in Suler, 2003.
34. Cited in Gwinnell, 1998: 32; Maheu & Subotnik, 2001: 3; Gerlander & Takala, 1997.
35. Cooper & Sportolari, 1997; Lea & Spears, 1995; McKenna et al., 2002; Merkle & Richardson, 2000; Schneider & Weiss, 2001: 63; Tidwell & Walther, 2002; Walther & Burgoon, 1992.
36. Hawaii Chat Universe, www.lovelife.com, Cyber Love Stories, "Lady Shelby," "Alice."
37. Berger, 1979; Tidwell & Walther, 2002.
38. Collings & Miller, 1994: 459.
39. Cited in Grounder Productions, www.grounder.com/cyber.htm.
40. Hawaii Chat Universe, www.lovelife.com, Cyber Love Stories, "Ladies beware."
41. Cooper et al., 2000; Cornwell & Lundgren, 2001; see also Joinson, 2003: 77–82; Schneider & Weiss, 2001: 14.
42. Whitty, 2002; Whitty & Gavin, 2001.
43. Bargh et al., 2002; McKenna et al., 2002.
44. www.wildxangel.come, "Stories ending in marriage," August 1998.
45. Buss, 1994: 44.
46. Stengel, 2000: 273; Whitty, 2002.
47. Joan Elizabeth Lloyd's website, www.joanelloyd.com/fbcheat.htm.
48. Joinson, 1998, 2003.
49. Adamse & Motta, 2000: 14.
50. Cited in Levine, 1998: 128.
51. Merkle & Richardson, 2000.
52. Cyber-Relations, www.geocities.com/Paris/6278/, Suddenly it stopped.
53. Hawaii Chat Universe, www.lovelife.com, Cyber Love Stories, "Me & Todd," "Love online," "Distant love," "Strawberry and Renfield"; Cyber-Relations, www.geocities.com/Paris/6278/, "Languages connect"; iVillage.com, emotional health, "Emotionally attached to cybersex partner."
54. www.infidelity-infidelity.com, Stories.
55. Joan Elizabeth Lloyd's website, www.joanelloyd.com/fbcheat.htm; Gwinnell, 1998: 72.
56. *Self-help Magazine*, www.shpm.com/articles/cyber_romance/cbrsxsrv.html.
57. *Self-help Magazine*, www.selfhelpmagazine.com/cgibin/cyber_survey.cgi? congo&monthMarch&year2002.

58. Cyberlove101.com, "I can't function till I check my email."
59. Bader, 2002: 266–269.
60. Gerstel & Gross, 1984: 15–17.
61. Rohlfing, 1995: 173.
62. Kirkendall & Gravatt, 1984: 51; Murstein, 1976.
63. Hess, 2000.
64. Gerstel & Gross, 1984; Rohlfing, 1995.
65. Joinson, 2003: 79–82; Rohlfing, 1995; Stafford & Reske, 1990; Stephen, 1986.
66. www.geocities.com/Paris/6278/, "Loving two people?"
67. Boym, 2001: xiii–xvi.

3 Emotions on the Net

1. For a more detailed discussion, see Ben-Ze'ev, 2000.
2. Buss, 1994; Metts et al., 1998.
3. *Self-help Magazine*, www.selfhelpmagazine.com/cgibin/cyber_survey.cgi?progo.
4. Lea & Spears, 1995: 228.
5. *Self-help Magazine*, www.selfhelpmagazine.com/cgibin/cyber_survey.cgi?progo.
6. Hawaii Chat Universe, www.lovelife.com, Cyber Love Stories, "Dream everlasting."
7. Joan Elizabeth Lloyd's website, www.joanelloyd.com/fbcheat.htm.
8. Gwinnell, 1998: 122–123.
9. Nussbaum, 2001.
10. Maheu & Subotnik, 2001: 5, 9.
11. www.infidelity-infidelity.com, Stories.
12. www.sexyads.net/tsearch.html.
13. Rusbult et al., 1986.
14. Lovingyou.com, Love at 1st type.
15. Joan Elizabeth Lloyd's website, www.joanelloyd.com.
16. Cited in Semans & Winks, 1999: 172.
17. Gilboa & Revelle, 1994.
18. Gwinnell, 1998: 104.
19. Joan Elizabeth Lloyd's website, www.joanelloyd.com/fbcheat.htm.
20. The citations are from iVillage.com, emotional health, "Can I trust Internet friend?"; Gwinnell, 1998: 153; Schneider & Weiss, 2001: 85.
21. Joan Elizabeth Lloyd's website, www.joanelloyd.com.
22. Reeves & Nass, 1996.
23. Joan Elizabeth Lloyd's website, www.joanelloyd.com.
24. Gwinnell, 1998: 69–70.
25. Joan Elizabeth Lloyd's website, www.joanelloyd.com.
26. Ben-Ze'ev, 1993, 2003a, 2003b.
27. Semans & Winks, 1999: 167; Hawaii Chat Universe, www.lovelife.com, Cyber Love Stories, "Sherri Hilts."
28. CollegeDates.com, "Not cheating?" December 15, 1999.
29. Canada Singles Connection, www.canadasingles.net, "Stories of Internet Adultery," March 1999.

30. Anil Ananthaswamy,"X-rated brains," *New Scientist*, May 25, 2002.
31. Cyber-Relations, www.geocities.com/Paris/6278/, Tidal waves.
32. Ben-Ze'ev, 2000: 175–181, 2003a.
33. P. Johnson, 1999.
34. http://SMH.com.au, January 27, 2003.
35. J. W. Moore, 2002: 43.
36. Joinson, 2003: ch. 1.
37. Capulet, 1998: 85–92, 102; Danet, 2001: 53–54; Rabin, 1999: 29–31; Shea, 1997; Lorryhew Cyberlove, www.e-my.net.my/kl/lorryman/cybersex.htm, Cybersex etiquette.
38. Stengel, 2000: 272.

4 Online imagination

1. See also Ben-Ze'ev, 2000: ch. 7.
2. Fitness & Fletcher, 1993.
3. Fitzpatrick, 1987; Murray et al., 1996: 1178; Rusbult et al., 2000.
4. Kant, 1797: section 47, 1803: 73, 78–79.
5. Lovingyou.com, "If this is a dream, let me sleep forever."
6. Cited in Adamse & Motta, 2000: 141.
7. Ibid.: 53.
8. Levine, 1998: 20.
9. Joan Elizabeth Lloyd's website, www.joanelloyd.com; Levine, 1998: 123.
10. Bargh et al., 2002; Semans & Winks, 1999: xiv.
11. Danet, 2001: 7–10; see also Whitty, 2003.
12. Cook & McHenry, 1978: 132–5; Levine, 2000; Tesser & Paulhus, 1976.
13. Joan Elizabeth Lloyd's website, www.joanelloyd.com/fbcheat.htm.
14. Cited in Levine, 1998: 124.
15. Cited in Young, 2001: 34–35.
16. Bader, 2002: 267.
17. Adamse & Motta, 2000: 139, 155–158.
18. Levine, 1998: 105.
19. Fromm, 1956: 52.
20. Cyber-Relations, www.geocities.com/Paris/6278/, Bryan & June.
21. Cited in Adamse & Motta, 2000: 135–136.
22. Joan Elizabeth Lloyd's website, www.joanelloyd.com/fbcheat.htm.
23. Adamse & Motta, 2000: 141–144.
24. Gwinnell, 1998: 28.
25. Cyberlove101.com, Story 20.
26. Dreyfus, 2001: ch. 4.
27. Joan Elizabeth Lloyd's website, www.joanelloyd.com/fbcheat.htm; www.infidelity-infidelity.com, Stories.
28. Cited in Schneider & Weiss, 2001: 54.
29. Cited in Semans & Winks, 1999: 172.
30. Ron Polland, "Internet romance: Mystique or mistake," Mistake 4, www.myloveneeds.com.
31. Seiden, 2001.
32. Ibid.

33. Ben-Ze'ev, 2000: 493–495; Gilovich & Medvec, 1995.
34. Tykocinski, 2001.
35. *Self-help Magazine*, www.shpm.com/articles/cyber_romance/cbrsxsrv.html.
36. Amichai-Hamburger, 2003.

5 Online privacy and emotional closeness

1. DeCew, 1997: 56–58.
2. Schoeman, 1992: 8, 1994: 78.
3. See also DeCew, 1997: 47–50.
4. C. D. Schneider, 1977: 49.
5. Sykes, 1999: 187.
6. Schoeman, 1994: 74.
7. See also Brin, 1998; Sykes, 1999: 241.
8. Fitzpatrick, 1987: 131; Vittengl & Holt, 2000.
9. Fitzpatrick, 1987: 131–132, 137.
10. Arendt, 1958: 47, 63; cited in C. D. Schneider, 1977: 41–42.
11. Joan Elizabeth Lloyd's website, www.joanelloyd.com/fbcheat.htm.
12. Jonathan Rauch, "Washington diarist: High lying," *New Republic*, April 20, 1998; cited in Sykes, 1999: 215.
13. Laurenceau & Feldman-Barrett, 1998.
14. Gwinnell, 1998: 78.
15. Joan Elizabeth Lloyd's website, www.joanelloyd.com/fbcheat.htm.
16. Cited in Sykes, 1999: 188.
17. Barbalet, 1998: 117–120.
18. Sykes, 1999: 10, 187.
19. Ibid.: 15–16; see also Baumeister, 1986.
20. Sykes, 1999: 16.
21. C. D. Schneider, 1977: 45.
22. See also Ben-Ze'ev, 2000: 182–184, 204–208.
23. Schulhofer, 1998: 60; the studies he refers to are Perper & Weis, 1987; Greer & Buss, 1994.
24. Schulhofer, 1998: 261–262.
25. Malamuth & Brown, 1994.
26. De Sousa, 1994: 28.
27. Biber et al., 2002.
28. De Sousa, 1994.
29. Brin, 1998; for a good discussion of his view, see Sykes, 1999: 238–245.
30. Etzioni, 1999: 214.
31. C. D. Schneider, 1977: 41.
32. Schoeman, 1992: 7; Sykes, 1999: 242–243.
33. Cited in Sykes, 1999: 22.
34. Ibid.: 5.
35. Ibid.: 192; see also 185–186.
36. Cyberlove101.com, Story 3, "The journey that leads to my new self."
37. Ben-Ze'ev, 2000: 512.
38. *Self-help Magazine*, www.selfhelpmagazine.com/cgibin/cyber_survey.cgi?progo.

6 Is it worth it?

1. See, e.g., *Metaphysics*, 1048b18ff., 1050a23ff.; *Nicomachean Ethics*, 1174a14ff. For further discussion and some relevant literature, see, e.g., Nussbaum, 1986: ch. 11.
2. De Sousa, 1987: 219.
3. Stengel, 2000: 17.
4. The notion of profound satisfaction is related to Aristotle's notion of human flourishing (*eudaimonia*). Human flourishing is something essentially dynamic, and fulfilling praiseworthy activities are its actual constituents. To engage in these activities is to be human. Human flourishing is not a temporary state of superficial pleasure; it refers to a longer period involving the fulfillment of the human species' natural capacities. Hence, it is most relevant for adults, who can fully exercise their natural capacities (see, e.g., J. M. Cooper, 1975: 89; Nussbaum, 1986: 6, and ch. 11; Stocker, 1990: 63). Csikszentmihalyi's notion of the optimal experience of flow is also relevant in this regard. He characterizes flow as "a self-contained activity, one that is done not with the expectation of some future benefit, but simply because the doing itself is the reward" (1990: 67). Someone who teaches children in order to turn them into good citizens is not engaging in such an activity, whereas someone who teaches them because she enjoys interacting with children is.
5. Nussbaum, 1986: 326–327.
6. Csikszentmihalyi, 1990: 53.
7. R. Brown, 1987: 24–30; Pitcher, 1965.
8. The research has been done by the Italian Institute for Interdisciplinary Psychology and is reported in *Ananova*, September 17, 2002.
9. *Ananova*, May 22, 2002.
10. *Ananova*, July 13, 2002.
11. Csikszentmihalyi, 1990: 100–103.
12. Gallup et al., 2002. Surprisingly, women who had sex with condoms were as depressed as those who abstained. The authors suggest that a chemical explanation may indicate that hormones and other chemicals in semen get into the woman's bloodstream and act like an anti-depressant.
13. Freedman, 1978; for further discussions on happiness, see Ben-Ze'ev, 2000: ch. 15.
14. Ben-Ze'ev, 2000: 456–458; Csikszentmihalyi, 1990.
15. Ben-Ze'ev, 2000: 450–452.
16. Cummins & Nistico, 2002.
17. Cummins & Nistico, 2002.
18. Langer, 1989; see also Ben-Ze'ev, 2000: 136–141.
19. Cummins & Nistico, 2002.
20. Ehrhardt et al., 2000.
21. www.marriedandlonely.org/married1.
22. Levine, 2000: 570.
23. Conley, 1999: 99.
24. Levine, 1998: 118, 2000.
25. Cyberlove101.com, Story 39, "An enchanting Belgian gentleman."
26. Lovingyou.com, "When we met."
27. Slater, 2002.

28. Hawaii Chat Universe, www.lovelife.com, Cyber Love Stories, "Christina," "Sweety."
29. Csikszentmihalyi, 1990: 49.
30. Hawaii Chat Universe, www.lovelife.com, Cyber Love Stories, "Maggie."
31. Wellman & Haythornthwaite, 2002: 28.
32. Ben-Ze'ev, 2000: 296.
33. Landman, 1993: 107–108.
34. Lovingyou.com, "Internet love can work."
35. Whitty & Gavin, 2001: 627.
36. Bargh et al., 2002.
37. Hawaii Chat Universe, www.lovelife.com, Cyber Love Stories, "Strawberry and Renfield."
38. Joan Elizabeth Lloyd's website, www.joanelloyd.com/fbcheat.htm.
39. Clanton, 1984: 15.
40. Cited in Adamse & Motta, 2000: 118.
41. Cited in Gwinnell, 1998: 28.
42. Cyber-Relations, www.geocities.com/Paris/6278/, "Love not lost."
43. Ibid.
44. Gwinnell, 1998: 100.
45. http://kampel.com/poetika/cyber.htm.
46. Gwinnell, 1998: 107.
47. Hawaii Chat Universe, www.lovelife.com, Cyber Love Stories, "Two married people, part 2."
48. Ben-Ze'ev, 2000: 126–131.

7 Flirting on- and offline

1. Ben-Ze'ev, 1994.
2. Danet, 2001: 25–26; Gwinnell, 1998: 25.
3. Cited in Levine, 1998: 19.
4. Hawaii Chat Universe, www.lovelife.com, Cyber Love Stories, "Pillow talk."
5. Lovingyou.com, "Where north meets south"; www.wildxangel.come, "Stories ending in marriage," "Campy & Notjustamom."
6. Illouz, 1997.
7. Cyberlove Seminars, www.bluejuice.com/cyberlove/story.html, Preparing for seduction.
8. Cyberlove101.com, Story 52, "Finding a partner on the Net?"; Canada Singles Connection, www.canadasingles.net, Stories of Internet Adultery, March 1999.
9. On the playful nature of cyberflirting, see Whitty, 2003; on the involvement of teasing in flirting, see Feinberg, 1996.
10. Miss Etiquette, Flirting etiquette, www.miss-etiquette.com/etiquette_advice.html. See also Feinberg, 1996.
11. www.cyber00.com/flirting/.
12. David N. Greenfield and Al Cooper (1998), Crossing the Line – On Line, *Self-help Magazine*, www.shpm.com/articles/cyber_romance/sexcross.html.
13. www.infidelity-infidelity.com, Stories.

14. The JFK Zone Forum, www.greenspun.com/bboard/fetch-msg.tcl?msg_id00Adsh.
15. Baym, 2002: 66.
16. Cited in Levine, 1998: 19–20.
17. Hawaii Chat Universe, www.lovelife.com/CLS/story124.html, Cyber Love Stories, "Dream everlasting."
18. The survey is reported in *Ananova*, June 13, 2002. On the value of flirting at the workplace, see also Spiegel, 1995; and Brenda P. Sunoo, "Flirting: Red flag or lost art," *Workforce*, June 2000.
19. Cited in Semans & Winks, 1999: 169.
20. Doering, 2002.
21. Capulet, 1998: 31.
22. Fein & Schneider, 2002: 144–145, 6.
23. Ibid.: 57, 95–98, 122–123, 127.
24. Ibid.: 81.
25. Ibid.: 50–51, 127.
26. Ibid.: 47–49.
27. Hometown.aol.com/VoodooCh1/duck.html.
28. Fein & Schneider, 2002: 37, 68, 87.
29. Lovingyou.com, "My unusual story but a wonderful real life one."
30. Baker, July, 1998.
31. Adamse & Motta, 2000: 135.
32. Wysocki, 1998.
33. See also Merkle & Richardson, 2000.
34. Lydon et al., 1997.
35. Baker, 2002; Byrne & Murnen, 1988; Dietz-Uhler & Bishop-Clark, 2001.
36. This claim is made by Allan Mazur from Syracuse University and is reported in "Think small if you want a man who won't run off with a younger woman," *New Scientist*, May 12, 2001.
37. McKenna et al., 2002.

8 Cyberlove

1. Ben-Ze'ev, 2000: ch. 14; Ortony et al., 1988.
2. Buss, 1994.
3. Etcoff, 1999: ch. 1.
4. Cited in Gwinnell, 1998: 98.
5. Hawaii Chat Universe, www.lovelife.com, Cyber Love Stories, "My soul mate."
6. Hawaii Chat Universe, www.lovelife.com, Cyber Love Stories, "Two married people."
7. Wallace, 1999: 138.
8. Cited in Gwinnell, 1998: 29–30.
9. The first quotation is from Lovingyou.com, "If it's the Lords will"; the second quotation is cited in Adamse & Motta, 2000: 55.
10. Capulet, 1998: 100.
11. Cited in Maheu & Subotnik, 2001: 36–37.
12. Scharlott & Christ, 1995.
13. Woll & Cozby, 1987; cited in Scharlott & Christ, 1995.

14. Cited in Gwinnell, 1998: 66.
15. www.chatcheaters.com/warning.htm, Warning signs of infidelity. The Cyberdating Home Page, www.cyberdatinghomepage.com, Story Archives 1.
16. Cyberlove101.com, Story 35, "Those who seek shall find."
17. Gergen et al., 1973; McKenna et al., 2002.
18. *Technology Review: MIT's Magazine of Innovation*, Forum – Love Online, October, ?2002.
19. Levine, 2000: 567–578.
20. Branwyn, 1993: 784; the former citation is from www.clitical.com/how_to/cybersex.php, Cyber sex.
21. Fromm, 1956: 28.
22. Cooper & Sportolari, 1997; Merkle & Richardson, 2000; Rheingold, 2000; Wysocki, 1998.
23. Epstein, May/June, 2002; Cole Kazdin, "Dr. Bachelor," www.salon.com/sex.feature/2002/07/01/epstein/index.html.
24. Schwartz, May/June, 2002.
25. Hawaii Chat Universe, www.lovelife.com, Cyber Love Stories, "Sherrie."
26. www.infidelity-infidelity.com, Stories.
27. Adamse & Motta, 2000: 107.
28. Joan Elizabeth Lloyd's website, www.joanelloyd.com/fbcheat.htm.
29. See, e.g., Brehm, 1992; see discussion in Levine, 2000.
30. Levine, 2000: 566.
31. Scharlott & Christ, 1995.
32. Murray et al., 1996; McKenna et al., 2002.
33. Lovingyou.com, "Keep wishing on a star."
34. Bargh et al., 2002; McKenna et al., 2002.
35. www.erotica-readers.com/ERA/I-Cybersex.htm, "Is cybersex adultery?"
36. Miller & Slater, 2000: 57.
37. Noller & Feeney, 2002: section 2.
38. The JFK Zone Forum, www.greenspun.com/bboard/fetch-msg.tcl?msg_id00Adsh.
39. Rusbult et al., 2000: 539.
40. Rusbult et al., 2000.
41. www.infidelity-infidelity.com, Stories; Lovingyou.com, "He opened my heart."
42. Levine, 2000.
43. Lovingyou.com, "Loving two people."
44. Buss, 1988; cited in Levine, 2000.
45. Lovingyou.com, "The man of my dreams"; Lust in Space, Story 53, http://members.tripod.com/~VixenOne/index.html.
46. Levine, 2000.
47. Lovingyou.com, "Man of my dreams"; "Nutty Irish guy and my English rose."
48. Cyberlove Seminars, www.bluejuice.com/cyberlove/story.html, "How we met online."
49. Gloria G. Brame: "How to have cybersex: Boot up and turn on," http://gloria-brame.com/glory/journ7.htm; Hawaii Chat Universe, www.lovelife.com, Cyber Love Stories, "Lady M," "Distant love"; Lovingyou.com, "Nutty Irish guy and my English rose."

50. Gladue & Delaney, 1990.
51. http://singles.wndmll.com/momhump.htm.
52. Ben-Ze'ev, 2000: 21–23; Buss, 1994: ch. 5; Etcoff, 1999: 234–235; M. M. Moore & Butler, 1989; Thompson, 1983:12.
53. Lea & Spears, 1995.
54. Cooper & Sportolari, 1997: 9.
55. Cornwell & Lundgren, 2001.
56. Neu, 2002.
57. Cited in Adamse & Motta, 2000: 111.
58. McKenna et al., 2002.
59. Ben-Ze'ev, 2000: 182–184.
60. J. Shaw, 1997: 29.
61. Ben-Ze'ev, 2000: 294.
62. Delilah (Deb Levine), Thriveonline.com, Online Love, "Husband's Online Friend is Getting her Jealous," April, 2000.
63. Hawaii Chat Universe, www.lovelife.com, Cyber Love Stories, "Sherrie."
64. Cited in Mary E. Behr, "High-tech sex," *PC Magazine*, September 4, 2001.
65. Hawaii Chat Universe, www.lovelife.com, Cyber Love Stories, "Maggie," "Forever and a day."
66. Capulet, 1998: 105; see also Joan Elizabeth Lloyd's website, www.joanelloyd.com/fbcheat.htm.
67. Cited in Adams & Crenshaw, 2000: 61.
68. Ibid.: 78.
69. Hawaii Chat Universe, www.lovelife.com, Cyber Love Stories, "Anonymous 2"; "Partners in passion"; Delilah (Deb Levine), Thriveonline.com: Online Love, "Cheating Online," June, 2001.
70. Cited in Semans & Winks, 1999: 170.
71. Ortega y, Gasset, 1941: 43, 76–77.
72. Cited in Semans & Winks, 1999: 171–172.
73. Sternberg, 1988, 1998: 3–15.
74. Sternberg, 1998: 8–9.
75. Ibid.: 10.
76. The above citations are from: Hawaii Chat Universe, www.lovelife.com, Cyber Love Stories, "Only one angel," "My true love, Rich," "Love online," "Sherri Hilts"; Cyber-Relations, www.geocities.com/Paris/6278/, "Loving two people?"; Match.com, Success Stories.
77. Cornwell & Lundgren, 2001: 208.
78. Gwinnell, 1998: 102–104.
79. Maheu & Subotnik, 2001: 6; Michael et al., 1994.
80. Sternberg, 1998: 29–35.
81. Folkes, 1982.
82. Adams & Crenshaw, 2000: 62.
83. Cyber-Relations, www.geocities.com/Paris/6278/, "Too broken to try again," "Two to tango"; Lovingyou.com, "My onc & only Babes."
84. Buss, 1994; Crouse & Mehrabian, 1977; Etcoff, 1999: ch. 3; Townsend & Levy, 1990.
85. The study has been done by Don Strassberg and Stephen Holty and is reported by Philip Cohen in *New Scientist*, February 14, 1998.
86. Adamse & Motta, 2000: 51.

87. McKenna et al., 2002.
88. Joan Elizabeth Lloyd's website, www.joanelloyd.com; Cyberlove101.com, Story 50: "The light in the distance."
89. Bader, 2002: 274; Boneva & Kraut, 2002; Boneva et al., 2001.
90. Boneva & Kraut, 2002; Boneva et al., 2001; Lefkowitz & Petterson, 2002.
91. Jackson et al., 2001; Weiser, 2000; Whitty, 2002.
92. Adamse & Motta, 2000: 47–54.
93. Glass & Wright, 1992; Lawson, 1988: 39.
94. Cooper et al., 1999; see also Goodson et al., 2000.
95. J. Schneider & Weiss, 2001: 83.
96. Bader, 2002: 265.
97. Cited in J. Schneider & Weiss, 2001: 104.
98. Portmann, 2001: 229.

9 Chatting is sometimes cheating

1. Joan Elizabeth Lloyd's website, www.joanelloyd.com/fbcheat.htm.
2. Ellis, 2001: 250.
3. Neu, 2002.
4. Joan Elizabeth Lloyd's website, www.joanelloyd.com/fbcheat.htm.
5. Portmann, 2001.
6. http://www.infidelity-infidelity.com, Stories.
7. *Ananova*, November 14, 2002.
8. Ellis, 2001: 246.
9. Ibid.: 251.
10. Fitness, 2001.
11. Maheu & Subotnik, 2001: 53.
12. Joan Elizabeth Lloyd's website, www.joanelloyd.com/fbcheat.htm.
13. Leiblum & Doering, 2002: 27–28.
14. Doering, 2000: 864.
15. Palac, 1998: 106; cited in Portmann, 2001: 237.
16. *Self-help Magazine*, www.selfhelpmagazine.com/cgibin/cyber_survey.cgi?progo.
17. Maheu & Subotnik, 2001: 9.
18. Dateable.com.
19. The last two citations are found in Schneider & Weiss, 2001: 2–3, 20.
20. The above citations are from Joan Elizabeth Lloyd's website, www.joanelloyd.com/fbcheat.htm.
21. Schneider & Weiss, 2001: 95; see also Young et al., 2000: 66.
22. Cited in Schneider & Weiss, 2001: 92.
23. Cited in ibid.: 97.
24. iVillage.com, "I'm married but I've been intimate with an old boyfriend online."
25. www.infidelity-infidelity.com, Stories.
26. Levine, 1998: 118, 125.
27. *Mainichi Daily News*, December 7, 2003.
28. Cited in Maheu & Subotnik, 2001: 68.
29. Cooper et al., 2002; Joinson, 2003: 141.

30. The last two citations are from Joan Elizabeth Lloyd's website, www.joanelloyd.com/fbcheat.htm.
31. Canada Singles Connection, www.canadasingles.net, "Stories of Internet Adultery," March, 1999.
32. J. Shaw, 1997: 29.
33. Joan Elizabeth Lloyd's website, www.joanelloyd.com/fbcheat.htm.
34. Schneider & Weiss, 2001: 92.
35. Cited in Adamse & Motta, 2000: 133.
36. Delilah (Deb Levine), Thriveonline.com: Online Love, "E-mail Betrayal," June, 2001.
37. Cited in Adamse & Motta, 2000: 134.
38. www.erotica-readers.com/ERA/I-Cybersex.htm, "Is cybersex adultery?"
39. *Self-help Magazine*, www.selfhelpmagazine.com/cgibin/cyber_survey.cgi?progo&monthApril&year2002.
40. Kurzweil, 1999; see also Marlene M. Maheu, "The future of cyber-sex and relationship fidelity," *Self-help Magazine*, selfhelpmagazine.com/booklet/index.html.
41. www.infidelity-infidelity.com, Stories.
42. *Sexual and Relationship Therapy Journal*, August, 2002; reported in NYPOST.com, August 26, 2002.
43. Joan Elizabeth Lloyd's website, www.joanelloyd.com/fbcheat.htm.
44. Cooper et al., 1999.
45. Kraut et al., 2002.
46. McKenna et al., 2002; Wallace, 1999: 156. For the view that on the Internet also, the rich get richer and the poor get poorer, see Kraut et al., 2002.
47. Adam Smith expresses this view in his *Reputation*; see Sykes, 1999: 241.
48. Delilah (Deb Levine), Thriveonline.com: Online Love, "Jealousy and Cybersex," June, 2001.
49. Young et al., 2000: 71; see also Cooper et al., 2000.

10 The future of romantic relationships

1. Stan Kelly-Bootle (2001), *Son of devil's advocate*. Retrieved online from: www.sarcheck.com/skb/soda0104.htm.
2. Montgomery & Baxter, 1998: 7.
3. Birch & Marlin, 1982.
4. Gaver & Mandler, 1987.
5. Cook & McHenry, 1978: 132–135.
6. Ben-Ze'ev, 2000: 430–433.
7. Buss, 1994; Metts et al., 1998.
8. Michael et al., 1994; Waite & Gallagher, 2001.
9. Various studies indicate this phenomenon. An extensive recent study was done by Dr. Graham Jackson from St. Thomas's Hospital in London, and is reported, e.g., in Health on the Net News, December 6, 2002, www.hon.ch/News/HSN/510681.html.
10. The research was conducted by Peter Gray at Harvard University and is reported in *New Scientist*, May 25, 2002.

11. In this chapter, unless otherwise indicated, all citations of people telling about their online affairs are from Joan Elizabeth Lloyd's website, www.joanelloyd.com/fbcheat.htm.
12. Almog, 2002.
13. www.erotica-readers.com/ERA/I-Cybersex.htm, "Is cybersex adultery?"
14. Forste & Tanfer, 1996.
15. Libby, 1977: Introduction.
16. D. R. Johnson & Post, 1996.
17. Almog, 2002; D. R. Johnson & Post, 1996.
18. Waite & Gallagher, 2001; see also, e.g., Freedman, 1978: ch. 5; Michael et al., 1994.
19. Waite & Gallagher, 2001: ch. 6.
20. Ibid.: ch. 13.
21. See, e.g., Browning & Miller, 1999; Clanton, 1984; Witte, 1997.
22. Axin & Thornton, 2000; Noller & Feeney, 2002: 1.
23. Lucas et al., 2003.
24. Ibid.
25. Glass, 1998.
26. Cited and discussed in Hirshman & Larson, 1998: 49.
27. Illouz, 1997: 39–42.
28. Waite & Gallagher, 2001: 200–201.
29. Bachrach et al., 2000.
30. Forste & Tanfer, 1996; Waite & Gallagher, 2001: 91.
31. Forste & Tanfer, 1996; Waite & Gallagher, 2001: 82.
32. Baumeister & Leary, 1995.
33. Waite & Gallagher, 2001: 46.
34. Gerstel & Gross, 1984: 62–66, 104–112.
35. Axin & Thornton, 2000; Bachrach et al., 2000; Forste & Tanfer, 1996.
36. Waite & Gallagher, 2001: ch. 3.
37. www.clitical.com/how_to/cybersex.php, Cyber sex.
38. Waite & Gallagher, 2001: 8.
39. Ibid.: 74.
40. *Ma'ariv*, March 3, 1996.
41. www.infidelity-infidelity.com, Stories.
42. Ibid.
43. Mileham, 2003 Joshua Quittner, "Divorce Internet style," *Time Magazine*, April 14, 1997; cited in Joinson, 2003: 83.
44. www.infidelity-infidelity.com, Stories.
45. Barak & Fisher, 2002.
46. Peris et al., 2002.
47. www.erotica-readers.com/ERA/I-Cybersex.htm, "Is cybersex adultery?"
48. *Business Wire*, February 8, 2001: "Modern love, 'Internet Style'"; see also Marlene M. Maheu, "The future of cyber-sex and relationship fidelity," *Self-help Magazine*, selfhelpmagazine.com/booklet/index.html.
49. Clanton, 1984: 15.
50. Amichai-Hamburger, 2002; Amichai-Hamburger & Ben-Artzi, 2003; Hamburger & Ben Artzi, 2000.

Bibliography

Adams, K. & Crenshaw, K. (2000). *The online dating survival guide.* United States: E-Solutions Press.

Adamse, M. & Motta, S. (2000). *Affairs of the Net.* Deerfield Beach, FL: Health Communications.

Almog, S. (2002). From Sterne and Borges to lost storytellers: Cyberspace, narrative, and law. *Fordham Intellectual Property, Media & Entertainment Law Journal,* **13**, 1–34.

Amichai-Hamburger, Y. (2002). Internet and personality. *Computers in Human Behavior,* **18**, 1–10.

Amichai-Hamburger, Y. & Ben-Artzi, E. (2003). Loneliness and Internet use. *Computers in Human Behavior,* **19**, 71–80.

Arendt, H. (1958). *The human condition.* Garden City: Doubleday.

Aristotle. *The complete works of Aristotle: The revised Oxford translation.* Ed. J. Barnes. Princeton: Princeton University Press, 1984.

Axin, W. G. & Thornton, A. (2000). The transformation in the meaning of marriage. In Waite, 2000.

Bachrach, C., Hindin, M. J. & Thomson, E. (2000). The changing shape of ties that bind: An overview and synthesis. In Waite, 2000.

Bader, M. J. (2002). *Arousal: The secret logic of sexual fantasies.* New York: St. Martin's Press.

Baker, A. (July 1998). Cyberspace couples finding romance online then meeting for the first time in real life. *CMC Magazine.*

(2002). What makes an online relationship successful? Clues from couples who met in cyberspace. *CyberPsychology & Behavior,* **5**, 363–375.

Barak, A. & Fisher, W. A. (2002). The future of Internet sexuality. In Cooper, 2002.

Barbalet, J. M. (1998). *Emotion, social theory, and social structure: A macrosociological approach.* Cambridge: Cambridge University Press.

Bargh, J. A., McKenna, K. Y. A. & Fitzsimons, G. M. (2002). Can you see the real me? Activation and expression of the "True Self" on the Internet. *Journal of Social Issues,* **58**, 33–48.

Baumeister, R. F. (1986). *Identity: Cultural change and the struggle for self.* New York: Oxford University Press.

Baumeister, R. F. & Leary, M. R. (1995). The need to belong: Desire for interpersonal attachments as a fundamental human motivation. *Psychological Bulletin,* **117**, 497–529.

Baxter, L. A. & Wilmot, W. W. (1985). Taboo topics in close relationships. *Journal of Social and Personal Relationships*, **2**, 253–269.

Baym, N. K. (2002). Interpersonal life online. In L. A. Lievrouw & S. Livingstone (eds.), *Handbook of new media: Social shaping and consequences of ICTs*. London: Sage.

Ben-Ze'ev, A. (1993). *The perceptual system: A philosophical and psychological perspective*. New York: Peter Lang.

(1994). The vindication of gossip. In Goodman & Ben-Ze'ev, 1994.

(2000). *The subtlety of emotions*. Cambridge, MA: MIT Press.

(2003a). The logic of emotions. In A. Hatzimoysis (ed.), *Philosophy and the emotions*. Cambridge: Cambridge University Press.

(2003b). Emotions as a general mental mode. In R. Solomon (ed.), *Thinking about feeling: Contemporary philosophers on emotion*. Oxford: Oxford University Press.

Berger, C. R. (1979). Beyond initial interaction: Uncertainty, understanding, and the development of interpersonal relationships. In H. Giles & R. St. Clair (eds.), *Language and social psychology*. Oxford: Basil Blackwell.

Biber, J. K., Doverspike, D., Baznik, D., Cober, A. & Ritter, B. A. (2002). Sexual harassment in online communications: Effects of gender and discourse medium. *CyberPsychology & Behavior*, **5**, 33–42.

Birch, L. L. & Marlin, D. W. (1982). I don't like it; I never tried it: Effects of exposure to food on two-year-old children's food preferences. *Appetite*, **4** 353–360.

Birnie, S. A. & Horvath, P. (2002). Psychological predictors of Internet social communication. *Journal of Computer Mediated Communication*, **7** (online).

Boneva, B. & Kraut, R. (2002). Email, gender, and personal relationships. In Wellman & Haythornthwaite, 2002.

Boneva, B., Kraut, R. & Frohlich, D. (2001). Using e-mail for personal relationships: The difference gender makes. *American Behavioral Scientist*, **45**, 530–549.

Boym, S. (2001). *The future of nostalgia*. New York: Basic Books.

Branwyn, G. (1993). Compu-sex: Erotica for cybernauts. *South Atlantic Quarterly*, **92**, 779–791.

Brehm, S. S. (1992). *Intimate relationships*. New York: McGraw-Hill Press.

Brin, D. (1998). *The transparent society: Will technology force us to choose between privacy and freedom?* Reading, MA: Perseus Books.

Brown, B. A. T. & Perry, M. (2000). Why don't telephones have off switches? Understanding the use of everyday technologies. *Interacting with Computers*, **12**, 623–634.

Brown, R. (1987). *Analyzing love*. Cambridge: Cambridge University Press.

Browning, S. L. & Miller, R. R. (eds.) (1999). *Till death do us part: A multicultural anthology on marriage*. Stamford: JAI Press.

Buss, D. M. (1988). The evolution of human intrasexual competition. *Journal of Personality and Social Psychology*, **54**, 616–628.

(1994). *The evolution of desire: Strategies of human mating*. New York: Basic Books.

Byrne, D. (1997). An overview (and underview) of research and theory within the attraction paradigm. *Journal of Social and Personal Relationships*, **14**, 417–431.

Byrne, D. & Murnen, S. K. (1988). Maintaining loving relationships. In R. J. Sternberg & M. L. Barnes (eds.), *The psychology of love.* New Haven: Yale University Press.

Cairncross, F. (1997). *The death of distance: How the communications revolution will change our lives.* Boston: Harvard Business School Press.

Capulet, N. (1998). *Putting your heart online.* Oakland, CA: Variable Symbols.

Chen, W., Boase, J. & Wellman, B. (2002). The global villagers: Comparing Internet users and uses around the world. In Wellman & Haythornthwaite, 2002.

Clanton, G. (1984). Social forces and the changing family. In L. A. Kirkendall & A. E. Gravatt (eds.), *Marriage and the family in the year 2020.* Buffalo: Prometheus Books.

Collings, N. L. & Miller, L. C. (1994). Self-disclosure and liking: A meta-analytic review. *Psychological Bulletin,* **116**, 457–475.

Conley, L. (1999). *Meet me online: The #1 practical guide to Internet dating.* Fayetteville: Old Mountain Press.

Cook, M. & McHenry, R. (1978). *Sexual attraction.* London: Pergamon.

Cooper, A. (ed.) (2002). *Sex and the Internet: A guidebook for clinicians.* New York: Brunner-Routledge.

Cooper, A., Delmonico, D. & Burg, R. (2000). Cybersex users, abusers, and compulsives: New findings and implications. *Sexual Addiction & Compulsivity,* **7**, 5–29.

Cooper, A., Scherer, C., Boies, S. C. & Gordon, B. (1999). Sexuality on the Internet: From sexual exploration to pathological expression. *Professional Psychology: Research and Practice,* **30**, 154–164.

Cooper, A., Scherer, C. & Marcus, I. D. (2002). Harnessing the power of the Internet to improve sexual relationships. In A. Cooper, 2002.

Cooper, A. & Sportolari, L. (1997). Romance in cyberspace: Understanding online attraction. *Journal of Sex Education and Therapy,* **22**, 7–14.

Cooper, J. M. (1975). *Reason and human good in Aristotle.* Cambridge, MA: Harvard University Press.

Copher, J. I., Kanfer, A. G. & Walker, M. B. (2002). Everyday communication patterns of heavy and light email users. In Wellman & Haythornthwaite, 2002.

Cornwell, B. & Lundgren, D. C. (2001). Love on the Internet: Involvement and misrepresentation in romantic relationships in cyberspace vs. actual-space. *Computers in Human Behavior,* **17**, 197–211.

Crouse, B. B. & Mehrabian, A. (1977). Affiliation of opposite-sexed strangers. *Journal of Research in Personality,* **11**, 38–47.

Csikszentmihalyi, M. (1990). *Flow: The psychology of optimal experience.* New York: Harper Perennial.

Cummings, J. N., Butler, B. & Kraut, R. (2002). The quality of online relationships. *Communications of the ACM,* **45**, 103–108.

Cummins, R. A. & Nistico, H. (2002). Maintaining life satisfaction: The role of positive cognitive bias. *Journal of Happiness Studies,* **3**, 37–69.

Danet, B. (2001). *Cyberpl@y: Communicating online.* Oxford: Berg.

DeAngelo, D. (2002). *Double your dating: What every man should know about how to be more successful with women.* Online: doubleyourdating.com.

DeCew, J. W. (1997). *In pursuit of privacy: Law, ethics, and the rise of technology.* Ithaca: Cornell University Press.

De Sousa, R. (1987). *The rationality of emotions.* Cambridge, MA.: MIT Press.
(1994). In praise of gossip: Indiscretion as a saintly virtue. In Goodman & Ben-Ze'ev, 1994.
Dietz-Uhler, B. & Bishop-Clark, C. (2001). The use of computer-mediated communication to enhance subsequent face-to-face discussions. *Computers in Human Behavior,* **17**, 269–283.
Dindia, K. (1998). "Going into and coming out of the closet": The dialectics of stigma disclosure. In Montgomery & Baxter, 1998.
Doering, N. (2000). Feminist views of cybersex: Victimization, liberation, and empowerment. *CyberPsychology & Behavior,* **3**, 863–884.
(2002). Studying online love and cyber romance. In B. Batinic, U. D. Reips, & M. Bosnjak (eds.), *Online social sciences.* Seattle: Hogrefe & Huber.
Donn, J. E. & Sherman, R. C. (2002). Attitudes and practices regarding the formation of romantic relationships on the Internet. *CyberPsychology & Behavior,* **5**, 107–123.
Dreyfus, H. L. (2001). *On the Internet.* London: Routledge.
Ebo, B. (1998). *Cyberghetto or cybertopia? Race, class, and gender on the Internet.* Westport: Praeger.
Ehrhardt, J. J., Saris, W. E. & Veenhoven, R. (2000). Stability of life-satisfaction over time. *Journal of Happiness Studies,* **1**, 177–205.
Eldridge, M. & Grinter, R. (2001). Studying text messaging in teenagers. CHI 2001 Workshop: Mobile Communications – Understanding users, adoption and design.
Ellis, A. (2001). Casual sex. In J. Portmann (ed.), *In defense of sin.* New York: St. Martin, 2001.
Epstein, R. (May/June, 2002). Editor as guinea pig: Putting love to a real test. *Psychology Today* (online).
Etcoff, N. (1999). *Survival of the prettiest: The science of beauty.* New York: Doubleday.
Etzioni, A. (1999). *The limits of privacy.* New York: Basic Books.
Fein, E. & Schneider, S. (1995). *The Rules: time tested secrets for capturing the heart of Mr. Right.* New York: Warner Books.
(1997). *The Rules II: More Rules to live and love by.* New York: Warner Books.
(2002). *The Rules for online dating: Capturing the heart of Mr. Right in cyberspace.* New York: Pocket Books.
Feinberg, L. S. (1996). *Teasing: Innocent fun or sadistic malice?* Far Hills, NJ: New Horizon Press.
Fink, J. (1999). *Cyberseduction: Reality in the age of psychotechnology.* Amherst: Prometheus Books.
Fitness, J. (2001). Betrayal, rejection, revenge, and forgiveness. In M. R. Leary (ed.), *Interpersonal rejection.* Oxford: Oxford University Press.
Fitness, J. & Fletcher, G. J. O. (1993). Love, hate, anger and jealousy in close relationships: A prototype and cognitive appraisal analysis. *Journal of Personality and Social Psychology.* **65**, 942–958.
Fitzpatrick, M. A. (1987). Marriage and verbal intimacy. In V. J. Derlega & J. H. Berg (eds.), *Self-disclosure: Theory, research, and therapy.* New York: Plenum.
Folkes, V. S. (1982). Communicating the reasons for social rejection. *Journal of Experimental Social Psychology,* **18**, 235–252.

Forste, R. & Tanfer, K. (1996). Sexual exclusivity among dating, cohabiting, and married women. *Journal of Marriage and the Family*, **58**, 33–47.
Freedman, J. L. (1978). *Happy people.* New York: Harcourt Brace Jovanovich.
Fromm, E. (1956). *The art of love.* New York: Harper.
Gallup, G. G., Jr., Burch, R. L. & Platek, S. M. (2002). Does semen function as an antidepressant? *Archives of Sexual Behavior*, **31**, 289–293.
Gaver, W. W. & Mandler, G. (1987). Play it again, Sam: On liking music. *Cognition and Emotion*, **3**, 259–282.
Gergen, K. J. (1991). *The saturated self: Dilemmas of identity in contemporary life.* New York: Basic Books.
Gergen, K. J., Gergen, M. M. & Barton, W. H. (1973). Deviance in the dark. *Psychology Today*, **7**, 129–130.
Gerlander, M. & Takala, E. (1997). Relating electronically: Interpersonality in the Net. *Nordicom Review*, **18**, 77–81.
Gerstel, N. & Gross, H. (1984). *Commuter marriage: A study of work and family.* New York: Guilford Press.
Gilboa, E. & Revelle, W. (1994). Personality and the structure of affective responses. In S. H. M. van Goozen, N. E. van de Poll & J. A. Sergeant (eds.), *Emotions: Essays on emotion theory.* Hillsdale: Erlbaum.
Gilovich, T. & Medvec, V. H. (1995). The experience of regret: What, when, and why. *Psychological Review*, **102**, 379–395.
Gladue, B. A. & Delaney, J. J. (1990). Gender differences in perception of attractiveness of men and women in bars. *Personality and Social Psychology Bulletin*, **16**, 378–391.
Glass, S. (1998). Shattered vows. *Psychology Today*, **31**, 34–42.
Glass, S. P. & Wright, T. L. (1992). Justifications for extramarital relationships: The association between attitudes, behaviors, and gender. *Journal of Sex Research*, **29**, 361–387.
Goodman, R. E. & Ben-Ze'ev, A (eds.) (1994). *Good gossip.* Lawrence: University Press of Kansas.
Goodson, P., McCormick, D. & Evans, A. (2000). Sex on the Internet: College students' emotional arousal when viewing sexually explicit materials on-line. *Journal of Sex Education and Therapy*, **25**, 252–260.
Graham, G. (1999). *The Internet: A philosophical inquiry.* London: Routledge.
Greer, A. & Buss, D. (1994). Tactics for promoting sexual encounter. *Journal of Sex Research*, **31**, 185–201.
Gwinnell, E. (1998). *Online seductions.* New York: Kodansha International.
Hamburger, Y. A. & Ben-Artzi, E. (2000). The relationship between extraversion and neuroticism and the different uses of the Internet. *Computers in Human Behavior*, **16**, 441–449.
Hampton, K. N. & Wellman, B. (2002). The not so global village of Netville. In Wellman & Haythornthwaite, 2002.
Hess, J. A. (2000). Maintaining nonvoluntary relationships with disliked partners: An investigation into the use of distancing behaviors. *Human Communication Research*, **26**, 458–488.
Hirshman, L. R. & Larson, J. E. (1998). *Hard bargains: The politics of sex.* New York: Oxford University Press.
Illouz, E. (1997). *Consuming the romantic utopia. Love and the cultural contradictions of capitalism.* Berkeley: University of California Press.

Jackson, L. A., Ervin, K. S., Gardner, P. D. & Schmitt, N. (2001). Gender and the Internet: Women communicating and men searching. *Sex Roles*, **44**, 363–379.

Johnson, D. R. & Post, D. (1996). Law and borders – the rise of law in cyberspace. *Stanford Law Review*, **48**, 1367–1402.

Johnson, P. (1999). *The philosophy of manners.* Bristol: Thoemmes Press.

Joinson, A. N. (1998). Causes and implications of disinhibited behavior on the Internet. In J. Gackenbach (ed.), *Psychology and the Internet.* San Diego: Academic Press.

(2001). Self-disclosure in computer-mediated communication: The role of self-awareness and visual anonymity. *European Journal of Social Psychology*, **31**, 177–192.

(2003). *Understanding the psychology of Internet behavior: Virtual worlds, real lives.* Hampshire: Palgrave Macmillan.

Kant, I. (1797). *Anthropology from a pragmatic point of view.* The Hague: Martinus Nijhoff (1974).

(1803). *Kant on education.* London: Kegan Paul, Trench, Trubner (1899).

Katz, J. E. & Rice, R. E. (2002). Syntopia: Access, civic involvement, and social interaction on the Net. In Wellman & Haythornthwaite, 2002.

Kellerman, A. (2002). *The Internet on earth: A geography of information.* Chichester: Wiley.

Kiesler, S., Siegal, J. & McGuire, T. W. (1984). Social psychological aspects of computer mediated communication. *American Psychologist*, **39**, 1123–1134.

Kirkendall, L. A. & Gravatt, A. E. (1984). Marriage and family: Styles and forms. In L. A. Kirkendall & A. E. Gravatt (eds.), *Marriage and the family in the year 2020.* Buffalo: Prometheus Books.

Kraut, R., Kiesler, S., Boneva, B., Cummings, J. N., Helgeson, V. & Crawford, A. (2002). Internet paradox revisited. *Journal of Social Issues*, **58**, 49–74.

Kraut, R., Patterson, M., Lundmark, V., Kiesler, S., Mukopadhyay, T. & Scherlies, W. (1998). Internet paradox: A social technology that reduces social involvement and psychological well-being? *American Psychologist*, **53**, 1017–1031.

Kurzweil, R. (1999). *The age of spiritual machines: When computers exceed human intelligence.* New York: Viking.

Landman, J. (1993). *Regret: The persistence of the possible.* New York: Oxford University Press.

Langer, E. J. (1989). *Mindfulness.* Reading: Addison-Wesley.

LaRose, R., Eastin, M. S. & Gregg, J. (2001). Reformulating the Internet paradox: Social cognitive explanations of Internet use and depression. *Journal of Online Behavior*, **1** (2).

Laurenceau, J. P & Feldman-Barrett, L. (1998). Intimacy as an interpersonal process: The importance of self-disclosure, partner disclosure, and perceived partner responsiveness in interpersonal exchanges. *Journal of Personality and Social Psychology*, **74**, 1238–1251.

Lawson, A. (1988). *Adultery: An analysis of love and betrayal.* New York: Basic Books.

Lea, M. & Spears, R. (1995). Love at first byte. In J. Wood & S. Duck (eds.), *Understudied relationships.* Thousand Oaks: Sage.

Lefkowitz, E. & Petterson, H. (2002). Communication with friends about sex-related topics during the transition to adulthood. Paper presented at the Society for Research on Adolescence meeting in New Orleans.

Leiblum, S. & Doering, N. (2002). Internet sexuality: Known risks and fresh chances for women. In A. Cooper, 2002.

Levine, D. (1998). *The joy of cybersex: A guide for creative lovers.* New York: Ballantine Books.

(2000). Virtual attraction: What rocks your boat. *CyberPsychology & Behavior*, **3**, 565–573.

Libby, R. W. (ed.) (1977). *Marriage and alternatives: Exploring intimate relationships.* Glenview: Scott, Foresman.

Lombard, M. & Ditton, T. (1997). At the heart of it all: The concept of telepresence. *Journal of Computer Mediated Communication*, **3** (online).

Lucas, R. E., Clark, A. E., Georgellis, Y. & Diener, E. (2003). Reexamining adaptation and the set point model of happiness: Reactions to changes in marital status. *Journal of Personality and Social Psychology*, **84**, 527–539.

Lydon, J., Pierce, T. & O'Regan, S. (1997). Coping with moral commitment to long-distance dating relationships. *Journal of Personality and Social Psychology*, **73**, 104–113.

Maheu, M. M. & Subotnik, R. B. (2001). *Infidelity on the Internet: Virtual relationships and real betrayal.* Naperville, IL: Sourcebooks.

Malamuth, N. M. & Brown, L. M. (1994). Sexually aggressive men's perceptions of women's communications: Testing three explanations. *Journal of Personality and Social Psychology*, **67**, 669–712.

Marx, K. (1869). *The eighteenth brumaire of Louis Bonaparte.* New York: International Publishers (1968).

McKenna, K. Y. A. & Bargh, J. A. (2000). Plan 9 from cyberspace: The implications of the Internet for personality. *Personality and Social Psychology Review*, **4**, 57–75.

McKenna, K. Y. A., Green, A. S. & Gleason, M. E. J. (2002). Relationship formation on the Internet: What's the big attraction? *Journal of Social Issues*, **58**, 9–32.

McKenna, K. Y. A., Green, A. S. & Smith, P. K. (2001). Demarginalizing the sexual self. *Journal of Sex Research*, **38**, 302–311.

Merkle, E. R. & Richardson, R. A. (2000). Digital dating and virtual relating: Conceptualizing computer mediated romantic relationships. *Family Relations*, **49**, 187–192.

Metts, S., Sprecher, S. & Regan, P. C. (1998). Communication and sexual drive. In P. A. Andersen & L. K. Guerrero (eds.), *Handbook of communication and emotion.* San Diego: Academic Press.

Michael, R. T., Gagnon, J. H., Laumann, E. D. & Kolata, G. (1994). *Sex in America.* Boston: Little, Brown & Company.

Mileham, B. L. A. (2003). Online infidelity in Internet chat rooms. Ph.D. Dissertation, University o Florida.

Miller, D. & Slater, D. (2000). *The Internet: An ethnographic approach.* Oxford: Berg.

Montgomery, B. M. & Baxter, L. A. (1998). *Dialectical approaches to studying personal relationships.* Mahwah: Lawrence Erlbaum.

Moore, J. W. (2002). *The Internet weather: Balancing continuous change and constant truths.* New York: John Wiley.

Moore, M. M. & Butler, D. L. (1989). Predictive aspects of nonverbal courtship behavior in women. *Semiotica*, **76**, 205–215.

Murray, S. L., Holmes, J. G. & Griffin, D. W. (1996). The self-fulfilling nature of positive illusions in romantic relationships: Love is not blind, but prescient. *Journal of Personality and Social Psychology*, **71**, 1155–1180.

Murstein, B. L. (1976). *Who will marry whom? Theories and research in marital choice.* New York: Springer, 1976.

Neu, J. (2002). An ethics of fantasy? *Journal of Theoretical and Philosophical Psychology*, **22**, 133–157.

Nie, N. H. (2001). Sociability, interpersonal relations, and the Internet: Reconciling conflicting findings. *American Behavioral Scientist*, **45**, 420–435.

Nie, N. H., Hillygus, D. S. & Erbring, L. (2002). Internet use, interpersonal relationships, and sociability. In Wellman & Haythornthwaite, 2002.

Noller, P. & Feeney, J. A. (eds.) (2002). *Understanding marriage: Developments in the study of couple interaction.* Cambridge: Cambridge University Press.

Nussbaum, M. C. (1986). *The fragility of goodness: Luck and ethics in Greek tragedy and philosophy.* Cambridge: Cambridge University Press.

(2001). *Upheavals of thought: A theory of the emotions.* Cambridge: Cambridge University Press.

Ortega y Gasset, J. (1941). *On love . . . Aspects of a single theme.* London: Jonathan Cape (1967).

Ortony, A., Clore, G. L. & Collings, A. (1988). *The cognitive structure of emotions.* Cambridge: Cambridge University Press.

O'Sullivan, P. B. (2000). What you don't know won't hurt me: Impression management functions of communication channels in relationships. *Human Communication Research*, **26**, 403–431.

Palac, L. (1998). *The edge of the bed: How dirty pictures changed my life.* Boston: Little, Brown.

Parks, M. R. & Floyd, K. (1996). Making friends in cyberspace. *Journal of Computer Mediated Communication*, **1** (4) (online).

Peris, R., Gimeno, M. A., Pinazo, D., Ortet, G., Carrero, V., Sanchiz, M. & Ibanez, I. (2002). Online chat rooms: Virtual spaces of interaction for socially oriented people. *CyberPsychology & Behavior*, **5**, 43–51.

Perper, T. & Weis, D. L. (1987). Proceptive and rejective strategies of US and Canadian college women. *Journal of Sex Research*, **23**, 455–480.

Pitcher, G. (1965). Emotion. *Mind*, **74**, 326–345.

Portmann, J. (2001). Chatting is not cheating. In J. Portmann (ed.), *In defense of sin.* New York: St. Martin.

Quan-Haase, A., Wellman, B, Witte, J. C. & Hamption, K. N. (2002). Capitalizing on the Net: Social contact, civic engagement, and sense of community. In Wellman & Haythornthwaite, 2002.

Rabin, S. (1999). *Cyberflirt: How to attract anyone, anywhere on the World Wide Web.* Harmondsworth: Plume.

Reeves, B. & Nass, C. (1996). *The media equation: How people treat computers, television, and new media like real people and places.* Cambridge: CSLI Publications and Cambridge University Press.

Rheingold, H. (2000). *The virtual community: Homesteading on the electronic frontier.* Cambridge, MA: MIT Press.

(2002). *Smart mobs: The next social revolution.* Cambridge, MA: Perseus.

Robinson, J. P., Kestnbaum, M., Neustadtl, A. & Alvarez, A. S. (2002). The Internet and other uses of time. In Wellman & Haythornthwaite, 2002.

Rohlfing, M. E. (1995). "Doesn't anybody stay in one place anymore?" An exploration of the under-studies phenomenon of long-distance relationships. In J. Wood & S. Duck (eds.), *Understudied relationships.* Thousand Oaks: Sage.
Rubin, Z. (1975). Disclosing oneself to a stranger: Reciprocity and its limits. *Journal of Experimental Social Psychology*, **11**, 233–260.
Rusbult, C. E., Johnson, D. J. & Morrow, G. D. (1986). Predicting satisfaction and commitment in adult romantic involvements: An assessment of the generalizability of the investment model. *Social Psychology Quarterly*, **49**, 81–89.
Rusbult, C. E., Van Lange, P. A. M., Wildschut, T., Yovetich, N. A. & Verette, J. (2000). Perceived superiority in close relationships: Why it exists and persists. *Journal of Personality and Social Psychology*, **79**, 521–545.
Savicki, V. & Kelley, M. (2000). Computer mediated communication: Gender and group composition. *CyberPsychology & Behavior*, **3**, 817–833.
Scharlott, B. W. & Christ, W. G. (1995). Overcoming relationship-initiation barriers: The impact of a computer-dating system on sex role, shyness, and appearance inhibitions. *Computers in Human Behavior*, **11**, 191–204.
Schiano, D. J. et al. (2002). Teen use of messaging media. CHI 2002 Conference: Human factors in computing systems. New York.
Schneider, C. D. (1977). *Shame, exposure and privacy.* Boston: Beacon Press.
Schneider, J. & Weiss, R. (2001). *Cybersex exposed: Simple fantasy or obsession?* Center City, MN: Hazelden.
Schoeman, F. D. (1992). *Privacy and social freedom.* Cambridge: Cambridge University Press.
(1994). Gossip and privacy. In Goodman & Ben-Ze'ev, 1994.
Schulhofer, S. J. (1998). *Unwanted sex: The culture of intimidation and the failure of law.* Cambridge, MA: Harvard University Press.
Schwartz, P. (May/June, 2002). Love is not all you need. *Psychology Today* (online).
Seiden, H. M. (2001). Creating passion: An Internet love story. *Journal of Applied Psychoanalytic Studies*, **3**, 187–195.
Semans, A. & Winks, C. (1999). *The woman's guide to sex on the Web.* San Francisco: Harper Collins.
Shaw, J. (1997). Treatment rationale for Internet infidelity. *Journal of Sex Education and Therapy*, **22**, 29–34.
Shaw, L. H. & Gant, L. M. (2002a). In defense of the Internet: The relationship between Internet communication and depression, loneliness, self-esteem, and perceived social support. *CyberPsychology & Behavior*, **5**, 157–171.
(2002b). Users divided? Exploring the gender gap in Internet use. *CyberPsychology & Behavior*, **5**, 517–527.
Shea, V. (1997). *Netiquette.* San Francisco: Albion (online).
Sherman, R. C. (2001). The mind's eye in cyberspace: Online perceptions of self and others. In G. Riva & C. Galimberti (eds.), *Towards cyberpsychology: Mind, cognition and society in the Internet age.* Amsterdam: IOS Press, 2001.
Slater, D. (2002). Social relationships and identity online and offline. In L. A. Lievrouw & S. Livingstone (eds.), *Handbook of new media: Social shaping and consequences of ICTs.* London: Sage.
Spiegel, J. (1995). *Flirting for success: The art of building rapport.* New York: Warner Books.

Stafford, L. & Reske, J. R. (1990). Idealization and communication in long-distance premarital relationships. *Family Relations*, **39**, 274–279.

Standage, T. (1998). *The Victorian Internet: The remarkable story of the telegraph and the nineteenth century's on-line pioneers.* New York: Walker.

Stengel, R. (2000). *You're too kind: A brief history of flattery.* New York: Simon & Schuster.

Stephen, T. (1986). Communication and interdependence in geographically separated relationships. *Human Communication Research*, **13**, 191–210.

Sternberg, R. J. (1988). *The triangle of love.* New York: Basic Books.

(1998). *Cupid's arrow: The course of love through time.* Cambridge: Cambridge University Press.

Stocker, M. (1990). *Plural and conflicting values.* Oxford: Clarendon Press.

Suler, J. (2003). *The psychology of cyberspace* (online, www.rider.edu/suler/psycyber/basicfeat.html).

Sunstein, C. (2001). *Republic.com.* Princeton: Princeton University Press.

Sykes, C. J. (1999). *The end of privacy.* New York: St. Martin's Press.

Tesser, A. & Paulhus, D. L. (1976). Toward a causal model of love. *Journal of Personality and Social Psychology*, **34**, 1095–1105.

Thompson, A. P. (1983). Extramarital sex: A review of the research literature. *Journal of Sex Research*, **19**, 1–22.

Tidwell, L. C. & Walther, J. B. (2002). Computer-mediated communication effects on disclosure, impressions, and interpersonal evaluations: Getting to know one another a bit at a time. *Human Communication Research*, **28**, 317–348.

Townsend, J. M. & Levy, G. D. (1990). Effect of potential partners' physical attractiveness and socioeconomic status on sexuality and partner selection. *Archives of Sexual Behavior*, **19**, 149–164.

Tykocinski, O. E. (2001). I never had a chance: Using hindsight tactics to mitigate disappointments. *Personality and Social Psychology Bulletin*, **27**, 376–382.

Vittengl, J. R. & Holt, C. S. (2000). Getting acquainted: The relationship of self-disclosure and social attraction to positive affect. *Journal of Social and Personal Relationships*, **17**, 53–66.

Waite, L. J. (ed.) (2000). *The ties that bind: Perspectives on marriage and cohabitation.* New York: Aldine de Gruyter.

Waite, L. J. & Gallagher, M. (2001). *The case for marriage: Why married people are happier, healthier, and better off financially.* New York: Broadway Books.

Wallace, P. (1999). *The psychology of the Internet.* Cambridge: Cambridge University Press.

Walther, J. B. & Burgoon, J. K. (1992). Relational communication in computer-mediated interaction. *Human Communication Research*, **19**, 50–88.

Weiser, E. B. (2000). Gender differences in Internet use patterns and internet application preferences: A two-sample comparison. *CyberPsychology & Behavior*, **3**, 167–178.

Wellman, B. & Haythornthwaite, C. (eds.) (2002). *The Internet in everyday life.* Malden: Blackwell.

Whitty, M. T. (2002). Liar, liar! An examination of how open, supportive and honest people are in chat rooms. *Computers in Human Behavior*, **18**, 343–352.

(2003). Cyber-flirting: Playing at love on the Internet. *Theory and Psychology*, **13**, 339–357.

Whitty, M. T. & Gavin, J. (2001). Age/sex/location: Uncovering the social cues in the development of online relationships. *CyberPsychology & Behavior*, **4**, 623–630.

Witte, J. (1997). *From sacrament to contract: Marriage, religion, and law in the Western tradition.* Louisville: Westminster John Knox Press.

Woll, S. & Cozby, C. (1987). Videodating and other alternatives to traditional methods of relationship initiation. In W. Jones & D. Periman (eds.), *Advances in personal relationships,* vol. I. Greenwich: JAI Press.

Wysocki, D. K. (1998). Let your fingers do the talking: Sex on an adult chat-line. *Sexualities,* **1**, 425–452.

Young, K. S. (2001). *Cybersex: Uncovering the secret world of Internet sex.* London: Carlton.

Young, K. S., Griffin-Shelley, E., Cooper, A., O'Mara, J. & Buchanan, J. (2000). Online infidelity: A new dimension in couple relationships with implications for evaluation and treatment. *Sexual Addiction & Compulsivity*, **7**, 59–74.

Index